PLAYING FOR LIFE

Billy Talbert's Story

By William F. Talbert

With Bruce S. Old
THE GAME OF DOUBLES IN TENNIS

With John Sharnik
PLAYING FOR LIFE

PLAYING FOR LIFE

Billy Talbert's Story

by

WILLIAM F. TALBERT

with

JOHN SHARNIK

WITH PHOTOGRAPHS

BOSTON · Little, Brown and Company · TORONTO

Portions of this book have appeared in *Sports Illustrated*.

Published simultaneously in Canada
by Little, Brown & Company (Canada) Limited

PRINTED IN THE UNITED STATES OF AMERICA

For Nancy,
Pike and Peter

A Note in Advance

THIS book may be described as an account of how I got to do some things I wanted to do, in spite of certain difficulties. The account would be incomplete without the mention of certain advantages, as well.

In Cincinnati, when I was starting my tennis career, I had the advice and assistance of individuals at the University, in the tennis association and in other quarters. Throughout my years in the game, while I have had my differences with men in the United States Lawn Tennis Association, I have also learned much and received valuable help from them. Wherever I've played — in this country and abroad — there have been people who made my experience more rewarding by their generosity. And my fellow members in the unofficial but very real fraternity of tennis players have always been quick to lend a hand in all kinds of circumstances. If not for all these people, I doubt that I would have had much to write about.

In connection with the preparation of this book I am indebted to Mrs. Gladys Heldman of *World Tennis* magazine, whose records were extremely useful in reinforcing my memory of tennis events.

Above all, I am affectionately grateful to my wife, Nancy, for being as helpful and understanding about authorship as she has been about tennis and diabetes.

W.F.T.

Contents

(Illustrations appear between pages 86–87)

	A Note in Advance	*vii*
I	My Kind of Magic	3
II	Talbert & Son	6
III	For the Rest of My Life	19
IV	On the Sidelines	30
V	Novice	37
VI	On My Own	49
VII	Breadwinner on Campus	63
VIII	The Circuit	74
IX	Default	97
X	A Hungry Tennis Player	111
XI	Where I Belonged	129
XII	Pick a Partner	150
XIII	The White Flannel Uniform	163
XIV	My Year	174
XV	Reunion and Recognition	182

x *Contents*

xvi   The Prize   193

xvii Nancy   205

xviii Setback   217

xix   Yanqui Goes Home   235·

xx   Grab the Brass Ring   240

xxi   Life and Diabetes   259

xxii Over the Hill   274

xxiii On Top Down Under   280

xxiv Gamble and Glory   291

xxv   The Way the Ball Bounces   304

PLAYING FOR LIFE
Billy Talbert's Story

I
My Kind of Magic

Most athletes swear by some personal kind of magic to keep themselves fit for combat. There are vitamin swallowers and rope skippers, abstainers from tobacco, aspirin, and any kind of food more complicated than a sirloin steak. Some golfers walk down the street squeezing a small rubber ball between their fingers to strengthen the grip. Left-handed pitchers, an especially nervous breed, have been known to make a fetish of always reaching for doorknobs with the other hand and always sitting with the left shoulder away from a window to ward off strains and drafts.

Before I set foot on a tennis court for the first time, on a spring day back in Cincinnati when I was fourteen, I already had a special routine of my own. It began, first thing in the morning, with a hypodermic needle, which I used to inject a substance called insulin under the skin of my thigh. There was nothing vague about its powers. Without it, I knew, I wouldn't have had the strength to swing my brand-new four-dollar racket. Without it, in fact, I'd have been more dead than alive.

The routine was the normal beginning of every day in the life of any person having the chronic physical disorder called diabetes. It still is. In a handful of extremely mild cases, antibiotic pills may take the place of the insulin. But for all the rest of us million diabetics in the United States and the millions of others all over the world, the hypodermic is the basic fact of life.

What was not in the least normal about my program was the tennis racket. At the time I started, there was no assurance — and, in fact, considerable doubt — that a diabetic could play and survive.

Whatever else changed in my life during the next twenty-five years, insulin remained the vital constant. On a late-December morning in 1957, I went through the same routine in a hotel room ten thousand miles from home in Melbourne, Australia. Wearing the traditional tennis flannels and a blue jacket with a team emblem on its pocket, I stepped into the bright sunlight of the Down Under summer and headed for a cluster of stadium-ringed courts. I was on my way to direct a group of robust American athletes in their campaign for the most international of all trophies, the Davis Cup.

I had gone before the huge Australian crowds as a player; now, a part-time athlete approaching forty, I was in my fifth campaign as a nonplaying captain. Never in all those times had I started in such an unfavorable position. We were underdogs of the lowest order, given probably less chance of winning than any United States team had ever had as it entered the climactic Challenge Round.

The fact that we were so lightly regarded bothered me a little; so did the necessity of the gamble that I had decided to take as our only possible hope of upsetting the odds. In the back of my mind were a couple of other matters unrelated to the day's big event. There was an important business problem, which I'd have to take care of that evening by cablegram to my office in New York. And there was the thought that at home, back across the international date line, today was Christmas, and I would have to settle for a transoceanic phone call to wish the season's best to my wife, Nancy, and our two small boys. There wasn't much room for the kind of worry that had dogged my invalid's steps back at the beginning, when I went to take my first uncertain swing at a tennis ball.

Twenty-five years of tennis had taken me a long way from invalidism — through all the tournament seasons, the international campaigns, the string of championships that had given me a trophy no player had been able to capture before. The early part of the route I had covered by hitchhiking because the bus fare was too rich for my blood; now it was all parlor cars, staterooms and de luxe flights.

In all that time, I had never been farther from diabetes than from my own skin. The hypodermic needle was just as vital as ever. It was just as true as ever that I couldn't live without it.

But what counted was the living — the excitement of a game, the lure of the gamble . . . the crowd, the band, the tennis officials and government dignitaries in their canopied pavilion . . . the freshly chalked lawn . . . and the Cup.

11
Talbert & Son

FROM the beginning — September 4, 1918 — or as close to it as I can remember, I had always been eager for life. In our Cincinnati North Side neighborhood, there were plenty of exciting things to do, and nothing to stop me from enjoying them. Any setback was only temporary.

At the age of seven, I had my first baseball glove. I took it across the street to the vacant lot where the kids chose up sides almost every spring afternoon. As the runt of the neighborhood pack, I had to make a nuisance of myself to get in on the action.

"Fatso, you catch and —"

"Shortstop!" I waved my mitt like a boy with the answer in arithmetic class.

" — and I'm gonna pitch this time."

"Shortstop!"

"I got my first baseman's mitt."

"Okay. Eddie, you wanna play second or third?"

"Can I play shortstop?"

The team scattered onto the field and began throwing the ball around, with more noise than accuracy. "We get our last licks — don't forget!"

"Hey, you guys," I yelled out, "where do I play?"

"Talbert, quit being a pest. Go play with the little kids, will ya?"

Some boys might have taken no for an answer and given up in tears. But I had other resources: my father. Calmly and logically, he could show me the way around any obstacle. He not only made it seem unmanly to cry; he made it unnecessary.

At the end of a week or so, I went back to the lot. I stood watching the game for a few minutes, then walked out to a spot just beyond the infield. Before long, the batter hit one past the flailing arms of the appointed shortstop. I snatched it and underhanded a throw, the way I'd been practicing it with my father all week. The second baseman smothered it like a pillow in a bedroom fight, wound up, and heaved it into the general neighborhood of first base.

"Double play!" I said, not very realistically. "Ford to Critz to Pipp!"

"Who?"

"Ford to Critz to Wally Pipp. Don't you even know the Reds' infield, for Pete's sake?" *I* certainly knew the Cincinnati Reds infield. I had already logged as much time in the Cincinnati baseball stands as some kids had spent in Sunday school. The team's personnel was as familiar to me as the names on the mailboxes in the lobby of our apartment building.

"The Reds!" said the regular shortstop scornfully. "They smell!"

"They do like fun!"

"Oh yeah!"

"Yeah!"

I was in. I was being treated as an equal. After that, when they chose up sides, I was included.

It was the kind of neighborhood that many men of my generation would probably recognize from their own boyhood. There was certainly nothing plushy about the apartments and small houses along our street. Neither was there anything about them to stir up a social worker's interest. It was the kind of place in which you grow up expecting no more than an interesting amount of trouble, and no special favors.

There were certain things you could count on: the Saturday movie, penny candy, a blue suit for church and a new pair of corduroy knickers for the first day of school every fall. Other things you knew you had to wait for, like a new bike for Christmas, when you got old enough.

Our apartment was pretty much like the others on the street: mohair davenport, with matching easy chair, in the living room; oilcloth-covered table in the kitchen. Through the lace-curtained windows you could see our Ford parked downstairs in the street.

If I had any advantage over the other kids in the neighborhood, it was my father. He was probably as available as any man in the modern history of parenthood. Being the only kid in the family, I had his close attention and the full benefit of his unusual working hours. He started on the job early in the morning, long before I was up; and he was usually home by early afternoon, when school let out and life really began.

Rezin Talbert worked for his father, a partner in the substantial livestock firm of Talbert & McDonald. Just where his unusual first name came from, I never did know. As I later came to realize, it wasn't the only thing Dad never got around to confiding in me, for all the time we spent together.

My grandfather I remember as a tall, impressive gentleman, living by himself in a hotel downtown. He was a widower with a courtly Kentucky-bred manner and an unshakably even disposition. The conversations I had with him, at the hotel or at his office, were always pleasant, and they always ended the same way. "Boy," he would say gravely, before turning back to the papers on his desk, "boy, save your money." It was a piece of advice he delivered with such deep sincerity I've always thought it was a shame he had to waste it on two generations of Talberts — my father and me.

My grandfather was gentle about everything he did and said — perhaps too gentle where his son was concerned. "Reese," as Dad's friends usually called him, didn't exactly get strapped into harness as a member of the family firm. He was left to run pretty much on his own. And there were other things he found more absorbing than the affairs of Talbert & McDonald.

In business, he didn't seem to have the taste for struggle. He was a quiet, serious man, who would often withdraw, after dinner, to a book or a crossword puzzle: he was an intense reader and probably one of the earlier devotees of word games.

These interests, though, seemed at odds with his physique — deep-chested, heavy-shouldered, though not much over average height — and with his face, weathered by outdoor work and also by outdoor play. They were the face and build of an athlete. At college (Transylvania, in Kentucky) Reese had pitched on the baseball team. He had also had a brief fling at professional ball, in the Texas League, before going home to settle uncomfortably into the family business. That role was like a painful masquerade. It still took sports to release the reckless, competitive streak that was a very real part of him.

Dad had much more than a reading knowledge of just about every form of athletics from handball to harness racing. Even though it meant taking time off from the job for a trip to Chicago, he was in the crowd at the second Dempsey-Tunney fight — the one in which Tunney had the benefit of a controversial long knockdown count and eventually won. I stayed home, but my heart was where Dad's money was — in Tunney's corner. Around our neighborhood that fight was a public cause, and a boy could make himself unpopular by rooting against the old champ, Dempsey. It was like rooting for the lions against the Christians. But Tunney, as my father said, was "a gentleman," and that made him worthy of any man's support.

Even when the real purpose of a trip was business — say cattle-buying for the company, in Indiana or Kentucky — Dad would still manage to work in the week end's big college football game, or somehow crowd in an afternoon at the race track. Time was not all he spent there, either. I could vouch for that, because often I was right there with him, trying to root a wrong horse home.

Sometimes my mother came along, too. She was a short, brown-haired woman, good-looking in an unspectacular way, with a Midwestern kind of chatty, neighborly quality. She was deeply absorbed in her family and she had a tendency to worry. It wasn't the ideal temperament for the wife of a horseplayer.

My father, on the other hand, could take a losing day in stride. "Well, Clara," he would tell my mother with a shrug, "if you knew how they were going to run, there wouldn't be any horse race."

That was just about the way he accepted everything in life, good or bad. It was Mother who did all the visible suffering for the family; Dad's feelings were private. It was part of being a gentleman to keep your griefs and your joys to yourself.

The quality of being a gentleman was important to Dad. It was one idea that my grandfather *had* been able to pass along. Around the Talbert house, manners were something you were expected to learn young, along with the use of the dictionary and the proper grip for throwing a curve. You always excused yourself before leaving the table, said "Thank you," and paid attention when you were spoken to. On picnics with other families — summer afternoons when we drove out to LeSourdsville or Indian Lake in the Ford, with a hamper of fried chicken and a jug of iced tea — you were expected to help hand the food around to the grownups before starting to gnaw on a drumstick.

All this was not explicit; it was understood. But occasionally the subject of how to conduct yourself in the company of other people came in for some interesting discussion around the house.

"Did Bob get off all right, this morning?" That was my mother, making dinner-table conversation. My visiting Uncle Bob — the Reverend Mr. Robert Talbert — was a minister in Cape Girardeau, Missouri.

My father nodded. "Caught the early train for St. Louis. . . . You know, Clara," he added after a moment, as if something significant had just struck him, "Bob is the only man I ever saw who knows just exactly how to wish somebody good-by."

"Why, what's there to that?"

"Well, did you ever notice — the way he does it, it really *means* something. It's almost like an art." Dad turned to me. It was one of his more communicative moments. "Wouldn't do you any harm to watch him sometime, Bill."

"Don't be silly," Mother said. "Any boy knows perfectly well how to shake hands and —"

"Not like Bob. It's something he happened to notice, he told me. If you dawdle around, the way most people do, you just make the other fellow feel awkward and uncomfortable. The thing to do is look a man in the eye, shake his hand firmly, just once, tell him 'Come back soon,' or 'Nice to have seen you,' and walk right away."

The first time I tried it, with a friend of my father's whom we met downtown, I whirled, walked into a fire hydrant, and drew a big guffaw. But I was convinced

that, as Dad said, everything was just a matter of practice.

My father seemed to put a lot of effort into the practice
of his own code of behavior. Not only was he a model of
courtliness toward the ladies who were often at our
house, chatting or playing cards with my mother, when
he arrived; but he also carried gentlemanly restraint to
an extreme. He was placid, reserved, a man of long si-
lences. Even when he was taking a bunch of us kids for
hikes through the park (always with a bat and ball), or
when he was driving a carload of us on some kind of
outing, he wasn't really with us — he was still somehow
remote and solitary. I never knew what sort of pain or
doubt of his own he might be holding back. I was only
dimly aware that, when I was a small boy, he had had
something called a nervous breakdown, and I didn't know
what that meant. It was somehow typical of him that,
after a while, he had simply made up his mind to leave
the hospital, and had walked out by his own choice.
It was typical of him that he never mentioned it after-
ward, and I suppose it was also typical of me that, even
much later when I was grown up, I never asked him
about that private part of his life.

I had a constant, unsatisfied craving to share his confidence; I settled for his company. When he was showing
me, during some of those afternoon hours together, how
to charge a ground ball or how to get your shoulders
behind the swing of a bat, he never became overenthusi-
astic with praise. Still, I could see he was pleased with
the way I handled myself. I was fairly quick, better co-

ordinated than most boys my age, and I had an instinct
for games — an ability to anticipate. As soon as the ball
left the bat, I knew which way to move for it.

Baseball was our common passion. Dad's free afternoons allowed us to become two of the most regular customers at Redland Field, the Cincinnati Reds' home
ground before it became Crosley Field and they became
the Redlegs. If, by any chance, Dad couldn't make it
himself, he'd often take me down to the gate and stand
there with me until we found some grownup who would
accompany me through the turnstile.

My father used to say that even the President of the
United States couldn't keep his son out of the ball park,
and that wasn't empty exaggeration. When Mr. Coolidge
paid a visit to Cincinnati, Dad offered to take me downtown to watch him arrive — might even arrange it so
I could get to shake the Presidential hand.

"Today?" I said, appalled at the whole idea. "Eppa
Rixey's pitching today!" It had to be somebody *really*
important before I'd pass up Eppa Rixey.

The magic that I found at the ball park was probably
a little different from the kind that most boys feel —
perhaps even brighter. I had the kind of appetite for the
game itself that other kids had for the hot dogs. What I
felt was the special quality of spring sunlight falling
across the infield, not just its warmth in the stands. I used
to listen for the sure ring of a ball hit truly. When Horace
Ford, the Cincinnati shortstop, dove and, in what seemed
to be a single perfect motion, scooped up a ball and
snapped it to Hughie Critz on second base, I could

almost feel the slight satisfying sting of the ball against my own palm. And I heard the cheers the way the players must have heard them. Even from my seat in the grandstand deck above third base, I was not so much a part of the crowd as part of the game. I lived all nine innings as if I were down there on the field with the players.

I knew what it was like down there because I also spent hours in the locker room, listening to the players talk about their special trade and their lives off the field. Sometimes it was my school pal, John Ogden, who took me behind the scenes; his father was a pitcher on the Reds' staff. Sometimes it was my father, who knew many of the ballplayers himself. Critz, Ford, Rixey, Charlie Dressen. . . . I knew them not just as heroes but as men. Like my own father, they talked about high rent and horses and poker; and they could admit to being baffled by a fastball, just as I was.

Whatever else Cincinnati may have been — market place, commercial center, river port — it was also a great sportsman's town; and my father, though not at all a gregarious man, seemed to know people in every field of the city's busy sports life. I grew up on speaking terms with athletes, feeling that my place was among them.

Once my father presented me to Sunny Jim Bottomley, a historic figure among major league first basemen. He was not a permanent member of the local sporting scene at that time, but a regular passer-through, as a player for the St. Louis Cardinals.

Mr. Bottomley was a huge, hearty man — the perfect figure of a professional athlete.

"How old are you, Bill?"

"Nine, going on ten."

"I suppose you're gonna be President of the United States some day?"

"No, sir."

"Oh, you want a real *big* job." He winked at my father. "What are you gonna be, then?"

"Infielder."

"After college," my father put in.

"Oh, sure," I said, "first I'm going to college, and *then* I'm going to be an infielder."

Mr. Bottomley laughed. "Okay, Bill. Just as long as it ain't first base you've got your eye on. I want to hold on to my job for a few years yet."

Maybe Mr. Bottomley didn't take the whole idea very seriously, but I did. Fireman, cop, soldier in General Pershing's army — none of those usual boyhood ambitions had ever touched me. I can't remember wanting to be anything, up to that point, but a major league shortstop. Because Sunny Jim, the ideal major leaguer, was left-handed, I learned to bat and throw lefty.

Baseball wasn't just recreation to me; it was the very center of life. I had trouble finding my stride in school until I discovered the sports pages. I learned to read in order to master the box scores. My first geography lesson was to learn the location of the major league cities, with the help of Dad and the atlas from the living room bookshelf.

Chicago, Illinois (the Cubs and White Sox), St. Louis, Missouri (Browns and Cardinals), New York, New York (Yankees and Giants). . . as baseball capitals, all these places took on a glamorous interest, and school stopped being a problem. For the rest of my classroom life, I never had to worry very much about grades; and long after I'd left school days behind, I found excitement in the name of any place far from home.

The name of Cape Girardeau, where my Uncle Bob lived, carried a special ring of adventure, the summer before my tenth birthday, because I was going there on my own. For weeks beforehand, I traced the railroad route in the atlas. Finally, armed with an impressive-looking ticket and a copy of *Baseball Magazine, I* was put aboard the train.

Bob was waiting for me when the train pulled into the dusty station at Cape Girardeau, then turned over to my Cousin Ike, his teen-age son, the job of keeping me entertained. Ike is now a psychologist at Texas Christian University, and I may well have been the one who drove him into that field. He spent much of that week trying unsuccessfully to talk me into going with him to the local tennis courts so he could play a couple of sets. That, however, was one sport at which I drew the line.

"Tennis?" I said, with unconcealed disgust. "That sissy game?"

When I got back home to Cincinnati, Dad had some plans for the two of us which were much more worth while. "Why don't we get in a couple of days' fishing before school starts?" he said.

I didn't need any coaxing. I loved the drive across the river and into the smoke-colored hills of Kentucky, Dad quiet behind the wheel, the creels rattling on the floor behind us. I liked the cold blue stream at the place with the fine rugged name of Kinnekenick, the way the reel came to life in your hands as a bass struck at the bait, the wonderful sense of triumph as you brought your prize in after what seemed like hours of struggle.

I did it by myself, the way Dad had showed me. He didn't reach out a hand to help, didn't offer a word of advice until the moment the line tensed, the rod bowed and I thought I would surely lose my bass. "Now!" Dad said sharply. I reeled in as fast as I could.

Afterwards, I walked back with my father toward the farmhouse where we were staying. I felt important and grown-up.

"Dad," I said, "what I was telling Mr. Bottomley that time . . ."

"*Mm?*" He lit a cigarette.

"I mean, when I get to be in the major leagues . . ."

"You just keep working at it, Bill."

"Uh-huh," I said. I quickened my step to keep up with him. "You know what I'm going to do? I'm going to get you and Mom tickets for every single game."

I had no doubt at all that it would work out just that way. After all, as long as you did what you were supposed to . . . as long as you tried hard and did it well . . . as long as you had your Dad around just in case you needed that one word of encouragement, that one gesture of support . . . how could anything go wrong?

For the Rest of My Life

I CAME bursting into the apartment one March afternoon, halfway between my tenth and eleventh birthdays, and headed for the kitchen — which in itself was nothing unusual.

"Mom!" I called out. "Paper's here!"

I unfolded the square I had picked up downstairs and handed her the front part, which contained nothing but another report on Admiral Byrd's expedition to the South Pole and a picture of the new President, Mr. Hoover. I spread the sports page out on the table.

"For heaven's sake!" my mother said. "Don't gulp your milk like that. You'll give yourself cramps."

I nodded. "Okay." Still panting, I poured myself another large dollop, then rinsed out the glass and drew a drink of water from the faucet.

She watched me closely. "What's the matter with you?"

"Thirsty." I started to wipe my sleeve across my mouth, but caught myself. I took out my handkerchief.

"Ogden and me want to go to the movies Saturday. By ourselves."

"That depends what's playing."

"William Boyd in *The Leatherneck*."

"A war picture?"

"I think it's cowboys." I returned the milk bottle to the icebox, leaving the wooden door open. "Anything good to eat?" Rummaging around, I took a couple of slices of last night's ham.

"Hey, want to hear a good one?" I said, buttering a slice of bread. "What did the tablecloth say to the table?" That was a great year for bringing home jokes and riddles. "Give up?"

She nodded.

"'Gotcha covered.'" I took a wolfish bite of ham sandwich. "Don't you get it? 'Gotcha covered.'"

"Bill, what's got into you?"

I put the sandwich down, surprised. "It's only a joke," I said.

"I know. I mean the way you're eating. You had a great big lunch, and . . ." She put her hand to my forehead — that automatic motherly gesture for all unusual occasions, like a case of sniffles or saying no to ice cream.

"I'm hungry," I explained.

"You're always hungry lately. And I've never seen anybody drink water the way you do. Do you feel all right?"

"Sure." I finished the sandwich. "What about the movie?"

Mother answered abstractedly, "I suppose so."

When Saturday came, I was just too tired for the movie. All week I had been that way. Even the usual afternoon ball game had seemed like too much effort. I climbed the stairs wearily and flopped down on my bed, exhausted.

Meanwhile, the peculiar habits that my mother had noticed continued. At school I never passed the drinking fountain in the hall without stopping, and I was always holding up a whole line of kids behind me because I couldn't seem to satisfy my thirst. At the dinner table, I ate like a castaway rescued by the French Line; yet I was losing so much weight that I had to keep hitching up the belt of my corduroys. At night, I could hardly wait to get to bed, but all through the night I kept getting up to go to the bathroom. Sometimes, when I got up, the light was still on in the kitchen, and I could hear Mom and Dad talking about me in worried tones.

One Friday afternoon, when I got home from school, they were waiting for me, dressed to go out. I put on a jacket and tie, and we drove downtown to the Union Central Building.

Feeling strange and scared, I was delivered into the hands of two doctors, who spent a lot of time asking me personal questions, thumping me in various places, drawing blood and taking a urine sample. "Dr. Walt," as I was urged to call the taller and older of the two, then patted my shoulder and sent me back to the waiting room.

I sat there between my parents for several years, leafing through the copies of *Liberty*, and wishing that doctors at least had enough sense to stock some decent reading matter, like *Baseball Magazine*.

A nurse appeared at the door, smiled briefly and motioned to my parents. Dad got up and followed her inside. Mother stayed with me, pretending to read her *Deline-*

ator, gripping the unturned pages so hard that her knuckles showed white. When we were finally called into the office, Mother gave a small, nervous sigh and hurried me in ahead of her.

Dad was sitting there, his face showing nothing. Dr. Walt got up from behind the desk and put his arm around me.

"Bill," he said, "your Dad's been telling us that you're a good soldier. He says you know how to follow orders."

I looked puzzledly at my father. I didn't understand. I wished they'd spoon out the awful-tasting medicine you got from doctors, and then we could go home.

"I'm going to have to give you some orders," Dr. Walt went on, "and you're not going to like them very much, I'm afraid. You're going to have to be very careful about everything you eat. There are quite a few things we can't let you do. Games, running around . . ."

He turned to my mother, as if this were something he'd been trying to avoid but knew he would have to arrive at sooner or later. "Mrs. Talbert," he said, "Bill has diabetes."

Mother gasped sharply and buried her face in her hands. Dad stirred in his chair, helpless and uncomfortable as always in the presence of any strong emotion. He cleared his throat. "What should we do?" he said.

"Well," Dr. Walt resumed briskly. He seemed relieved to get on with the business at hand. "The first thing we've got to do is get this young man into Children's Hospital. That's where we'll start working out the insulin — find out just how much he's going to need. Let's see . . ." He consulted the calendar on his desk. "We'd better get him in on Monday. Meanwhile, plenty of rest — that's going to be one of the important things from now on. And a special diet, of course."

He turned to my mother. "Don't worry about all those details just yet, Mrs. Talbert. We'll give you all the help you'll need. The important thing is to start learning — all three of you. . . . Because," he finished quietly, "this is something you'll all have to live with."

Mother bit her lip. "How long will it be, Doctor?"

The doctor hesitated. This was the point that he must have always come to, sooner or later, with other children and their parents.

"Mrs. Talbert," he said, "there is no such thing as a cure for diabetes."

In the history of medicine's conquest of diabetes, 1928 was an early date. It was only seven years before that science had found a remedy enabling the diabetic to stay alive. A normal kind of existence was still beyond any patient's expectations. When a mother was told that her child had diabetes, it meant that life had suddenly shriveled down to a narrow, hollow shape. From now on, each day would be confined by constant dangers.

Since then the remedy has been developed further and the shape of life has expanded, although there is still no cure for diabetes. Even its cause remains a mystery.

A number of clues have been collected over the years; a number of deductions have been made from them and a few possibilities have been ruled out. Diabetes is known to occur most often not among children but in the middle-aged. It is far more common among overweight people than thin or average ones. Statistics indicate that it can be inherited if there have been cases on both sides of the family. In my family, there had been no diabetes that we knew of, on either side, and I certainly wasn't a fat boy. I couldn't have "picked up" diabetes anywhere, because it isn't contagious; it's nothing you can catch from another child at school or another man at the office, from a drinking glass or a used towel. As far as doctors know, it isn't caused by poor diet.

Actually, diabetes isn't a disease at all; it's what might be called a biological fault.

Normally, the human body makes efficient use of all foods. The proteins, contained mainly in meat, eggs, milk and some vegetables, provide growth and replacement of tissues. The carbohydrates, concentrated most highly in sweet and starchy things like bread, potatoes and candy, are converted to simple sugars in the intestinal tract and stored as the body's chief source of energy. Fats, found mostly in meat and dairy products, are built up as a reserve source of energy.

In the diabetic, however, the body is unable to make maximum use of foods, especially of carbohydrates. Instead of converting and storing the sugars fully, it passes some of them on, through the bloodstream, into the kidneys. Beyond a certain capacity, the kidneys cannot hold them, and excrete them in the urine.

Starved for energy, the body keeps demanding more food; but unable to use it, the body tires. Eventually it starts seeking energy from the alternate source — fats. But when fats are used, they give off an acid; and if too much acid is produced, the result is a condition known as acidosis, in which the diabetic symptoms grow worse.

Until the early 1920's, there were only a couple of things a doctor could do for a diabetic. He could put him on a near-starvation diet, keeping him away from anything containing sugar or starch. At the same time, the doctor could keep him inactive, so the body would need little energy and would not have to use its fats. Even so, unless the diabetic condition was only slight, it was only a matter of time before the condition deteriorated. Fatigue gave way to a deep lassitude, then to coma, and finally to death.

People still die of diabetes or from complications of it, but ever since 1921 the picture has been brightening. That was the year a Canadian surgeon named Frederick Banting and a medical student named Charles Best, working together, discovered the substance that helps convert foods in the digestive system. This is the hormone called insulin, a chemical produced by a gland called the pancreas, which is located behind the stomach. Subsequently, it has been found that several other glands also influence the effectiveness of insulin. These are the adrenal glands, the pituitary and the thyroid. When the pancreas fails to produce enough insulin, or when the insulin is somehow nullified by the action of the other glands, the sugar content of the blood and urine increase, and the symptoms of diabetes appear.

Banting and Best discovered, however, that if you

extract insulin from the pancreas of slaughtered beef or pork and inject it into the bloodstream of a diabetic, his body can make more efficient use of carbohydrates. The sugar content of the blood will drop and the symptoms will diminish.

To science the discovery made by Banting and Best was considered so important that they were rewarded with Nobel prizes. To diabetics, 1921 ranks pretty close to 1492 among the memorable dates of history, Banting and Best rate as popular heroes, and insulin is probably the most important single word in the language. It means, after all, the difference between life and death.

The session at Dr. Walt's office had warned me vaguely that something was about to change. In the next couple of weeks at Children's Hospital the new pattern took shape. There was a strange, dreary new way of looking at everything.

Food, for instance. It was no longer something that either you liked or was good for you. Now it was a form of treatment. There were lists and categories as important and as rigorous as "The Early Explorers and Their Countries" in social studies.

There were the "Foods to be Eaten in Moderation" — mostly things like cauliflower, asparagus and eggplant, all the less starchy vegetables, which no ten-year-old was apt to go overboard for, anyway. There were the foods you could really load up on — exciting dishes like clear broth and unsweetened gelatin. Above all, there were the "Foods to be Shunned" — namely cake, ice cream, almost any sweets; the things a ten-year-old considers the staff of life. Sugar, as the doctors were explaining to my parents during regular educational sessions, had to be rigidly limited to the amounts that the insulin could take care of.

That was a serious blow, but I was prepared to make the best of it.

"Candy and stuff — that isn't too good for you, anyway," I assured the dietitian, who was, at the same time, coaching me. "If you only eat the things that are good for you, you can run the bases twice as fast."

"Running bases?" The nurse who was plumping the pillow behind me gave me a stern, first sergeant's glance. "Now, we can't have any of that, young man. Plenty of rest — that's what we're going to need from now on."

Rest, my parents were being told, was still an important part of the formula. On his low-sugar diet, a diabetic had to save his energy.

It was all one long lesson in arithmetic — almost like going to school in a classroom with beds instead of desks. Meals were not so much food to be enjoyed as figures to be added and subtracted. There was a printed sheet called a calorie chart, with figures on it for everything — the sugar content of various-sized portions. There was also a set of portable scales, placed before you at every meal, and as inescapable as a knife and fork. Every spoonful of food had to be weighed, gram by gram, before you dared to swallow a bite. But the most shocking new fact of life was the insulin injection, three times a day.

"Now, this is our syringe, where the insulin goes. And here, on the end, is our needle." The nurse paused, holding the wicked-looking instrument in mid-air. "Bill, are you paying attention?"

"Yes, ma'am." I eyed the needle warily.

"Now, we just stick the point into the skin — gently, the way you've seen the doctor do it. . . . Now," the nurse concluded, handing me the syringe, "let's see you try it — on Andy, here."

Andy, the lucky stiff, couldn't feel a thing. He, or rather, it, was the rag doll the hospital staff used to teach young diabetics how to give themselves insulin injections. Which is something like teaching a drunk to take up milkshakes — you can't expect him to enjoy it. I kept wondering how I was ever going to be able to stick that needle into my own thigh.

As in school, too, the hospital routine was crowded with tests — constant examinations of the blood and urine, to measure the sugar content. This morning, the sugar was up, so your before-breakfast insulin dosage was increased. On the next test, in the afternoon, would the sugar be down — and would it be down far enough?

In my mind, sugar — that innocent, tempting stuff that you used to swipe in cubes from the kitchen cupboard — began to take on the shape of the devil. It seemed to me I was locked in an endless wrestling match with it, and the tests told who was winning — it or me. Each day, I waited for the results with all the apprehensiveness of a horseplayer waiting for news from the track.

Three weeks of waiting, three times a day. Then, finally, the event that I had begun to think would never happen.

I sat on my hospital bed, my legs dangling over the edge, Mother and Dad in the visitors' chairs beside me. We were all watching the doctor's face as he glanced over the latest test results.

"You've got your sugar down now. You seem to be in pretty good shape." He gave me an approving smile. "Good work, Bill!"

I felt as if I had just beat out Bill Terry for the National League batting championship, or at least got a 100 in spelling.

What the doctors had now found was the balance between the food I needed and the insulin required to digest it — the amount of insulin I would have to take every day in order to stay alive. I was ready to leave the hospital, to take up a kind of life different from everything that I had known before. The new facts of life were already pretty clear to me: From now on, I would have to learn to stick myself with a needle. I would have to do it, not just once in a while, but every single day. I would have to keep doing it, not just for months or for years, but all the rest of my life.

The most important change of all was one that, I could tell, had struck my father pretty hard. As we started home together — my suitcase in the back seat with Mother; Dad and I up front — I tried, in my turn, now, to find the word that would help him.

"Dad," I said, "even if I can't play baseball any more, maybe someday I can write about it."

That was the only time I can remember seeing my father cry.

On the Sidelines

THE DAY I went back to school, there was a little welcoming speech from the teacher, assuring me that all the boys and girls in the fifth grade were glad to see me back. Privately, there were also a lot of awed questions about what they do to you in a hospital. My social status was roughly that of wartime GI released from several years in an enemy prison camp.

The role of returned hero lasted exactly two hours. It ended when the bell rang for recess, and we marched out to the daily interclass games. At that point I fell back to what soon became my permanent position: I was the boy who sat and watched.

One day, after school let out for the summer, I sat in the sun on the front steps of the house. John Ogden came by, dressed in a slightly oversized pair of khaki scout pants.

I held up my bag of marbles. "Play you a game," I offered.

"I don't feel like it," he said. "We're going on a camp-out. You want to come?"

"I don't know."

"We're going to sleep over. All night!"

I thought about asking permission, but I realized there wouldn't be much point in it. "Can't," I said. "I have to hang around and take my insulin."

Ogden squinted at me in disbelief. "Are you still sick?"

"I'm not sick," I said. "I'm just diabetic."

The distinction was lost on him.

"Boy, can't you ever do anything?"

"Sure," I said, without conviction.

"Like what?"

I held up the bag of marbles again. "I told you, I'll have you a game."

"I don't even have any with me."

"I'll lend you some," I offered eagerly. "Or we could play for funs."

"I'm tired of marbles." He shifted from one foot to the other. "Well," he said finally, "I better go."

I settled for a game with Dad, later that afternoon, on the living room rug.

The daily game, in the living room or outdoors, was something Dad had started, soon after my return from the hospital. Even in this remote form of sports he had a knack, which I soon picked up. Considering all the time I had to practice, it wasn't surprising that I had become the most accurate shooter in the neighborhood — when I could get somebody to play with. Most kids, like Ogden had more exciting things to do. Pretty soon they stopped asking me to join them.

We moved, that fall. The neighborhood was much like the old one: apartment houses, small homes, a park where the other kids played ball in the afternoons. The only reason we made the change was diabetes. Now we were closer to school. The walk home seemed less of a risk. There was a high school, too, only a block away. When the time came, I would still be able to come home for my noontime insulin shot and for lunch. I would not have to run the daily hazards of eating out, at the school cafeteria. An invisible spoonful of shortening in a sauce, a few unknown grams of sugar — anything you couldn't actually see and measure might upset the balance between diet and insulin.

It was a year before I finally undertook the great adventure of eating a meal away from the scales and our own kitchen. By then Mother, Dad and I all knew the food lists by heart. With constant practice I had acquired the knack of sizing up portions and weights at a glance. I could measure out 150 grams of dried apricots by hand; I knew just what size orange or how large a serving of broccoli I could substitute for them without exceeding my quota of sugar. I was as proud of my skill as a boardwalk weight-guesser.

Even so, eating out seemed like too much of a gamble to take without hedging, so we went to a cafeteria, where everything was on display and I could make my own choice, item by item.

It was a big event for me. I carried my tray to the table like a trophy. With a wonderful sense of daring, I worked my way through soup, meat, vegetables and salad, lingering over each dish to stretch the experience to its fullest. But as I started my dessert of unsweetened grapefruit, my courage started to drain. I left the dessert half-eaten, and fidgeted for my coat. I couldn't wait to get home. And when Dad turned the key in the door, the first thing I did was to rush for the bathroom, to test for sugar.

Sugar was still a *bête noire*. Once or twice a day, a few drops of urine, diluted in a solution, had to be boiled and examined for the color that showed the presence of sugar and the amount. Even if I managed to escape the tell-tale sign at home, there was always the threat that it might show up in the tests the nurses made on our visits to the hospital clinic every month or so. Each visit was an event I looked forward to with nothing but dread. All through my schoolboy years, I knew kids who were afraid of failing tests in spelling, English, history, math; I lived in fear of flunking a urine test.

By the time I was ready for that daily one-block walk to high school, I had spent almost four years as a diabetic, and I had come to accept it as a way of living. It wasn't, after all, anything you could really complain about. I felt no pain, not even the fatigue I'd had back at the beginning. In fact, as time went on, as insulin and diet took control of the problem, I felt no less fit, no less full of energy than I had back in the days when I was running loose with the rest of the kids.

That was the only thing that really bothered me: I felt okay; I wasn't any less capable than the other guys of fielding grounders or swinging a bat or (a sport that was beginning to take on a certain appeal) chasing girls head-long off the pier at Indian Lake. But however I felt, and whatever I wanted to do, there was that standing rule that warned me: "You're a diabetic. Stay under wraps." I had to think of myself as different.

In my forced retreat from life, I had taken one important thing with me: my love of baseball. Even though it was at best a poor substitute for a real game, I still enjoyed tossing a ball back and forth with Dad. As a spectator, I spent even more time than before at the Cincinnati ball park.

One day, between seasons, a piece of exciting news came rocketing around the circle of fans in the freshman class: Sunny Jim Bottomley had been traded to the Reds! From now on, I wouldn't have to wait for the Cardinals to come to town. Sunny Jim and his murderous bat would be on display at Redland Field every home game of the season.

On opening day, the Pittsburgh Pirates came to town, and Dad and I were out there to see Sunny Jim's debut in a home-team uniform. We sat in a box right down on the first base line, where we could watch him at close range. Although Cincinnati lost, its new first baseman performed heroically: he had the solidest hit of the game — a lofty triple — and scored the Reds' only run.

As Cincinnati went out in the ninth inning, and the final score was posted, a pack of kids broke from the stands and intercepted Sunny Jim on his way to the dressing room. He stopped to sign their score cards.

"You want to go over and say hello?" Dad suggested.

"He won't remember me, will he?"

"He'll remember the name. Bet he'll get a kick out of seeing you again."

I climbed over the low railing in front of the box. The green turf felt wonderful underfoot — fresh and lively. Instead of heading for the cluster of fans around Sunny Jim, I walked out to the infield, and started down the first base line. A groundskeeper growled at me, "All right, kid, let's clear the field." I paid no attention to him.

I ticked the bag tentatively with my foot, and stood there for a moment. Then, for no special reason, I started, at a trot, toward second base. As soon as I did that, something curious happened: all restraint seemed to leave me; I felt free and weightless. Now, like a little kid, I broke into a run — something I hadn't been allowed to do for years.

I heard somebody yell behind me — it may have been Dad, maybe one of the field police — but I didn't stop. I rounded second at full tilt, automatically touching it with my left foot, to save steps — a vestige of my baseball training, years before. Nothing seemed important except to run, and keep on running. I touched third without breaking stride, and raced for home, as if I were carrying the winning run in a world series. A few yards from home, I flung myself recklessly into the dirt, feet first, and slid joyously into home.

A cop pulled me to my feet. He must have been chasing me down the line. The stragglers in the stands seemed to have enjoyed the performance — they laughed and cheered as I dusted myself off, grinning with a mixture of satisfaction and embarrassment.

Dad came over, wearing a worried look, and took me off the policeman's hands.

"That was a kid stunt," he said. "You know they don't want fans running all over the field."

"I know."

"Especially you. You're not supposed to do things like that."

"I couldn't help it," I said. "I just felt like it." Grim as he was trying to sound, he didn't really seem angry.

In the car, on the way home, he kept glancing at me. "You feel all right?" he asked.

"Sure," I said, with some conviction. "I feel fine."

He spent one of his rare smiles. "I'll bet you do." We pulled up at a stop light, and he shook a cigarette from a pack and lit it. "Be sure you get that dirt off your clothes before your mother sees you."

He didn't say any more about it. All the way home, he seemed to be working something over in his mind.

V

Novice

IT took my father a couple of weeks to reach his decision and carry it out. In that time — in his unemotional, down-to-work fashion, and without saying a word about it to Mother or me — he found a way to redirect the whole course of my life.

That afternoon, Dad came home late. "I had to make a couple of stops downtown," he explained. Deadpan, without so much as a hint of the bombshell that he was about to explode in the Talbert household, he put a bulky, odd-shaped package in my hands. "I brought you something," he said simply.

I tore the wrappings loose.

"A tennis racket," I said. Wrapped with it was a single white tennis ball. I held them, the racket in one hand, the ball in the other, not knowing quite what to make of the gift. Tennis was one sport in which neither of us had ever shown any special interest.

"Well, what do you say?" Dad asked.

I looked at him, puzzled. "Oh. Thanks, Dad." I glanced around the apartment, wondering where I was expected to hang these pieces of sporting bric-a-brac.

"I mean how would you like to learn the game?"

"You mean *play* tennis?"

"Reesy!" my mother said, in a tone as shocked as if Dad had invited me to a stag party at a shady hotel. "That isn't funny."

"I'm not trying to be funny, Clara. I've —"

"You can't be serious. You know Bill is sick."

"I'm not sick," I said automatically. "I'm just dia —"

"Well, he isn't *helpless*," my father broke in. "Damn it, Clara, haven't you even noticed? Do you think he *enjoys* sitting around all day, while the other boys run around doing things? Do you think that's his idea of fun? He's a strong, healthy kid."

For Dad, that amounted to an oration, and for him to raise his voice above the level of offhand comment was rare enough to startle Mother into tears.

"Healthy!" she said, sniffling into her handkerchief.

"All right," Dad said. "He has to take his insulin, he has to watch his diet. That doesn't mean he's an invalid, Clara." He turned to me. "Am I right, Bill? Wouldn't you like to do something, for a change?"

"Sure," I said, rather tentatively.

"How about some tennis, then?"

Much as I had been yearning to cut loose, as I had for just those few careless moments at the ball park, still the habit of thinking of myself as an invalid wasn't easy to cast off so suddenly. Neither was the prejudice I had expressed once, years before, when my Cousin Ike had tried to introduce me to tennis. Tennis wasn't a game that filled college stadiums or downtown ball parks, that made the big headlines on the sports page, that boys learned before they could read. Everybody recognized the names of Babe Ruth and Lou Gehrig; but who had ever become famous with a tennis racket?

"There's no fun in tennis," I said.

Dad picked up the racket and bounced the ball on the strings, thoughtfully. "It's better than just sitting around," he suggested.

I considered that. "I'll try it."

"Please be sensible," Mother said. "Both of you." She dabbed her eyes. "Reesy, let's talk to the doctor about it. If he says yes, then . . ." She made a gesture of resignation. I'm sure she thought that this condition would dispose of the whole question. She knew that, as far as the doctors were concerned, exercise for diabetics was forbidden.

"I was trying to tell you, Clara," Dad said firmly. "I've already talked to the doctor. That's where I went this afternoon."

It was Dr. Walt who, some years after, told me about the scene that had taken place in his office earlier that day.

Together, Dad and Dr. Walt went over the records of my visits to the clinic and to the doctor's office during the last four years. Dr. Walt had to agree that I'd been doing very well. Except for a couple of minor incidents, just after I left the hospital, I had had no bad times.

"The only trouble is," Dad said, pointing to the sheaf of records, "that's no life for a fourteen-year-old boy. You know how kids are at this age, Doc — full of beans, always wanting to do things."

"What do you think he'd like to do?"

"You know what I mean. Bill's always been interested in sports."

Dr. Walt began to pace the office. "Reese," he said, "I think you understand the problem in that."

It was the old story: exercise required energy, energy required sugar, and sugar was the great bugaboo to the diabetic. By careful control of diet, I was being allowed to take in just enough sugar to maintain life at a quiet, inactive pace. The carefully regulated insulin injections were enabling me to use that sugar safely. Wasn't that enough?

"No," my father said flatly.

Dr. Walt looked at him for a moment. "I agree with you," he said.

Quite a few doctors, it seemed, were beginning to think that diabetics were being held back unnecessarily. Insulin, after all, had introduced an entirely new factor into the problem — a means of control. So far, it was being used mainly as an item of equipment in an impersonal kind of chemistry, to hold down the sugar level of the blood. But didn't this mean the diabetic himself now could do things forbidden to him before?

Possibly, Dr. Walt said, but there would be risks. It was fairly easy to determine the amount of energy, and therefore of sugar, a person needed to perform the routine motions of daily life — getting dressed, walking certain limited distances, doing ordinary jobs. It was a much different matter trying to predict the rate at which energy was used, and sugar burned, in any kind of sport. If a game ran especially long, or the play ran especially hard, a diabetic would be using up his energy at a fast rate, and the insulin might be left with no sugar to work on. He would then run into a second major hazard — the one at the opposite extreme from diabetic coma. This is the condition called insulin reaction, the effects of which come on more suddenly and can be just as dangerous.

There was only one way to work out a new equation of insulin, diet and that third, alien factor, exercise. This was on the basis of individual experience. Even then, the results wouldn't be foolproof. The diabetic would have to learn to recognize the danger-signs of insulin reaction himself, and take prompt countermeasures.

He would also have to take prompt, efficient care of routine cuts and bruises, the normal attrition of sports, because, in the opinion of some doctors, diabetics are more susceptible to infection than most people.

"In other words," Dr. Walt summarized, "there isn't a lot I can do for Bill. But if he's willing to work at it, there may be something he can do for himself."

"If it's sports," Dad assured him, "or anything that gives him a chance to move around, he'll work at it."

"If I were you," the doctor said, "I'd try him on tennis."

Any form of athletics, from tournament archery to three-legged racing at a Fourth of July picnic, has its satisfactions. But for someone looking for a sport that he can practise regularly and over a long period of years, tennis offers special advantages. In the first place, it has the two basic requirements of sport: it's highly competitive and it's physically challenging. You have to react to every single ball hit from the other side of the net, whether you're playing singles or with a partner. And when you've finished a few sets, you know you've been using muscles that aren't normally required in signing office memos or doing dishes.

At the same time, you don't actually need tremendous speed or agility to get some fun out of the game, which means you can keep up the habit of playing long after your baseball, football or basketball years are behind you. At any public court you are apt to find men of fifty-five or sixty hitting away at a tennis ball, and the late kings of Sweden and Norway, Gustav and Haakon, were both still ranging the courts well into their eighties.

Above all, tennis doesn't require rounding up a couple of teams every time you want an hour or so of competitive exercise. Neither can you play the sport alone, as in swimming. You need just one other person — and for a diabetic, it's a good idea to have someone around while exercising, in case you should run into trouble.

For all the encouragement Dad had got from the doctor, my mother was sure we were headed for nothing *but* trouble, that first day when we walked across the street to the park and the public tennis courts. She couldn't even bear to face the trial, herself. Dad and I left her at home, still full of doubt and foreboding.

Dad, on the other hand, was his usual calm self. His advice to me was brief and simple: "You just keep your eye on that ball," he told me, as if this were no more eventful than one of our old-time batting-practice sessions, and nothing were any different from where we'd left off, four years before.

In the afternoons, the courts at Coy Field were in the custody of a tall, muscular guy of about twenty, named Roy Fitzgerald, a University of Cincinnati football player to whom the job meant a few weekly dollars toward his college expenses. He also had a personal interest in tennis and a sound knowledge of its fundamentals, which he didn't mind passing on to the younger kids who used the courts. Dad put me in his hands.

"Now," Roy said, after showing me how to take a firm grip on the racket, "I'm going to tell you the first three things to remember about this game. First, you want to watch the ball. You have to hit it before you can put it away. Then, when you do hit it, your feet should be parallel to the net. Don't be facing the net, the way some kids always want to do. Finally, start your swing with the racket-head below the ball, not coming down over it. Watch me now. Always step into that ball. Get your shoulder into the swing."

"Like when you're batting," I offered, "in baseball."

"Right. You get over on the other side of the net, now, and we'll try a few."

I bounced the ball on the asphalt surface and swung. The ball arced across the steel net.

"Level that swing," Roy called across, sending it back. I ran up, checked myself, brought the racket around, and again managed to connect.

From the beginning, the satisfaction was enormous. Compared with the narrow surface of a baseball bat, the fat area of a tennis racket was a pleasure. In baseball, you were lucky if you connected once out of three or four times. With this unfamiliar weapon, I found I could hit the ball nine times out of ten.

"This is easy," I said to my father, as I stopped to pick up a stray ball.

From across the net, Roy grinned. "A couple more and we'll knock off." He hit one down the sidelines to my right. I ran for it, hit it back to him, then had to reverse myself immediately and dash for the opposite side of the court, as his return headed for the farthest corner. With a lunging effort, I brought my backhand around, missed and fell full-length on the hard surface.

As I lay there, catching my breath, Dad tensed forward from the park bench where he was sitting, but relaxed as I got to my feet.

"You all right?" Roy said. He jumped the net.

"Sure," I said, hitching up my trousers.

Dad walked over, deliberately, and checked my elbows, hands and knees. No blood. "Not as easy as you thought," he said, "is it?"

"I should have got that one," I said.

Roy laughed. "Come around tomorrow and we'll really give you something to run for."

I looked at my father.

"No reason you can't," he said.

As we headed back toward the house, I noticed that the ground around his bench was littered with cigarette butts. He must have smoked a pack in the hour I'd been on the court.

That was early in May. Every day after that, as long as

the weather was anything better than pouring rain, I
went over to Coy Field, armed with my racket, tennis
balls, and a few lumps of sugar. That was the emergency ration Dr. Walt and I decided to try — a quick
way of raising the blood sugar when exercise had burned
it too fast, and therefore a quick, crude defense against
the risk of insulin reaction. I had been startled when Dr.
Walt proposed it. Sugar, after all, was something to be
scared of. But I was willing to try anything. Sometimes,
after I'd been run around the court especially hard by
Roy or one of the teen-aged regulars who played there,
I would feel my breathing become quick and shallow,
my control of strokes becoming suddenly erratic. A lump
of sugar, or its equivalent in a bar of chocolate, I found,
would bring me back to normal within a matter of minutes. I was encountering no serious trouble, and for the
first time in years I began once again to look forward to
every new day with the old eagerness.

If there is such a thing as a natural — if tennis players
are born, not made — then I wasn't it. Even though I had
outgrown the "runt" classification, I still didn't scare anybody just by walking onto the court. Nor did the ball
explode when I hit it. I had all I could do to put a shot
where I wanted it.

"Bring that left hand back!" Roy kept telling me.
"With the racket — right on it! Wait a minute, wait a
minute. Come on over here and I'll show you again."

I walked up to the net and tried, once more, to get the
hang of using the left hand to guide the racket on the

backswing, before letting the right hand make the actual stroke.

"You've just *got* to get that down right," Roy said, "if you ever expect to play this game."

I kept working on that troublesome swing, backhand and forehand. I was anxious to learn, and I felt comfortable, if not at all masterful, with a racket in my hand. The more I played, the more resemblances I found between tennis and baseball. My infielder's instinct — the ability to anticipate the direction and pace of the ball as soon as my opponent hit it — was a good basis on which to learn any kind of game. And the backhand — the stroke that gives almost all young players fits of frustration . . . at least I could understand the principle of it, which was much like learning to bat left-handed.

The strokes kept giving me trouble, but the difficulties didn't spoil my desire to play the game. When Roy called a Saturday practice session for the Coy Field boys' team, or scheduled a match against one of the other parks on a school holiday, some of the team members might favor a movie or some other attraction. I was always at the courts, and — at first probably by default — Roy put me on the team. By mid-summer he had me playing as his Number 2 man, which meant that in the matches against the other parks, I was put up against their second-best player. Just before the big match of the season, Roy told me he was moving me up to Number 1.

At the age of not quite fifteen, barely emerging from the shell of invalidism, I wasn't the cockiest youngster afoot. The prospect of squaring off against the toughest player in town gave me no real pleasure. I hardly slept that night, and I played the match at least half a dozen times in my mind before I even reached the court. When I took my usual test in the morning I found that I had fretted myself right into trouble. The whole diabetic balance was out of whack, something that can happen from nervous strain as well as from improper diet or slipping up on an insulin shot. I felt terrible.

Sick or well, I wasn't good enough to win. Somehow I managed to stick it out, and even made it close. When it was over, Roy introduced me to a man in tennis clothes who had been watching from behind the wire fence. I recognized the name as one that I had heard around our house in connection with business, politics and sports in Cincinnati.

"You played a real fighting game, boy," he said. He looked me over appraisingly. "How old are you?"

"Fifteen — pretty near."

He nodded. "You look pretty wiry. I guess you'll grow some too." I wondered if Roy had said anything to him about the diabetes. I hoped not.

"You're going to enter the city tournament, aren't you?"

"I guess so," I said, mopping wearily at my face with a towel.

He glanced down at my cheap racket. "You'll wear yourself out swinging that fishnet. Here." He put a handsome new racket into my hand. I plucked at the expensive gut with my fingers and marveled at the resonant twang. "Why don't you see how this one feels to you? If you like the weight and the grip, you're welcome to use it."

I should have won that tournament. With Dad, Roy

and the donor of the racket cheering me from behind the fence, I had the finals right in the palm of my hand. In my first season of tennis, I was about to win a championship. Then, casting aside my usual careful game, I started swinging that handsome new racket with a reckless sense of power. In two more shabby sets I threw the match away and walked off the court a loser.

Ashamed of myself, I handed the racket back with a murmured "Thank you very much." I had been given my first glimpse of the rare generosity that tennis, above all other sports, seems to inspire in people who love the game, and I hadn't lived up to it.

On the way home, I couldn't even look Dad in the face. Then and there, I made up my mind to give up tennis, not knowing this was a decision every player makes about as often as a smoker swears off cigarettes.

The next morning, when the sun was bright, the air still, and the courts starting to fill with players, I couldn't stay away. I was beginning to shake the languor that diabetes had imposed on me. I had found something I could do, and I wanted to learn how to do it well. At some cost, I had already learned a couple of valuable lessons, which I would never forget: Never change a winning game. And never let a poorer player get the upper hand. There was nothing wrong in being beaten by a better man, and there could even be much to gain from an honorable loss. But there was no honor in knowing that you could have won a match if you had only tried.

On My Own

IF YOU think of tennis as strictly a warm-weather sport, then you've never met a real tennis nut. There are always a few around any public park, and Coy Field was no exception. I became one of the hard-shelled specimens.

Unwilling to let one season go and impatient for the next to start, we bundled up in heavy sweaters and took down our rackets on days when other young sportsmen were carrying footballs or ice skates, if they went out at all. Even snow was no obstacle; we just carried shovels over to the park along with our tennis rackets and cleared the courts.

When spring came, I was ready for the high school team tryouts. I made the grade as Number 1 in both singles and doubles. I didn't have a losing match all season. The next year's record was almost as clean. I was already established as one of the leading high school players in the state.

But tennis, as the game in the sports page headlines, doesn't mean school or even college teams, playing before crowds of undergraduates and alumni. The real game consists of the annual tournaments for individual players. These are events officially recognized by the ruling body of amateur tennis, the United States Lawn

Tennis Association. They are held at and sponsored by the various private clubs that make up the USLTA through their membership in its regional organizations. These tournaments are the mainstream of the sport.

Some of the clubs and their tournaments are known throughout the country to people who have never swung a racket: the Newport (Rhode Island) Casino and its annual Invitation Tournament; the River Oaks Invitation at Houston; the USLTA Singles Championships, the biggest tennis event of all in this country, held at the end of every summer at the West Side Tennis Club in Forest Hills, New York. You may have played some fine tennis at school, in college, or in the public parks of your home town; but until your name has appeared in the results of events like this, you are not a tennis *player*.

If you want to make the jump from team to tournament play, you don't start right in at Houston or Newport. "Invitation" means just that; you have to be asked, or at least file an application, which the club's tournament committee may or may not find acceptable. Your credentials are the record which you have built up gradually by playing in smaller, relatively little known tournaments close to home, where the competition is slower and where some one on the committee has heard of you. At the very least, he knows somebody in your home town who can vouch for your qualifications.

At sixteen, I was eager to try my wings in tournament competition. I had just won the state high school doubles championship with my teammate Richard Rihm, a skinny kid with a vast shock of curly hair. My record had come to the attention of the Ohio Valley Tennis Association, and a couple of men from that organization had shown an interest in me, encouraging me to keep working on my game and offering me the use of the courts at their own club in Cincinnati. Their backing was enough to guarantee Rihm and me admittance to a tournament coming up at a club in Chillicothe. It was a challenging event; a number of older players well-known in the area would be entering, including some of the players on the powerful Kenyon College team. But Chillicothe was seventy-five miles away, and that raised problems for both Rihm and me.

In my two years of tennis, I had always played under some sort of chaperonage. Most of the time Dad had been on hand, and if not Dad there was always the school coach. That took some of the edge off my mother's fears. If I should have an insulin reaction on the court, then at least there was always an adult on hand who understood my problem and would know how to handle it. There was also some assurance that I would be able to sterilize my needle properly for the insulin shots and that I would be eating the right food.

If I wanted to take the next step in tennis, however, I would have to take it by myself. To play a tournament like Chillicothe meant a whole week away from home. And that much time wasn't the only thing Dad couldn't spare. A week away from home would cost money. The tournament committee would give us some sort of allowance for meals, but there was still the problem of bus fare and a place to stay once we arrived.

The year was 1935. At that point of the depression, it wasn't easy to raise money for a trip like that in many families, including Rihm's. Mine had problems of its own. My grandfather, having bought out his partner a few years earlier, had become sole operator of the livestock firm. His gentle instincts had got the better of him in making decisions for the company; the firm was in trouble. Now, suffering progressive blindness, he had been forced to turn the business over to Dad, who was poorly equipped to handle it. In the Talbert household, where money had never been available by the fistful, things were getting pretty tight. Even forgetting the diabetes, I couldn't ask Dad for the bus fare, let alone a week's expense money. Rihm was in the same boat.

Neither of us said anything about the tournament to our families beforehand. The day before it was scheduled to open, we each slipped out of the house with a tennis racket and suitcase, leaving notes for our parents to explain where we'd gone. We rendezvoused at a midway street corner and began thumbing our way to Chillicothe.

The hitchhiking business was so bad that a couple of hours later, at some remote crossroads, we were thumbing both ways at once; we would just as gladly have taken a ride back to Cincinnati. Yet we finally landed in Chillicothe that evening and presented ourselves at the only address we knew — the home of the tournament committee chairman. He hardly knew us, except by name, but he couldn't have been more friendly.

"You boys had your supper?" he said, sizing up our dusty clothes.

Rich and I glanced at each other.

"Well, you probably wouldn't mind a snack, anyway," he added quickly. "Might as well stay here with us to-night, too. Tomorrow, we'll fix you up with a couple of cots at the club."

Although, as we could see, he and his wife had finished dinner not too long before we landed, they made a gesture of joining us at the table. Hungry as I was, I had to eat cautiously because my insulin schedule was uncertain. "Is anything wrong?" our hostess asked me. "Your partner seems to be enjoying it." Rihm was, in fact, eating ravenously.

"No," I assured her, "it's fine."

"I guess," she said to her husband, "William's afraid there won't be enough for tomorrow."

I flushed. "Oh, no," I said. "It's only . . ." I hesitated. "Would I be troubling you too much if I asked for some boiling water?"

As the wife of a tournament committee chairman, she was apparently well prepared for the demands of tennis players in training, which are sometimes rather eccentric. "Of course," she said sweetly. "A cup? With lemon?"

"No, thank you," I said. "A pot. Not right now," I added hastily. "I mean I just wanted to be sure I'd be able to boil a hypodermic needle."

Having got myself in that deep, I had to go on and explain about the diabetes. It took some talking on my part to persuade her that I was physically fit to play in her husband's tournament, and even then she kept eying me as if she expected me to drop at any moment. Her husband relieved her — and discomfited me — by promising to have a doctor at the courts. It was a relief when we moved to the dormitory that had been set up at the club, where our host made some arrangements in the kitchen to enable me to sterilize my needle.

In the next few days, Rihm and I kept wishing he had arranged some other liberties for us in the kitchen, because eating turned out to be more of a problem than we'd anticipated. The tournament committee gave us daily food money: 20 cents for breakfast, 25 cents for lunch, 35 cents for dinner. Eighty cents went a lot farther in those days, but nobody with an average athlete's appetite could have made enough money on the deal to be accused of professionalism. In my particular case, the diabetic diet called for a lot of protein — and even at 1935 prices, you couldn't get much of a steak dinner for 35 cents.

Toward the end of the week, rescue arrived: My folks drove up from Cincinnati and took us to dinner. We ate like a pair of orphans turned loose on a Christmas feast. It must have put a serious dent in the family budget. Before we left for home, my father also made sure I took care of another matter, at some expense to himself. He took me to a florist shop and had me send some flowers to the woman who had been my hostess that first night in town.

"If you're going to be traveling," he said, you'd better learn how to be a guest."

On the court, Rihm and I gave the folks a pretty good show for their money. We won the junior and men's doubles. In singles, I reached the finals of both classes, and in both I was murdered by one of the Kenyon College guys — a thick-set, somewhat erratic but hard-hitting player named Morey Lewis. Counting the mixed doubles, which I won in partnership with a girl I met at the tournament, I was a finalist in all five events. With my arms full of trophies, my parents couldn't very well fault me for having taken off on a risky adventure.

After that, I didn't have to sneak out of the house to get to tournaments. Diet remained something of a problem, but I managed. And the difficulties about hypodermic needles and other matters of diabetic routine decreased as I became less self-conscious about them.

I found that if I treated the matter casually, myself, no special fuss was apt to be made. The request for facilities to sterilize a needle became routine. Nobody offered to station a doctor at the courts, because I didn't seem to need one. Few people seemed to know much about diabetes, and those who did apparently felt that I knew what I was doing. If it was all right with my parents, it was okay with them. My mother never really stopped worrying. If she had been at the courts very often she'd have found even more to worry about, because I played with abandon. In one tournament I played nine sets in a single day — two singles matches and an almost interminable doubles in which nearly every game went to deuce, or tie score, time after time. The local press commented on my "remarkable stamina." That, I thought to myself with considerable pride, was something not often said about a diabetic before.

As long as my mother didn't know too much about

what I was doing, and as long as I could catch a ride and make some arrangements with the tournament committee for my keep, I was free to play. Dad's only word of restraint was an admonition, during my senior year at high school: "Don't forget about your books, Bill. When you want to get into college next fall, they're going to be looking at more than your tournament record."

I didn't overlook the books. From the earliest time I could remember, it had been understood around our house that college was one of the most important goals of a fellow's life. My report card looked pretty good, but I was more pleased with my tournament record. I won the state high school singles championship, and was sent East to play in the National Interscholastic Championships. That gave me my first taste of grass courts — luxurious and springy after the local asphalt and clay; my first sight of Forest Hills, where the tournament was held; and my first close look at a champion — Fred Perry, the great English player, a model not only of tennis form but also of personal dignity and charm. Perry dressed, looked, talked and acted as a hero should.

That tournament also gave me my first view of New York, a place where things seemed to be happening all the time, where everybody you met seemed substantial and important. It was, I was sure, the place you went to live once you had "arrived." I had a long way to go. I was knocked out in the first round.

On my own, that summer, I managed to get to most of the club tournaments in Ohio. Amost every week end, I'd come home with a trophy or two, and from one tournament I brought home all of the five I was eligible to compete for: junior and men's singles; junior, men's and mixed doubles. I was becoming what's known in the trade as a regular mughunter, and the apartment in Cincinnati began to be overcrowded with silverware — cups, trays, plaques of all shapes and sizes.

By hometown standards it was an impressive record. By tennis standards it didn't count for a great deal. Occasionally the small tournaments were illuminated by the presence of a real tennis star like Bobby Riggs, Frank Parker or Bitsy Grant; sometimes the field would contain a couple of really talented youngsters like Don McNeill and Joe Hunt, both already marked as future champions. When that happened, I went home empty-handed. Shoved to the sidelines in an early round, I would only too happily serve as ball boy for the semifinalists and finalists. From that vantage point I could study the winning kind of game. After the match I would hurry to catch up with the players on their way to the locker room.

"The way you hit your forehand volley — is this the grip?" Sometimes I'd get nothing but a brush-off, but sometimes I'd get a valuable lesson.

One fact that impressed me was that the players who won most consistently were the ones who emphasized control rather than power. It would be especially true on our Midwestern clay courts, where the ball's bounce was slower and gentler than on grass or concrete; on clay the power hitters would find their best shots being returned. Eventually, because the harder they swung the less they could control the ball, they would hit a shot into the net or out of court and would wind up beating themselves. Time after time I saw the flamboyant Californians, accustomed to hard courts, equipped with a big, scary serve and a murderous instinct, mowed down by the patient players like Riggs and Grant, who never tried to do more than they were capable of.

Even when I was still in the running during a tournament, I spent a lot of my time between matches on the sidelines. I liked to watch tennis and think about it as well as play it. I also found that, by studying an opponent before I was to play him myself, I could often spot patterns in his game that could be exploited.

That all-important sense of anticipation, I noticed, could be used two ways. If you could anticipate your opponent's shots, half the battle was won. If you could also throw off your opponent's sense of anticipation, you would really have him. The element of surprise could be a potent weapon.

There was one highly rated boy named Arthur Nielsen who gave me terrible trouble on the courts. Nielsen had good, strong ground strokes, but, I noticed after losing to him several times, he wasn't too confident of his volley. The next time I played him, I threw him a quick series of psychological curve balls. To begin with, although I won the toss, I chose to receive instead of taking the normal choice of serving. Next, I returned each of his first four serves in an identical and unorthodox manner: I dropshotted every one, which brought him tearing into the net, to a position from which he would be forced to use the volley. The fifth time, as he came rushing in, I lobbed the ball over his head. He stopped in confusion, started back, swung at the ball and missed it. After that he couldn't do anything right. I beat him 6–1, 6–1.

By outmaneuvering opponents when I couldn't out-stroke them, I managed to win my share of matches. Against the established players, even though I wasn't winning, I was beginning to make things close.

After one match, in a tournament held at the Kenyon College courts, a man from the college athletic department walked me back to the dressing room.

"What're your plans for the fall, Talbert?"

"College, you mean?" I shrugged. "I don't know for sure. Somewhere here in the state."

"Ever think about Kenyon?"

I had, because besides having an excellent academic reputation, that Ohio school was then beginning to produce some well-known tennis players — Don McNeill was on the Kenyon team, for instance, along with Morey Lewis. The trouble was that it was also known as an expensive school, much favored by rich men's sons. I wasn't in the least sure the Talberts could pay the freight.

"Well, we've looked into your grades," he said. "I think we can get you a scholarship — maybe help you out with a spare-time job, too."

"Thanks," I said. "I'll talk to my father."

When we sat down around the dining table, not long after that, to make the decision, we had more than the Kenyon offer to weigh. Ohio State had also entered the picture. At State, I had been assured, I'd be able to live

and take my meals at the Stadium Club, with the football players — which would eliminate a couple of sizable
expenses.

Dad was curiously noncommittal about the whole
thing. All through the discussion, he seemed abstracted.
I figured he was trying to avoid influencing my decision.
After a lot of inconclusive talk, we finally agreed that just
before the opening of the semester, we'd drive up to
Kenyon and look the situation over more closely. If it
seemed workable, I'd stay. Otherwise, we'd go on to OSU.
It was the kind of window shopping an athlete can do,
especially in the Middle West, and it could be done even
more easily back in those days when fewer families could
afford college for their sons.

One morning early in September, I packed my clothes,
and Dad, Mother and I loaded into the car for the drive
up to Kenyon. We hadn't gone more than a few blocks
when Dad happened to notice a friend of his walking by,
and pulled over to the curb to say hello.

"Clara, Bill, you know Mr. King, don't you?"

Mother nodded. "Sure," I said. "How's the team going
to be this fall?" Dana King was the football coach at the
University of Cincinnati.

"Fair," he said, with the habitual caution of all football
coaches. "If we're lucky, we'll win a few." He looked
at the luggage in the back. "Going on vacation?"

"No," Dad said. He explained the purpose of our trip.

"Kenyon?" King said. He uttered the name with a tone
of disbelief, as if we'd told him I was going to enroll at

Heidelberg or the Academy of Fine Arts in Rome. "You don't have to leave home to go to college. What's the matter with the University of Cincinnati right here in town? Bill, what are you going in for?"

"You mean for a major? Economics, I think."

He waved an arm expansively toward the university buildings, only a mile or so away. "We've got a great Econ department — good as any in the state. That's a fact, Reese. And don't forget, he could live at home."

From my family's point of view, I was aware, the idea had a very definite appeal. Living at home, whatever I may have thought of the idea, would not only save money but would also keep my diabetic's schedule under the parental eye for another few years.

"I think Mr. King's got a point, Bill," my father said, turning to me. "How about it?"

I was somewhat disappointed. I'd built up an enthusiasm for Kenyon in the last few weeks. But in the last analysis, family decisions were Dad's. Even with a scholarship, after all, it was he who would be paying most of the bills.

Dad turned the car around and drove home, and I hung my clothes back in the closet. A few mornings later, I got ready to leave the house for the beginning of my college career — just a streetcar ride from home. As I sat down to breakfast, Dad and Mother, who had been discussing something earnestly between them, suddenly became quiet.

"Before you go, Dad," I said, "could you write me a check for the fees? I think, with books and stuff, it's supposed to be around a hundred dollars for the term."

Dad tugged at his lip. "I'm afraid I can't give it to you," he said softly.

"They want you to pay it when you register."

He looked away from me.

"Bill," he said, "we haven't got it. We haven't got a damn dime."

Breadwinner on Campus

I WAS JOLTED. I had had no idea of just how bad things were. No money to throw around on tennis trips — that was no disaster. No money for something as important as college, the goal my father had picked for me himself — that meant we really must be in trouble. And in all this time Dad had never said a word about it.

"Well," I said, after a moment, "I guess I'd better forget about college and find a job." I pushed my chair back from the table.

"Oh, Reesy," Mother said reproachfully.

"Now hold on, Bill," Dad said. "A fellow's nothing any more without a college degree."

"They won't let you in without the money," I said. "If I went to work now, I could put some aside. Maybe I could go next term."

My father lit a cigarette, somewhat unsteadily. "Why don't you speak to Granddaddy?"

"Ask *him* for the money?"

"A hundred dollars. It isn't so much."

It's more than we've got, I thought. The idea of going to anybody for money didn't make me too happy. The way I'd been brought up, it wasn't easy to ask for favors.

"Couldn't *you* talk to him?" I said.

My father exhaled the smoke from his cigarette slowly. "I wish you'd do it, Bill." It was something I'd never seen before: my father, the man of such deep inner resources, unable to cope with life.

I went downtown right away to see my grandfather at his hotel. When I told him, hesitantly, what had happened, he didn't seem surprised. "Poor Reese," he said, shaking his head. He stared at me emptily through eyes that by now had become completely sightless. Then he pulled himself erect from his chair. "Well, boy," he said briskly, "I suppose you're in a hurry to get started. Now, if you'd kindly fetch my hat . . ."

He took my arm and directed me down the street to the bank. At the counter, he drew out a check book. The teller placed a pen in his hand and guided it to the signature line.

My grandfather handed me the cash. "No need to count it," he whispered to me. Even helpless in his blindness, he preferred to trust the people he dealt with. I waited for his usual parting advice to save my money, but in the circumstances I suppose he considered it ungentlemanly. All he said was, "Work hard, boy."

From the time I walked past the registrar's desk, that afternoon, my big worry at college was not whether I'd pass the course but whether I'd last it, financially. Most of the time it seemed less like a program of learning than a kind of steeplechase, with me clearing the hurdles just a step or two ahead of the man with the bills — and sometimes behind.

In the mornings I hurried through a classroom schedule crammed together in order to leave my afternoons free for work. At two o'clock I'd check in at my receptionist's job in one of the university administrative offices; out at five, home to my insulin injection and dinner; then on to my evening job, manning the parking lot at the adult extension division of the university. From time to time I could also pick up a little extra cash at odd jobs like waiting on tables and selling programs at football games. During one semester, when the race against debt became just too close for comfort, I dropped out of school altogether and took a steady job as a bank messenger. Dad was terribly bothered by that decision, but when we got to the question of an alternative, the conversation just died, and Dad withdrew to the privacy of his own thoughts. The truth was that my college expenses weren't the full extent of the problem; we needed the money to keep the household going. It wasn't coming from Dad's business.

Tennis — and the university's athletic department — made it a little easier for me to go back to college than it might have been. As a player wanted for the college team, I was given a crack at some of the better-paying student jobs, scheduled so as to leave time for team practice and matches. The bookwork got done somehow.

Other parts of campus life didn't interest me terribly. I had as much as I really wanted.

"Talbert," Bob Kistner said to me one night, as he wheeled his Chevy into my street, "I think we've just lost our franchise in the stagline. And it's nobody's fault but yours, Romeo."

"Romeo!"

"That's you, boy. The next time either of us shows up at a fraternity house dance without a date, they're going to bar us at the door."

"I behaved like a law-abiding citizen," I said defensively. "I didn't get loaded on that glass of ginger ale — which is more than some of the boys can say. Didn't take a swing at anybody — "

"You know what I'm talking about," Kistner said. Bob, a slim, sandy-haired fellow, was a pre-med student a year or so ahead of me at the university, though we happened to have a couple of economics courses in common. "I'm talking about the brunette whose ear you were bending most of the time. The fraternity brother who brought her thinks you were cutting him out."

I wasn't used to being taken so seriously as competition. Girls were remote, elevated creatures, to be talked to because that was part of the tribute they expected.

"And I made the mistake of defending you," he added.

"Well," I said, trying not to seem too pleased, "shows you how unappreciative some guys are. I was just trying to make him look good."

"Oh, sure."

"I figured two or three dances with me and she'd realize just how well off she was with him." I stopped to think for a moment. "She really was something, wasn't she? Where do you suppose they find them like that?"

"I don't know, but next time you'd better find your own."

I put my knees up against the dashboard. "Hell," I said, "even if I could afford to take a date to one of those things I wouldn't want to. I'd rather lone-wolf it."

Neither Kistner nor I actually belonged to a fraternity — Bob because, as he said, he had his hands full with his courses, and getting into the medical school was nothing a man could take for granted. I had nothing against the fraternity system myself; it just didn't seem to fit in with the program of a guy working his way; and besides, I felt no great desire to add my name to the membership list of any club.

"What's the difference?" I said to Kistner, when the subject of joining came up. "I like the guys just as well without swearing it in blood. We can go to the dances, anyway. Why get involved?"

Bob laughed. "You're a real old Republican, aren't you?"

"My old Kentucky granddaddy would die of shame if he heard you say that."

"I mean the old rugged individualist," Kistner said. "The way you hate rules and regulations — You just don't want to go through all that junk of having a bunch of guys tell you what to do and when to do it, and how a good fraternity brother ought to behave."

"Rules — " I said unenthusiastically. "I've had enough of them thrown at me since I was ten to last me the rest of my life."

It may have been that; it may have been just that I

had lost the habit of traveling with the crowd at an early age, and had never really reacquired it. When I was younger, my rigid health program had taken me pretty much out of circulation, socially. My role as the neighborhood sick boy had made me self-conscious. The diet and the absolutely regular hours, built around the injection schedule, created some awkward situations. After a school dance, for instance, when the gang adjourned to the drugstore for ice cream or hamburgers, I used to sit nursing a cup of black coffee (sugarless; no value on the calorie chart), with an uneasy eye on the clock. Staying up late might put too much of a drain on the insulin. Or it might mean oversleeping in the morning, and a dangerous delay in the morning injection.

Tennis had relaxed my attitude toward the rules, of course; and getting around to a few tournaments, where dances were usually a part of the club program, had broadened my social life. I was starting to find that, for the sake of an occasional late evening, I could bend the rules a little without great harm, just as I had done on the tennis court.

That was another side of life, however. That was tournament life, something that happened only during the summer. During the college term, I was a guy with a job — or, rather, jobs. As far as fraternity-house life and steady dating were concerned, I didn't have the money and I didn't have much time.

It was even hard to work in an evening for The Panther, who was worth any red-blooded U.C. man's time.

Her real name was Louise, but everybody knew her as

The Panther. It had something to do with the wonderful sinuous way she moved. By acclaim, she was the most beautiful girl in the university, always being voted queen of something or other.

I considered her the perfect flower of American womanhood; and like every other man on the campus I made my feeble efforts to catch her attention. I'd follow her out of the college library and try to start up a conversation. I had no fears of getting out of my depth, financially or socially, because I hadn't the slightest intention of daring to ask her for a date.

The Panther's thinking must have run along the same lines. Her response never went beyond a cool hello.

One day, however, as I emerged from the library beside her, she turned to me and said sweetly, "I didn't know you were the tennis player."

"There are all sorts of things we don't know about each other," I said with what I thought was a debonair tone. "Maybe it's time you gave us a chance to find out." It was a bit of snappy dialogue I must have picked up at a club dance somewhere during the last tournament season.

"No, seriously. I saw the write-up about you in the *Record*. You must be awfully good."

The story in the college paper had been very flattering. It recorded my latest victories as Number 1 man on the varsity, along with a few successes I'd had in summer tournaments. It didn't mention the ones that got away.

"How would you like to take me to the Gibson next Friday, for dinner and dancing?"

I froze — of chagrin as much as surprise. The Gibson Hotel was the local equivalent of the Stork Club or El Morocco — a place to take a date on the most special, and expensive, of occasions.

"It's free," she said. "That was my prize for being elected Queen last week. And I can invite anyone I want as my date for the evening."

I began to breathe again, but not without difficulty. Friday night was no different from any weekday night: I had a job. At dinnertime, when the Campus Queen would be waiting for her escort, I was scheduled for my nightly duty as janitor at an office building downtown. And I couldn't afford to give that up. Given the chance of a lifetime — an evening with the most beautiful girl in the world, or at least in Cincinnati — I was going to pass it up in favor of a stimulating evening sweeping up offices and baling wastepaper.

Bob Kistner came to the rescue, only too gladly. That Friday he called for The Panther in his respectable Chevrolet, brought her my flowers and escorted her to dinner. At 11:30 that night, after winding up my janitorial duties and shucking my work clothes, I turned up at the Gibson and relieved him from duty.

The janitor's job was one that I shared with four or five football players. Sometimes there were special duties, like moving furniture and rearranging offices, which kept us working overtime. Once, when we reported for work, we were armed with sledgehammers and crowbars. The night's mission was to knock down a heavy masonry wall, in order to merge two small offices into a single large one.

I came dragging home about seven the next morning, covered with plaster dust, my hands and arms cut by wire lath. My mother looked at me despairingly. It had been only a few years before that a long walk home from school had seemed like dangerous overexertion. Tennis was something she still held under suspicion. Now, I could see, she pictured me dropping unconscious some night under a bale of paper or a heap of broken-out plaster.

"Don't worry so much," I told her. "I ate some oranges and a sandwich."

"Do me a favor, Bill. Get some easier kind of work."

"The easy ones don't pay so well," I said. "There are plenty of guys at school who only wish they could get this one." I stretched my arms contentedly, wincing just a little with the effort. "Besides, it was fun."

I went in to wash and get ready for my morning injection. As I passed the telephone table in the hall, I stopped to look at the mail stacked there. All bills. One from the phone company, with an ominous footnote. Ditto the owner of our apartment house. Even the grocer: there were bills from two different stores in the neighborhood, both heavily stamped *Past Due*. I gritted my teeth.

I went back to the kitchen and took what money I had out of my pocket, keeping enough for a couple of days' lunches and handing the rest to my mother. "Maybe we can pay one or two of those bills," I said, "before Dad sees them."

I took considerable pride in my role of buffer for Dad, warding off some of the blows that came in each day's mail. As a boy I had always counted so heavily on his support, and now it made me feel like a man to be able to return it. I kept thinking that somehow this had brought us closer, and that he must feel it himself. Things that he had never been able to say to a boy, I thought, he might be able to confide in me as a man.

If he felt that way, however, he kept it to himself. When we were home together (not so often, any more) we talked impersonally — about my courses, the university tennis team's prospects, the suddenly rising fortunes of the Cincinnati Reds.

Just the same, I found a tremendous personal satisfaction in the idea that I was paying my own way. The years of being watched over — by the doctors at the hospital, the nurses at the clinic, my own family — made any taste of freedom sharp and wonderful. This was one more step toward escape from all the scary restrictions that had once hedged me in. First it had been tennis, now school and work. I could handle it, and there was nothing like this feeling of being competent, able to take care of a situation.

I didn't always take the life of a working student in stride. There were times, as I hustled from job to library and on to job, when I felt terribly pressed — especially because, for all the hours I was putting in, I was always on the brink of financial crisis. The stack of unpaid bills at home never seemed to get any smaller.

I was lucky to have the tennis to take my mind off these day-to-day concerns. On the court, I felt a release that was more than just physical. Wearing tennis clothes, it didn't matter whether I had a dime in my pocket. In that one field I was a match for anybody at the college. As a student, I was doing well but not spectacularly; for campus politics I had no ambitions and no room on my schedule. Tennis was the one thing that made me feel like an individual among the several thousand young men and women who milled about the Cincinnati college buildings every day. It was the one thing that had made me worthy of being noticed by the Campus Queen, the only reason for having my name in the college paper.

The tournaments I had played so far, however, were minor-league stuff. It was in the East that tennis players made their records. Those were the tournaments that really counted when the annual men's rankings were made, at the end of each year. This was where the game was really played, and where, if you took yourself seriously as a tennis player, you had to go to prove yourself.

As a twenty-year-old college student, with a few local trophies to my credit but no national standing in the sport, I had reached a crossroads. If I really wanted to be a tennis player, not just a rehabilitated invalid getting his exercise on the court, I had to take the step now. Somehow or other, in spite of diabetes and the expense, I had to find a way of going to play the Eastern circuit, the climactic schedule of summer tournaments in the main arena of tennis, where every match counted.

The Circuit

Just before the Fourth of July, in 1938, Bob Kistner and I headed east in his Chevy. I had qualified for the National Intercollegiate Championships, at the Merion Cricket Club in Haverford, Pennsylvania. The tournament wasn't one of the events on the Eastern circuit proper, but for a good many ambitious college players in the past it had been a gateway to the circuit. I was hoping it might prove the same for me.

Kistner went along not only as pilot, friend and sharer of expenses, but also as a sports fan with a genuine interest in tennis for its own sake. He was a frustrated athlete who had had to resign himself to a spectator's role because of bad eyesight, and he seemed to enjoy the chance to identify himself, through me, with the playing end of sport. I liked having him along; he was a fine traveling companion, and it was good to be able to count on one rooter, at least, when you were playing in strange territory.

In the week-long tournament at Haverford, I gave my claque only two or three days' worth of cheering. I had a couple of routine victories, then a spectacularly easy one over a Stamford University player — 6–0, 6–0; or, in the trade term, "love, love." After that I was put out by Bill Murphy of the University of Chicago, one of the seeded players — the favorites in the tournament.

For the rest of the week, I sat in the stands with Bob, watching the field narrow down to the ultimate winners — Frank Guernsey of Rice in singles; Lew Wetherell and the ubiquitous Joe Hunt of Southern California in doubles. Between matches, I hung around the locker room, asking some of the other players for advice on my grips and strokes. I was still searching for a better way to do everything on a tennis court. By now, among the fellows who knew me from tournaments around home, it was a standard locker-room gag.

"Damn it, Talbert!" one of the boys said to me in a tone of exasperation, only half-kidding. "How come you're such a lousy tennis player? You've already got Frankie Parker's back hand, Rigg's lob, Allison's volley. Now you want Hunt's serve! Why, with that combination of strokes, you ought to be the best player in the whole damn country!"

There was quite a bit to learn at Merion, and not all of it on the court or in the locker room. Even though the national collegiates weren't a major tennis event, Merion itself was one of the big league tennis clubs. It was, in fact, one of the original breeding grounds of American tennis — the site of some historic matches between the earlier greats of the game, of Davis Cup matches and also of national championship tournaments before the events were moved elsewhere. At Merion you could see the real difference between the Eastern circuit and the small-time tournaments I'd played in the Midwest. It provided a handsome vista of what tennis really had to offer.

The difference didn't lie just in the keenness of competition, the superior quality of the players — although that was true enough. But more than that, there was something rich and heady in the atmosphere. Merion was a repository of Philadelphia's Main Line traditions. The clubhouse, the lawns, the people themselves had that patina of security — the tone that comes with social position established and reinforced over a period of generations. It was that special tone of "Eastern casualness." In the mellow sunlight of Merion, the girls in their light skirts and cashmeres seemed gayer and prettier; the men in their dressed-down flannels and seersuckers seemed suave and knowing. There was a wonderful sense of leisure being used with good taste and decency. People seemed to have the time, the means and the ability to enjoy each other's company.

There were club dances and private parties — a great holiday fling for the sons and daughters of Merion members, home from their colleges for the summer. Most of us tennis players came from homes nothing like the great Main Line houses, and from public courts that had little in common with Merion's tailored grass, but they took us in like blood brothers.

Along with the collegians who made up most of the crowd at the matches, there were also a number of adult members, their guests, and LTA officials on hand out of perennial custom, to look over the new crop of college talent. They were in the position of unpaid scouts, keeping their eyes open for the "hungry" tennis player — the boy who not only had the skill to win but also the driving need to win, because nothing else would satisfy him.

I heard that one of these visitors, a man named Winchester, was on the tournament committee of the Baltimore Country Club, where the Maryland State Championships were to be held the following week. I ambushed him in the clubhouse, introduced myself, and asked if he could arrange to get my name into the field at Baltimore.

He looked me over analytically. "Talbert. I saw you against that Chicago fellow, didn't I? Fourth round?" He appeared to be measuring me against some invisible standard. "We've got a pretty full draw, but let me see what I can do."

A little later, out of the corner of my eye I caught him nodding in my direction while talking with one of the Merion club officials. Eventually, he came over and told me, in a friendly way, "We've got room for you in our tournament, Talbert. About arrangements, I guess we can put you up with some of the other boys at one of the Johns Hopkins dormitories. There's a cafeteria not too far away where you can take your meals."

That was a genteel way of letting me know that I wasn't important enough to expect accommodations at the club itself, to say nothing of a hotel in town.

"By the way," he added, "I hear good things about you."

I listened eagerly, thinking that perhaps, underneath

the flaws in my game, someone had spotted the makings of a future winner.

He smiled and shook my hand. "People here tell me they consider you a fine gentleman."

I suppose he meant that I'd kept my eyes open wider than my mouth. I hadn't argued with the officials' decisions on the court, and I hadn't made a fool of myself at the parties afterwards. It wasn't the kind of praise I was looking for, but I couldn't help realizing what it meant — that here, as at home in my own family, things were expected of you above and beyond the ability to swing a tennis racket.

At the end of the week at Merion, I shook hands with Kistner, told him to give my folks my regards when he got back to Cincinnati, and then hopped a bus for Baltimore.

Tennis can hardly be called "a gentleman's game" any more — not in the stuffy sense of the term. Long before I took up the game, it had stopped being the exclusive property of the rich. It is played far more commonly on concrete and asphalt playgrounds than on private lawns. Kids who have to peddle newspapers to buy their first rackets have become stars in the sport. And the eight or ten thousand people in the stands at a climactic Davis Cup match or United States championship singles final include a fair proportion of cabdrivers, office secretaries, hardware store clerks and others who certainly don't clip coupons for a living.

It's true that the clubs, their members and their officialdom in the LTA sometimes seem to insist on certain standards of behavior that aren't required in, say, a football game between the Detroit Lions and the Chicago Bears. But that, I think, is because to these people tennis is more than just a sport — it's a function of society. And a tennis tournament is more than a series of games played on a lined court — it's a social event in which the obligations of host and guest, they feel, ought to be maintained.

The clubs that act as hosts are made up of rich and powerful families. Many of these people genuinely love the game; nearly all of them enjoy watching it; even those few who may be bored by it, personally, respect it as something that has been going on for so long, among the right people and in the right places, that it couldn't be dispensed with, any more than the opera or the Junior League.

"Tennis week" — the week of a tournament at any of the old Eastern clubs — is usually the high point of the summer social season. It's at the time of the Casino Invitational, for example, that some of Newport's most festive débuts are held. An invitation to a house party at Southampton is all the more prized if the date falls during the Meadow Club tournament. All along the Eastern circuit, hostesses are apt to plan their most elaborate soirées for the time when the tennis players are on hand. As the players move along the tournament route, like strolling minstrels visiting courts, the doors of the summer houses swing open, the guestrooms start to fill, the orchestras strike up that peculiarly thin music reminiscent of expensive hotels, and the terraces light up to full lantern power.

The players themselves are the lions of this society. The game is their cachet, admitting them to places they might never reach with their other credentials. The circuit is a fantastic kind of melting pot. It's where a young man whose parents speak broken English and who has never worn a tie at the dinner table could find himself seated, at dinner, with the daughter of an Ambassador or a Supreme Court Justice — and possibly near His Excellency or Mr. Justice himself. Or where a fellow working his way through school by baling wastepaper on a janitors' gang, whose folks might or might not be able to pay the next month's rent, could find himself accepted without prejudice in this sort of company. All you had to do was recognize that there were some obligations on the guest's side, too.

The day I was eliminated from the tournament at Baltimore, Mr. Winchester came around to offer his sympathies.

"You fellows were up against a tough pair," he said. "Mulloy has been playing well this season."

I nodded. "They really blasted us off the court." Gardnar Mulloy, an easygoing, muscular giant with a crew cut, was already a veteran of several years on the circuit. The powerful game he played, as partner of a player named George Toley, had been too much for me and my teammate, Izzy Bellis of Philadelphia. That was a quarter-final match — the third-from-the-last round. I had been put out of the singles earlier.

"You'll do better next year," Mr. Winchester assured me. "Where are you going from here?"

"I don't know," I said. "I'm trying to get into Seabright, but I haven't heard from them yet."

"That's not for another week or two. How would you like to go on to Easthampton in the meantime? They've sent down a call for a few fill-ins." He winked. "I guess the ladies up there have been after the committee to get them some extra men."

I hitched a ride to Easthampton with two other players — Jack Bushman, a dark, wiry guy from Louisiana State University; and Billy Gillespie, a boy just out of one of the Eastern prep schools. We made the trip in high spirits, flushed with our first taste of the circuit, and ready for anything waiting for us on the Maidstone Club courts. We all did well, too. It took Frank Shields and Sidney Wood, still one of the great teams, to keep Gillespie and me from winning the doubles.

Off the court, however, we weren't quite prepared to meet the tony standards of the Long Island South Shore. The night of the tournament dance at Maidstone, I walked in with my eye peeled for a spectacular blond girl I'd been introduced to at the matches that afternoon. As soon as we started to dance, I felt a hand on my shoulder. It was one of the club officials, and he wasn't cutting in.

"I'm sorry, Mr. Talbert," he said. "I'll have to ask you to leave the floor."

I looked at him in astonishment, wondering what I'd done.

"Dinner clothes required," he said quietly.

I glanced down at my well-pressed, hard-earned, but definitely nonformal dark suit. "I didn't know," I said uneasily. "None of us brought any dinner clothes up from Baltimore." (I didn't mention that, as far as I knew, none of us owned any, in Baltimore or anywhere else.)

"Terribly sorry," he said, "but it's always been one of our rules."

I had to sit out the rest of the evening, but even from the sidelines, it was a good party.

When I got to Newport, a few weeks later, and found myself invited to one of the débutante parties that kept the resort lighted up nightly, I borrowed a suit of dinner clothes. I didn't want to miss out on anything.

It was a magnificent affair, in a house of magnificent size. A half-dozen of us young circuit neophytes went in convoy, all in borrowed or rented black-tie. We all trailed up to the entrance behind a boy who had appointed himself our leader and social mentor, his credentials consisting of a couple of years at Princeton.

The door was swung open by a splendid-looking gentleman in a tailcoat. Our leader gave him a broad smile, shook hands warmly, introduced himself, and then presented each of us (each dutifully smiling, each offering a firm hand) to the man at the door — the butler.

En route from Easthampton to Newport, there were a number of other stops on the circuit, but it wasn't just a matter of catching rides from place to place. The Seabright invitation I'd been hoping for never did come through; Southampton also turned me down. Too many of the top players were starting to drift back from Wimbleton and the other European tournaments, and there just wasn't room for many newcomers. I headed instead for Ocean City, New Jersey, and a tournament that the ranking players were bypassing. I not only got into the draw but actually won my first Eastern title. Two titles, in fact — since I not only took the singles cup, but also got my name on the doubles trophy with Jack Bushman as my partner.

After one of the late-round matches, when I went back to my room at the rambling old shore hotel where we were being boarded, I found a note bearing as its letterhead the name of one of the handsome yachts moored in the basin not far from the club. "Please join us for cocktails," it said, above a signature well known in seaboard society.

That evening, I sat luxuriantly in a deck chair gently rolling with the Atlantic swell, keeping an eye out for the white-liveried mess boy who was making his way among the guests, taking their orders for Scotch and soda.

"Scotch and soda," I nodded, when my turn came.

I turned to my doubles partner. "Bushman," I said, "I don't know about you, but I never want to go home." I took a pull at my glass. "I'll bet I could even learn to like Scotch and soda."

A couple of days later we were traveling by bus and counting every dime it cost.

All summer long it was like that: a perpetual seesaw from the depths of uncertainty to pinnacles of luxury — and down again. Leaving a tournament party that had been served by butlers to a company that had arrived in chauffeur-driven cars, I'd be wondering whether I'd have enough fare to get to the next tournament; whether I'd be considered good enough to qualify for it, in the first place; whether I'd have a place to stay and be able to eat well enough to stave off the threat of a diabetic attack.

The next day, somewhere, a gate would open. There was, it seemed, always somebody eager to help you with a ride, or lodgings, or a call to the next club's tournament committee — just as in those earliest days in Cincinnati there had been someone ready to offer me a decent racket for a boys' tournament in the public park. This kind of generosity seemed to be an inherent part of tennis, a tradition of the game.

At one tournament — the Eastern Grass Court Championships in Rye, New York — I spent the first night stretched out on the soggy turf of the polo field, along with a few other lodging-less young players on tight budgets. The next day, a couple I had met at an earlier tournament showed up and invited me to stay at their luxurious Westchester County house, a few miles away.

It required acts of private generosity like that to take up the slack in the system, and people who loved tennis seemed to consider it a duty to help. Among us young players who were caught in the slack unless and until help came, there was a healthy amount of griping about the setup, but there were certain realities of the situation which had to be faced — as some of the veteran players occasionally reminded us.

"The tournament committee knows most of you guys are making the tour on a shoestring," one of the veterans assured a group of us at a house party. "They know you haven't got the dough for a hotel and decent meals. But they've got just so much dough to spend, themselves, on players' expenses. And, you might as well face it, most of it goes for the big boys — Budge, Mako, Riggs, guys like that. Say you're the committee chairman of some big tournament — Southampton or Newport. You need those players. If you can't get them, you've got no tournament."

I indicated "No thanks" to a butler passing a tray of canapés.

"Don't forget," somebody put in, "you can't have a tournament with just three or four top guys. You need a lot of other players to fill up the draw.

"There are always plenty of 'other' players around. Guys like you, just dying to play because that's the only way you can build up a record. You need the committee. They know you'll come, with or without being put up, as long as they'll let you in."

Sometimes, as one of the "other" players dealing with the tournament committees, I found that concessions had to be pried out of them, round by round. Once, for instance, I started playing a tournament with no expenses paid at all. After winning my first-round match, I was told I could take lunch at the club — a sandwich and milk. When I won again, the offer was raised to lunch plus a room at a local hotel. After a third-round victory, I was given the full treatment — the hotel room and all my meals.

Unfortunately, that system also worked in reverse: some clubs would keep you only as long as you kept winning. The day you were eliminated from their tournament, your meals and lodgings were cut off. At one of these strictly business events, having been knocked out in an early round and having no place else to go, I was able to stay on only by switching roles, from player to official. In exchange for my services as linesman, I was given my meals for the rest of the week.

This, then, was the tennis life, life on the circuit — this curious mixture of struggle and comfort. Surrounded constantly by the atmosphere of the life *de luxe*, still, whenever I walked onto the court, I was literally fighting for my supper.

By the time I reached Newport, in mid-August, I was a recognized, if undistinguished, young member of the tennis troupe. What victories I had won had been against players of no more than second rank, in matches that had stirred no great attention. I had yet to find a corner of the limelight.

If I was going to find it at all, Newport was a likely place. The field of players entered there was the most brilliant of the season so far. Budge, the American champion, who had lately added the championships of Wimbledon and Paris to his string, was there to make his first American appearance of the summer. Entered along with him were most of the other members of the country's top ten: Mako, Sidney Wood, Frank Parker, Elwood Cooke, and the unrelated Hunt boys — Joe and Gilbert. In the

As a young mughunter (age: 19) on my first trip east, I managed to collect this one trophy — for winning the Atlantic Coast tournament at Ocean City, New Jersey. Everywhere else on the Eastern circuit that summer, I found the going rough.

Atlantic Studios

Myron Davis — LIFE © *1941* TIME, INC.

First act of all young travelers on the tennis circuit: looking over the draw. In this crowd of eager young at the 1941 Southern Championships in Louisville, I had to poke my head (the crew-cut one, center rear) over a couple of shoulders to size up my prospects. In the following seasons I saw a lot of the three players at the left: Eddie Alloo, Gardner Larned and Pauline Betz.

Photo from European

Victory in the 1945 National Doubles at Forest Hills
gave Gardnar Mulloy and me our second leg on the
twin trophies. The next year we took the cups home
with us for good.

Photo by Max Peter Haas

int for our side in the 1948 Davis Cup Challenge Round, on a risky angled shot
to the alley. In this match at Forest Hills, Mulloy and I (far court) beat the
ıstralian team of Billy Sidwell and Colin Long for the point that clinched the
Davis Cup for the United States.

Photo by Max Peter Haas

Secretary of State Dulles initiated 1955 Challenge Round at Forest Hills with gesture of good wishes to the Australian and American captains. *At the right:* Australian Ambassador Sir Percy Spender.

Tom Hutchins — Life © *1954* Time, Inc.

Davis Cup rivals met on court at Sydney, Australia, in 1954, before the largest crowd ever to watch a tennis match —26,000. From my left: Tony Trabert, leading singles player; Harry Hopman, Australian captain; and Lew Hoad, his tiger. Trabert's victory started us off on our unexpected recapture of the cup.

Bringing home the bacon. Nancy brought our sons Pike
(then 5) and Peter (3) to the airport, to make the 1954
homecoming of the Davis Cup a family reunion.

Conference with Tony Trabert during a change of court in the 1955 Challenge Round at Forest Hills. Strategy didn't work: the Australians beat us, 3-2.

Alfred Eisenstaedt — LIFE © 1955 TIME, INC.

Photo by Max Peter Haas

Losers (U.S.A.) share equally with winners (Australia) when the Davis Cup is filled with champagne. At the 1955 banquet, from my left: Ham Richardson, Gil Shea (behind him), Harry Hopman; Ken Rosewall; Rex Hartwig, Lew Hoad, Tony Trabert, Neale Fraser, Vic Seixas (obscured), and Ashley Cooper.

Husband-and-wife doubles at a New York City court. A woman's place, as Nancy demonstrates when she gives up her usual one in the gallery, is right up at the net with her partner.

Discussing shots — tennis and diabetes — with a group of young patients at a camp operated by the New York Diabetes Association.

Running backhand drive from the baseline, during a 1946 match at Kooyon Stadium in Melbourne, Australia.

doubles, the current championship team of Budge and Mako were joined by powerful combinations, including the great team they had lately displaced — Wilmer Allison and John Van Ryn.

Tennis fans from all along the Eastern Seaboard were drifting in to watch the combat. The hotels were full, and the great monumental houses were aglow. There were luncheon parties scheduled for every afternoon, and dinner parties every evening. In the air there was a steady hum of excitement that was part tennis, part social. The conversation swirled back and forth from Budge and Mako to Brenda and Gloria — the Frazier girl and the Vanderbilt girl, who were the objects of most of the excitement off the courts. The New York press — sports page and society page — was there in full force to record the campaign on both fields.

Bushman and I checked in at the big attic dormitory above the Casino, where about 40 players were being lodged on cots. The place was alive with the kind of steady pandemonium you'd expect of any large pair of rooms in which several dozen young fellows had been thrown together. It was like an army barracks with the sergeant called away. A pillow fight and a wrestling match were already in progress. One small guy had been hoisted bodily onto a huge chandelier by a group of playful colleages, and was being swung gently back and forth while he clung to his perch like a frightened parrot, screaming useless protests. Another group was huddled together conspiratorially, drawing up a scheme to plant a live lobster in the bed of a keeper of late hours.

"Hey, Talbert!" somebody yelled as we came in. "D'you see the draw yet?"

"No," I shouted, ducking as the chandelier creaked by. "We just got in."

"Well, don't bother to read past the second round."

My heart fell a notch. I'd been hoping to last long enough to make a decent impression. "Who did I get?" I asked.

"Gil Hunt, you lucky so-and-so. And is he hot lately!"

"Tough luck," Bushman said.

"Don't count me out yet, boy," I told him. "Anyway, there's still the doubles. Maybe we've got an easier draw there."

But when we went downstairs, a little later, to look at the draw for ourselves, the picture became even gloomier. We were matched against Allison and Van Ryn.

I laughed. "It's a good thing you brought your lucky rabbit's foot. We might have drawn Budge and Mako."

I managed to give Gil Hunt a run for his money. I started fast, pressing the attack, and won the first set. In the second, he came back strong. Then we fought out the final one, point by bitter point. Once, I had him backed against the wall — a couple of good shots would have earned me the match — but I couldn't quite bring them off. He slipped away from me, turned and over-powered me. It ended 7–5, 2–6, 7–5 in his favor, but the gallery was all mine as I left the court.

When Bushman and I walked on for our doubles match, I was less concerned with winning the gallery than with making an impression on our opponents. Wilmer Allison and John Van Ryn were historic names in the game of doubles. They had won the national championship twice and had played together in a number of memorable Davis Cup matches. Just being on the same court with them was something to live up to.

Good doubles is one of the most exciting of all spectator sports. It is full of action. The game is made up of sudden moves and countermoves, brilliant offensive thrusts and surprising recoveries. The very essence of the game is close-range combat, with all four players firing at each other face to face at the net.

From the player's standpoint, the game is full of challenge, yet a great many tennis players have gone through the motions of doubles play without really enjoying it or even understanding it. They fail to recognize the special nature of the game. Some approach it as nothing much more than a singles match in which you have to share your end of the court with another player. Tilden, great as he was as an individual performer, played poor doubles, by his own admission. Ellsworth Vines and Bobby Riggs were no great shakes at the team game, either. Frank Kovacs, equipped with a natural tennis talent probably as great as any player in the history of the game, never got the hang of doubles at all.

On the other hand, there have been players who never really distinguished themselves in singles but were brilliant on the doubles court. Van Ryn was one. George Lott was probably the supreme doubles player. By watching Lott play in some pro exhibitions I had noticed that the game could be directed into wonderful patterns and situations like nothing in singles play, and that it had requirements of shot-making and tactics all its own. It was not so much a game of power as of angles, demanding the keenest of anticipation and quickness of reflex.

Lott, I used to notice, would concentrate on getting his first shot into play, whether it was service or return of service. He never tried to score with the first blow. He gave no points away. His was a game of court position and movement. If his partner was drawn off the court by a sharply angled shot, Lott would automatically be moving toward the center, where the next one was almost sure to come. Watching Lott play doubles, I had seen it as a game in which a player like me, short on power but equipped with a pretty good ball sense, could distinguish himself.

Allison and Van Ryn played a beautifully co-ordinated game. In a typical maneuver, Van Ryn would force a member of the opposing team out of position with a low, sharply angled drive, or would force him into a weak return by hitting low down the middle. As the return came back, Allison would move across the net, cut off the return with a volley and punch it murderously into the opening his partner had set up. Sometimes Allison would "poach," moving across the center line into his partner's territory to make his volley. When that happened, Van Ryn would be backing him up, covering the spot Allison had left, in case the volley was returned.

Against such a pair of practiced campaigners, Jack Bushman and I had no plan except to try to stay in the game. Tempting as it might be to try to pound Van Ryn's service back for an outright winner, I made my returns low and short, hoping to force an error or a weak return from him as he came charging to the net. I lobbed over Allison's head instead of trying to pass him. I measured my own serve carefully, sacrificing speed to make sure the first one would be in, twisting high to the backhand side. At the net, Bushman played his volleys beautifully down the middle, leaving the alleys alone until the opening was sure. He scrambled for shots that seemed impossible to retrieve and somehow sent them back.

We reached 4–4 — a crucial point in a set. If we won the next game, they would have to win three to take the set. It was my turn to serve. I put the ball in play each time with great deliberation, careful not to waste a point by committing faults. Bushman guarded the net perfectly, and when Allison slapped back a careless return, Jack hammered it away for the winning point.

With the score now 5–4 in our favor, Van Ryn served. We lobbed, caught Allison going the wrong way on a "poach," lost a couple of points on our own errors. It was our advantage, and set point — one more needed for us to win the set.

Van Ryn drove deep to my backhand. I put up a lob, realizing as I started forward toward the net that it was short and too low. Allison started back for it but hesitated just a fraction of a second too long and had to let it bounce. Van Ryn, coming up behind him, took it on his forehand and drove it right down the middle. I was there. I brought my racket around sharply, timed the ball just right, and volleyed right back between them for the winning point.

The umpire called out, "Game and set, Bushman and

Talbert." I tried to avoid gazing up in delight as the score, 6–4, was mounted on the post beside the court. Some spectators began to leave other matches on the neighboring courts as word of an upset-in-the-making went around. They began to drift away again as the second set went on. Allison and Van Ryn had got down to work. We were outmaneuvered and overpowered completely.

In the third set, Jack and I righted ourselves and fought back all the way. But we couldn't quite make it. Van Ryn pulled off a couple of beautiful placements, and Allison hit an unreachable smash that finished us. It ended 4–6, 6–1, 6–4, and we were out of the tournament.

When the New York papers arrived, next day, I turned to the sports pages of the *Times*. There was a big headline on the Newport tournament, and somewhere down in the story was the note that "William Talbert of Cincinnati, a young newcomer, surprised with the all-around soundness of his game." That was the first time my name had appeared in the New York press except as a line of small type in the tournament scores.

Wilmer Allison said it with less restraint, that same evening. As I was taking a stroll through the Newport streets, I met him, leaving his hotel in dinner clothes. "Let me tell you," he said, "you were one hell of a tennis player on that court."

Even as a loser, I was in my glory. But still a loser.

A week or so later, the seesaw hit the down side again, and this time it seemed to be stuck there. The application I had made with Bushman for the national doubles at

Boston was turned down. There were no other tournaments going on, and even if there were, I wouldn't have been able to play. I was scraping bottom on my meager cash reserves. I had reached the end of the line.

Tired and disappointed, I boarded a bus for Cincinnati. I was, after all, just another would-be tennis player —one of the also-rans and never-quites who couldn't make the points that counted, couldn't win the big match; who get weeded out along the circuit. I arrived home absolutely broke.

"How do you feel?" my mother asked anxiously.

"Fine, fine."

"We saw the write-up in the New York paper," my father said. He looked fatigued. "How are things, Dad?" I asked.

It took him a moment to answer.

"Oh, fair enough." He drew a cigarette out of a pack and began rummaging about the house for a match.

I hadn't been home for more than a few hours when a telegram came for me. It was from the local tennis association, and I had to read it through several times before I could be sure I understood it. What it said was that I had been chosen for something called the Junior Davis Cup Squad, and that I was invited to report to the Merion Cricket Club in a few days.

I called one of the local officials.

"That's right, Bill. We just got word from the national committee. We've been getting good reports on you, you know, all along the circuit this summer."

"I appreciate it very much," I said, honestly. To myself, realistically, I had to discount some of the flattery. The LTA, I knew by now, was subject to the kind of internal politics of any large organization. There were regional branches to be appeased, regional officials whose personal influence sometimes shaped decisions. The fact that I had been chosen as one of a national group of some fourteen young players didn't necessarily mean that I was one of the fourteen *best* young players in the country — I couldn't believe my record during the summer had been *that* impressive. It could have meant no more than that, in order to keep the Midwestern tennis crowd happy, it had been found desirable to include a player from that area on the squad. And I was the regional choice.

Nevertheless, the telegram did mean *something*. Even if I might not be that good, at least they thought my game had some merit. I wasn't going to pass up an honor and an opportunity just because of some shadowy doubts that may, after all, have been false. There was another reason, though, that did stand in my way — the money problem.

The Cincinnati tennis official had an answer for that.

"Suppose we advance you, say . . . twenty dollars? Could you get by with that? You'll be put up once you get to Merion, you know."

"I'll get there," I said.

The Junior Davis Cup Squad was something new — a device to encourage young players, to single out possible future material for the Davis Cup team itself, and to bring some of this young talent under closer inspection. Joe Hunt was the star of the group, of course; Don Mc-

Neill was brought to Merion, too; and so was a spindly California high school boy named Jack Kramer, a hungry tennis player if there ever was one. Jake, as we all called him, not only couldn't wait to get on the court for our daily practice and coaching sessions — once on, he kept straining for the net like a leashed hound, always on the offensive.

One of the attractions of being named to the junior squad was the chance to watch the "varsity" members — Budge, Mako and Riggs — at practice, and then to see them perform in the climactic event of the tennis year: the challenge for possession of the Davis Cup.

The Challenge Round that year was played just a few miles from Merion, at the Germantown Cricket Club. When the American team, defending the trophy, and their Australian opponents strode onto the court, all impeccable in their white flannels, they were surrounded with an atmosphere of drama that I had never felt even in the most important of tournaments. The flags and the anthems of the two countries gave the matches an air of solemnity and importance. The tension in the stands and on the court; the polish of the tennis and the manners — these things made every point exciting.

I had seen and talked to the American players. I had read and heard about the Australians — Jack Bromwich, with his curious two-handed shot, and Adrian Quist, with his elegant style. But in this setting they seemed even more than tennis players. The Davis Cup team emblems on their white shirts were badges of national honor.

When Budge beat Quist in three straight sets on the

final day of the matches, and the Americans happily reclaimed the huge, ornate, silver punch bowl, I felt a surge of pride and desire. To play for the Davis Cup — that would be something better than any tournament victory or national ranking.

When I went back to Cincinnati and another year of college, I found myself a campus hero and an acknowledged man of the world. I could declare with an air of authority that Brenda was a vivacious beauty — great fun to talk to and even prettier than in her newspaper pictures. I could report to my clothes-conscious pals that at Merion or Newport, even in the summertime, you never wore a shirt-collar spread outside the lapels of a jacket. With only mild exaggeration, I could describe how it felt to get bounced from the dance floor of an exclusive Long Island club, and to try to hold down a couple of Scotch-and-sodas against the swell of a yacht's deck.

I was glad to be home, glad to see my folks — and dismayed that there was nothing I could seem to do either to get my father out of his deepening business troubles or to unlock him from his isolation.

In the next couple of months, things became worse. My grandfather died, leaving my father to manage the affairs of Talbert & McDonald completely by himself. It was only a short time before the inevitable happened. The company collapsed, and my father was out of business.

I X

Default

WHILE Dad floundered — taking a job with another live-stock firm, losing it, drifting briefly to still another, drinking a little too much in between — I wrestled uneasily with my studies and finances. My luck in picking up jobs was still with me. I caught on as a clerk at Dunlap's, a local menswear shop owned by the Schaengold brothers, Dick and Bob. Clerking at Dunlap's had become a kind of off-season tradition for Cincinnati athletes. Leo Durocher, for one, had worked there during his tenure as shortstop for the Reds. It may have been the start of his reputation as a dandy.

I had always liked clothes, had noticed what people wore at places like Newport and Southampton, and I enjoyed selling. Before long, I was making as much as sixty or seventy dollars a week, just working four or five hours a day. It was a lot of money in those days. Whatever I could squeeze out of it, after my college bills were paid and the household running expenses taken care of, I put aside toward the beginning of the next tennis season and my next tour of the circuit.

That's what really kept me going. The worse the family situation became — financially and psychologically — the more attractive tournament life seemed. Home, college, even the job, were just steps on a dreary treadmill. Tennis was freedom, the only real fun.

"It may be fun," Bob Kistner said, "but it isn't really freedom. You'll always have to take your needles, you'll always have to watch your diet. In a way, tennis only makes the diabetes problem tougher. You've got to watch yourself all the closer."

Kistner spoke with some authority now. He had been admitted to the university's medical school. But that didn't mean he had all the answers.

"I got through the circuit all right, Doc," I reminded him. "I was only in trouble a couple of times — and then, it wasn't really bad at all."

Kistner shook his head. "You think you've developed some kind of immunity," he said. "You run around the courts all day, and then you stay up late at night — I watched you at the intercollegiates, don't forget. How long has it been since you checked with the doctor?"

"I don't need to check with the doctor. I'm sugar-free. I'm in good shape." I watched him, scowling behind the wheel of his car. I laughed. "You med-school guys really kill me. You read something about diabetes in a ten-year-old medical textbook, and you're ready to write off the patient on the spot."

We drove silently toward my house. "It isn't the diabetes that worries me," I resumed after a while. "The real trouble is, I'm just not a good enough player, when you get right down to it. I love the damn game, Doc. I love the life. It's like being sprung from a jail sentence

— getting away from the bills and the frets at home. And from trying to figure out how you're going to pass Money and Banking 2 if you don't cut work for a day or two to bone up for the exam. And how you're going to pay next term's tuition fee if you *do* cut work. And juggling the tuition fee against the rent."

I pounded my hand into my fist. "Damn it!" I said. "I want something more out of life than that! And I can get it out of tennis, at least for a while. If . . . "

"If what?"

"If I'm good enough so they'll *invite* me to play their tournaments . . . so I don't have to keep scrounging around for some club that'll agree to let me in. I want to be *asked*, like Budge and Riggs. Expenses paid . . . No worry about whether they'll put me up — that way, I'm right back behind the same old financial eight-ball. I don't give a damn about the diabetes. I've just got to be a better tennis player, that's all!"

When summer came, I took my small hoard and went east again. It was like breathing out of a cocoon — a change from off-campus beaneries to summer-house butlers, from life on the run to life at ease. In fact, it was easier than the year before. Tournament committees at least knew me; I had a record, such as it was, from the season before. I was accepted at all the places where I had been turned down the last time.

I still had no really outstanding victories to my credit, but I was playing better. I wasn't losing many matches to the also-rans, and I was giving some of the better players a hard time, especially in doubles. Bushman and

I got into the national doubles championships at the Longwood Cricket Club, in Boston, where we took the first two set from Parker and McNeill, one of the top-seeded teams, before they wore us down.

I was beginning to feel at home on the circuit. People at the clubs knew me. The older players, who had been somewhat standoffish before, seemed more cordial. I got helpful advice about things I'd been doing wrong on the court, encouragement about things I was doing well.

"Not bad," said one of the veterans as I left the practice court one morning before a tournament match. He looked me over with the air of a prep school upperclassman sizing up a new boy. "At least you *look* like a tennis player. Socks match, shirt's clean, and you're not wearing one of those two-tone basketball jackets like those rustics from Texas. Where are you from, Talbert?"

"Cincinnati."

"Let's see, that's in one of our Middlewestern states, isn't it? How come you're so civilized?"

"A season on the circuit does wonders for a man," I said drily.

He laughed, in a friendly way that changed my mind about him. The air of eastern snobbery, I realized, was just an act, which he expected to be understood that way. He meant nothing very seriously. Everything he did was part of a continuous performance.

Jimmy DeFay was a tall, dark-haired, impeccable fellow in his middle twenties, who had been around the circuit for several years. He had pulled off just enough wins in the important tournaments to establish a ranking for himself in the top twenty players of the country, without ever showing much evidence that he would climb much higher. Or that he especially wanted to. It didn't seem to matter. People liked him. He made a place for himself everywhere.

The things that happened when Jimmy DeFay was around were always fun. That was his element. During a tournament at Orange, New Jersey, he and I were invited to a dinner party at the home of one of the club members. There were a few young people there, tennis players and others, and also some older, very social types, who filled the long drive with a variety of elegant cars. Jimmy drove up in a horse-drawn hack — I don't know where he'd dug it up. Everyone was delighted. Later on, a few of us piled in for a ride, with Jimmy holding the reins — a little unsteadily but well enough.

In the course of the evening, somebody asked him if he was related to the DeFays of Boston.

Jimmy looked at her stonily. "I'm one of the *original* DeFays," he said. "We go back to the fourteenth century. And," he added, "we haven't improved a bit."

He was always doing that — striking a pose and then, with a few words, shattering it himself. He happened to come from New England, but the patrician manner was just something he had picked up for its entertainment value. I never did learn much about his family but knew he didn't have a cent. He was making the tour on a shoestring almost as thin as my own.

That was why I was surprised when, at Newport, some weeks later, he asked me to join him and a couple of girls he'd invited on an evening's drive over to one of the other shore resorts, an hour or so away. I knew he didn't have a car — we had come up to Newport together as passengers in another player's jalopy. But when Jimmy came by to pick me up, that evening, he was behind the wheel of a gleaming new Cadillac convertible.

"You've modernized," I said. "I thought you were a horse-and-buggy man."

"Some local people I met asked me to take this wreck off their hands for a few days," he said airily. "It was cluttering up their grounds."

I shook my head in wonder.

"Talbert," he said, "you don't seem to have the hang of this tennis-player thing. We are the gladiators, the court jesters — in more ways than one. Did you ever take Shakespeare or medieval history? You do and you'll see the way it works. All we're supposed to do is keep the noble lords and ladies amused. That gives us privileges ordinary people don't get." He patted the wheel of the Cadillac. "Use your privileges, Talbert. Use your privileges."

I let Jimmy's advice and example go with no regrets. I felt I was doing about as well as my record in gladiatorial combat deserved, and maybe even a little better.

I was invited to Merion again that year, to join the Junior Davis Cup Squad. Once more it was the Australian team that reached the Challenge Round, only this time against an American group weakened by the loss of Don Budge, who had turned professional. When the Challenge Round ended, Australia had the Davis Cup.

There was an air of dismay on the American side, deepened by world events. Just as the matches were starting, ominous news bulletins had begun to come over the radio: Hitler's Panzers had invaded Poland. Europe was at war.

Someone remembered that in 1914 the Australians had also taken the cup away from the United States, and it was five years before we even had another chance to get it back.

"Oh, well," one of the other players said, "it won't last five years this time, for sure. The British aren't fooling around with Hitler any more. They mean business. And don't forget the French — they have this Maginot Line."

It all seemed very remote, and meanwhile, at Merion, I had become engaged in a small private war of my own. The issue seemed desperately important at the time.

The junior squad that year was limited to eight players, as against the fifteen or so chosen the year before. That made relations within the group closer, and competition among us more intense. We were all looking for every opportunity to display our skills — and improve them — for the officials in charge. . . . All, that is, except for a compact, jaunty young Californian named Frederick R. Schroeder, Jr., a new member and a tennis player of outstanding potential — no less an authority than Bill Tilden considered him even more promising than Kramer.

I came in from the practice courts one afternoon, and found Ted Schroeder already in his street clothes.

"For Pete's sake!" I said angrily. "I waited two hours for you out there this afternoon!"

"I couldn't make it," he said. "I was busy."

"Busy with what? Hanging around Kramer and Hunt, over on the team courts? They don't want you around all the time. They're just too polite to tell you to beat it."

"They don't seem to mind. Anyway, that's my business, Talbert, not yours."

"The hell it isn't my business! You're forgetting — there are just eight guys on this squad, and when you don't show, it's odd man out. I didn't even get to play at all today, on account of you, and that wasn't the first time you've pulled that stunt." I swiped viciously at the air with my racket. "The next time I do get you on a court, I'm going to keep you there all afternoon. I'm going to run you around until you drop!"

That was the beginning of the one real feud I ever became involved in, during all my years of tennis. We left Merion feeling none too comradely toward each other. When we met again on the circuit, we picked up where we left off.

That season gave me my first national ranking in the men's class — Number 21 out of the thirty or so players regarded by the LTA as good enough to list. At the end of the year, I was invited to play in the Sugar Bowl tournament, the winter sports festival in New Orleans.

Dad encouraged me to accept. "You've been working

pretty hard all fall," he said. "It'll do you good to get away."

I had been half-hoping he would say something to indicate that he'd rather have me around for the Christmas holiday. It might have been an occasion for some of the family intimacy that had all but disappeared from the household. Yet, at the same time I was relieved — not only because I missed the tennis and tournament life whenever I was away from it, but also because I knew, inside, that my father was prepared to make no concessions to the season. He might be concerned about Mother and me — he brooded constantly, in a kind of lonely paralysis — but there was no sign that he enjoyed us.

Before I left, I tried one small seasonal gesture toward making us a real family. Besides getting a couple of small individual Christmas presents for my mother and father, I bought some sort of large family game, thinking we would all use it together. Summoning all the holiday spirit I could muster, as I brought the package into the house, I pushed open the door and yelled, "Merry Christmas, everybody — a little early!"

"Hello, Bill," my mother answered tonelessly.

"What's the matter?" I glanced around. "Dad here?" She shook her head.

"Where'd he go?"

She sat down wearily in a kitchen chair. "Florida. He went to sell the car. He says he can get more for it down there."

"Couldn't he have waited? We had enough to get by

for the holidays." The commissions on Christmas shopping at Dunlap's had made my latest pay check a pretty
substantial one.

My mother didn't answer. I could see she knew as well
as I did that Florida wasn't really an objective for Dad
— only an excuse. He had given up trying to cope with
the family problems. He was running away from
them.

"Did he say when he'd be back?"

She shook her head, then said cheerily, "You go ahead
on your trip, Bill. I'm going to have myself a real nice
holiday — no cooking Christmas dinner, for a change.
I've already been invited over to the neighbors, and I
told them I'd go."

The next day I left for the Sugar Bowl, by a somewhat
roundabout route. First, I stopped at Baton Rouge, Louisiana, to pick up Jack Bushman at college. Together, we
went on to St. Petersburg, Florida, where Jack's family
lived, and where I had been invited to stay with some
friends of theirs.

It was a strange, lonely Christmas. I took a long walk,
feeling lost in the incongruous summery warmth and the
green foliage along the streets.

My father is somewhere down here, I thought. I might
even bump into him, right on the next block. Would we
have anything to say to each other? Would he even be
glad to see me?

How could a man have been such a giant in a boy's
world — a world of games and fishing — and such a loss
in the world of men? Why, when he had always been

able to show me how to do things, couldn't he seem to do things for himself? Not that it mattered so much. I loved him just the same. I was anxious to help him. And it hurt to think that this was all he thought of my help — to escape it. What I didn't take into account was his pride.

I kept trying to fit the pieces together: ambition and responsibility; my strong feelings for my family and my revulsion from what it had become — three separate individuals who couldn't seem to be happy together. Meeting resistance whichever way I shifted these elements around, I went back to the Christmas party I'd left, drank a little and stayed up late.

I wrestled with the problem all the way back to New Orleans and fell into my hotel bed exhausted, only to wake up in the middle of the night with a racking headache. I was painfully shaving when Jack poked his head in that morning.

"Shake a leg, Willy! We've got a match, fella." He stopped, staring at my reflection in the mirror. "Hey, what happened to you? You look as if you found an all-night poker game."

"I had some trouble sleeping," I said, not exaggerating a bit. I drew a glassful of water from the sink and swallowed it with a grimace. "Phew! How do you drink the water down here?"

"With bourbon whisky, mostly. Go easy, though. I prefer my doubles partners sober — at least on court. You can make up for it when you get back to Cincinnati."

I buttoned my shirt as briskly as I could. "I'm not going back," I said.

I had finally figured it all out. I was through with Cincinnati, with home and college. From New Orleans, we were scheduled to go on to play one or two tournaments in Florida, on the winter circuit. Only, I had decided, I wouldn't stop at that. I would keep going on the circuit, and somewhere along the way I'd find some small club that needed a tennis professional. When I did, I'd take the job. It wouldn't pay much, probably, but enough so I'd be able to send some money home. That seemed to be the only solution — the only way I could keep playing tennis and earn a living and stay away from the mess at home.

As time approached for the matches, I began to dread the effort of even swinging a racket. My head was pounding. My insides felt like the engine room of a foundering tanker.

Somehow I managed to struggle through the doubles match, never really knowing the score, unable to care that we lost. When it came to my singles match, I didn't even get onto the court. I went up to the officials' table and defaulted to my opponent. Then I went up to the press section of the stands and buttonholed a news-agency reporter.

"You could do me a tremendous favor," I said. "I just had to default my match, and if my mother reads that in the papers back home, she'll start worrying what's wrong with me. It'd save a lot of unnecessary trouble if you could fake a score."

He thought it over. "I guess it won't hurt anybody if I do. These results get scrambled up, anyhow, by the time the printers get through with them."

Bushman caught up with me at the hotel. "You look like hell," he said. "Have you had anything to eat?"

I shook my head. "Can't. This water down here has my stomach all messed up." I flopped back on the bed and shut my eyes.

I sweated out a couple of more days of misery, getting out of bed only long enough to force down an occasional glass of milk and a sandwich. My bleary mind was functioning just well enough to grapple with my normal concern — diabetes. Since I was hardly eating, I reasoned, there was little food in my system to absorb insulin, so I cut down on my normal dosage.

I passed up the New Year's party which for most of the participants was perhaps the main attraction of the Sugar Bowl festival. I just couldn't make it. Nor did I think I'd be able to reach Tampa, the first stop on the Florida circuit. I made the trip by auto with Charley Hare, the former British Davis Cup player who had lately come to live in this country. It was six hundred miles of torture.

Again, at Tampa, I defaulted, enlisted the help of the press to cover myself at home, and retreated to my hotel and a series of nightmares.

That was the last I could remember. What followed was something I was in no condition to be aware of. It was told to me later by a man whose entry on the scene was one of the most vital strokes of luck I ever had.

The man was Ray Peo, a Cleveland businessman and

tennis fan, who happened to be in Florida at the time. Knowing me from his club's tournament at home, and hearing that I had come to play at Tampa, he stopped in at the hotel and asked for me. When the desk rang my phone, there was no answer. Peo decided to wait until I showed up. After a while, Charley Hare came in and Peo found out I hadn't been seen around the courts all day.

"Bill's been feeling rather under the weather," Hare said. "Says the water hereabout has been giving him quite a bit of trouble."

Peo persuaded the desk clerk to let him into my room. I was in bed, where I'd been since the night before — unconscious.

"Water, nothing!" the doctor at the Tampa hospital told Peo after they'd unloaded me from the ambulance. "This boy's in an advanced stage of diabetic coma. Probably been coming on gradually for days, if not longer. A few more hours, and I don't think we'd have been able to save him."

A Hungry Tennis Player

IN four or five days at the Tampa hospital, enough insulin and nourishment were pumped into me to bring me around. Just about able to move under my own power, I boarded a train for Cincinnati. Before I left, one of the tournament officials tried to put some money into my hand for a Pullman berth. I couldn't accept it, though, having contributed absolutely nothing to his tournament but a small cloud of trouble. I sat up in the coach, dozing, reading and reassembling my thoughts. My plans had come to a quick, brutal end, but there was nothing to do about that, at least for now.

When I got off the train at the Union Terminal in Cincinnati, my mother nearly fainted. I had lost about twenty pounds, and hotel rooms and hospital beds — even Southern ones — had proved no place to pick up a healthy suntan.

"Better let me take your bag, Bill." I turned to the familiar but unexpected voice. Dad was standing there, as if trying to decide how to join the family group. He had come home a few days before, having found no sanctuary. So here we both were, limping back from our separate attempts to escape.

In a way, I had actually lost ground in my attempt. I now had to go back to the beginning as a diabetic, back through the mill of tests under a doctor's care. What was needed was a complete analysis of my relapse, and a complete reassessment of my diabetic needs. That presented a slight difficulty in itself. I had been breezing along independently for such a long time, without bothering about checkups, that the only doctors familiar with my case were Dr. Walt and the staff at Children's Hospital. The only practical thing was to go back there again — at twenty-one, probably the oldest "child" on their records. In an adult-sized bed, specially installed for me, I felt like Gulliver among the Lilliputian tots in the ward.

During the couple of weeks I spent there, I learned to be grateful for their company. It was the first time I could really relate my own experience with physical trouble to somebody else's. Naturally I felt a special kinship with the young diabetics in the ward. The years of growing up, wrapped up in myself like any adolescent, and then the years of striking out on my own as an athlete, had kept me from any close association with other diabetics. Now I found some comfort in getting to know youngsters whose problems were the same ones I'd met.

"Here's the way I gave myself an injection the day I went out on the court to play . . ." I searched for the most impressive name I could muster . . . "to play Bobby Riggs." I turned to a sad-looking eight-year-old with tousled red hair. "You've heard of Bobby Riggs, haven't you?"

He shook his head.

I hitched up my punctured ego. "Bobby Riggs is a champion tennis player. Red, how are you going to see how to take an insulin injection with your hair falling down over your eyes? What you need is a haircut."

Red held still when I cut his hair. In the next day or two the other boys began to line up for their turns under the shears. They joined in a couple of games we devised to relieve the boredom of hospital life, bouncing and tossing a ball around the ward. And they watched me more and more attentively when I showed them how to use the hypodermic needle.

As the one adult patient in the place, I also had the company of the doctors and nurses on a social basis. They invited me to join them for coffee in their lounge.

"I ought to resent you," one of the nurses told me one day, "the way those children pay attention to everything you tell them. It's all I can do to make them even look at the hypodermic."

"They're probably scared to death of me. Don't forget, I'm the biggest boy in the ward."

"You know it isn't that at all. It's because you do something for them that none of us on the staff do — you use the needle on yourself." She stacked the used coffee cups on a tray. "They trust you because they can see that you're really one of them."

I liked being trusted, and yet there was something that irked me about being considered "one of them." I would rather have won their confidence as a tennis player, if I could, than as a fellow diabetic. Diabetes was something to get away from, not to be bound to. As far as I was concerned, the hospital was just an unfortunate interruption to my life as a tennis player.

Even my mother realized by now that I had gone much too far beyond invalidism to turn back willingly. She suggested a compromise.

"I'm not going to try to talk you out of playing tennis altogether," she said to me one day during visiting hours. "I know it means too much to you. But you can see there was some reason for me to worry — now, wasn't there?"

"Mom," I said, "I couldn't talk you out of worrying any more than you could talk me out of tennis."

"Well, what's wrong with playing just once in a while, for fun? You don't have to make a whole life out of it."

I sorted out my words carefully before I answered. "I've been thinking the whole thing over," I told her, "and I'm sure that what happened to me down in Florida proves only one thing. You have to use your head about diabetes — more than I've been doing. Honestly, that's all it proves."

"You won't stay home this season?"

"The circuit's half the fun. Ninety per cent of it. The things I do out there, the people I meet — how would I ever have any of that if I didn't play the tournaments?"

"You won't give it up?" she said again.

"I'd just as soon give up insulin."

"That's a silly thing to say."

"That's the way I feel about it."

Although my father, sitting at the other side of the bed, had stayed out of the debate, I could sense that he

understood and was still with me. He had only one
reservation.

"Don't give up college, either," he said finally. "You
just can't understand how important it is. Your mother
spoke to the dean's office, and they're willing to let you
re-enter if you make up the work you've missed. I . . ."
He hesitated, as if he weren't sure whether to commit
himself. "I'll try to give you more help than I have."

I was sure he meant it, but the good intentions didn't
pay off. I went back to classes — and back to my jobs.
Mother began to do some sewing for other ladies in the
neighborhood, as a way of bringing a little more cash
into the household. Dad got a new job — and lost it.
I began to look forward to the summer circuit and freedom. This time, I was determined to be better prepared
for tennis — as a diabetic and as a player.

Not that I could really separate those two sides of my
life. In fact, what I had learned most surely at Tampa
and, afterwards, in the hospital, was that the two were
inextricably connected. My success as a player would
always depend, in the long run, on my success in mas-
tering the facts of my own faulty biology. And the more
I worked on improving my game for the summer tournaments, the more I kept coming back to diabetes as the
key to the problem.

Obviously, in the past I hadn't really mastered diabetes; I had only survived it, day by day. In New Orleans,
I had failed to recognize the signs of a really serious
attack. And when it came, I had done exactly the wrong
thing. Several wrong things, really.

I had been under stress — upset about the problems at home. I may have picked up a cold in the change of climate. Either of those things alone could have thrown the normal balance out of kilter. But instead of sweating it out by myself in a hotel room, instead of trying to juggle the amount of my insulin dosage, I should have gone straight to a doctor. A diabetic has to find a doctor who is expert in the problem (as not all are); having found one, he must depend on him. That, I told myself, was an absolute rule for even the most nonchalant cuss or the most independent-minded one.

I spent a great deal of time with Dr. Walt now, talking over what I thought I had learned and trying to learn more. He seemed pleased to see me after several years, though disappointed that it was trouble that had brought me back. He had been using my experiences in tennis as a pattern of treatment for some of his other patients and as an example to encourage them in getting away from the invalid's attitude toward life.

"You'd better find a new example," I told him, "because I'm beginning to think I've been going at this whole thing wrong."

He was willing to listen. "I've always found I had something to learn from my patients," he said. "You're a lot closer to diabetes than I am."

"Well," I said, "all these years I had the idea that the most important thing was to be sugar-free. You know how it starts, when you first go into the hospital — all the tests and the scales and the warnings about sugar. A low sugar count in your tests gets to be the biggest thing in life."

"It's hard to get over the ideas you learn at the beginning," Dr. Walt agreed. "A lot of doctors still feel that this is the only safe way to handle diabetes. But . . ." He shrugged. "It's something you can certainly overdo."

"Well," I said, "I don't think I really ever have got over that guilty feeling. Even after you started me playing tennis. When I took a lump of sugar or some candy, the way you told me to, it was just an emergency measure — something to do only if I got in trouble, when I could feel an insulin reaction coming on." I leaned forward in my chair. What I wanted to say was something on which I needed a doctor's assurance.

"The truth is that, as long as I've taken my insulin, I think I'm much better off if I do have a little too much sugar — I mean, what you and the doctors at the hospital used to *say* was too much. My sugar count ought to be a little too *high* before I start playing a match. Then I won't be so apt to run the risk of an insulin reaction. There won't be so much chance of an emergency."

I leaned back. "I don't know about any other diabetic. That's just the way it seems to make the most sense for me."

It made sense not only for my future as a diabetic but also for my future on the tennis courts. When I began to think back over some of the matches I might have won and hadn't, I could see that the old habits of thinking about diabetes had been holding me back. How many times had there been when, on some crucial point, I hadn't been able to move quickly enough, or bring my racket around sharply enough? That was because my sugar level — my source of energy — was already a little too low. I might not be in any serious trouble yet, from the medical standpoint, but I might have taken an unnecessary loss in the game. In a moment or two, I might take a lump of sugar or a bite of chocolate to offset the situation, but by that time I might already have given up a couple of important points in the match.

The answer, it seemed clear, was to be biologically prepared for the crucial points before they came. That meant always having sufficient sugar in my system to keep my game up to par. And that, in turn, meant also having enough insulin in my system to keep the sugar from getting out of hand.

The doctor had the beginning of a solution to the problem. A new long-lasting form of insulin had been developed just a year or two before — protamine zinc insulin. Once injected, it released its effects slowly, over a period of twenty-four hours. It was, I realized as soon as I began to use it, a blessing of the proportions of the original discovery by Banting and Best. It simplified the cumbersome old routine of using the needle two or three times a day. One injection, first thing in the morning, would take care of me until the next day.

Now the question was to find the right combination of diet that would keep this insulin "occupied" in the body at all times and still leave enough of a sugar reserve to carry me through a tennis match. What I had to do now was to fill in the other factors to make up a new and more effective diabetic equation for myself as a tennis player.

There was some guidance from a few things I'd learned in freshman biology — and before that, in my diabetes-clinic schooling with my parents. I knew, for example, that different kinds of food were digested by different chemical processes. Insulin burned some of them fast (the sweet and starchy carbohydrates). On others (the proteins, mainly in meats and fish), insulin worked more slowly. Maybe I ought to be eating a different combination of foods — heavier on protein or carbohydrate. Probably I ought to be eating them according to a different time schedule, to allow for the new insulin, the different rates of digestion and also for the sugar-burning effects of tennis.

With the doctor, that winter and spring, I kept going over the results of the tests I was taking. Between visits I read books and articles he lent me, and others that Bob Kistner brought me from the medical school library. The bull sessions between Kistner and me took on an odd clinical tone. Metabolism — the process by which the body converts food into energy and growth — became one of our favorite topics of conversation. We argued the ins and outs of carbohydrates and proteins almost as heatedly as we used to argue about girls and the merits of major league ball players.

"You know," Bob said, after one rousing session, "if I ever do get my M.D., I just hope I don't have any patients like you. If I prescribed aspirin, you wouldn't take it unless I drew you a complete chart of aspirin metabolism — even if there is no such thing."

"You've got me all wrong, Doc. All you'd really have to

do is show me how it affects the forehand volley after three sets on a hot afternoon. That's what I'm really interested in — the metabolism of the tennis player."

The metabolism of tennis figured not only in my attempts to work out an effective diet but even in my ideas about the strategy and technique of the game.

My experience on the fast Eastern grass courts hadn't changed the basic fact about tennis that I had noticed on the slower Midwestern clay. On grass, the hard-hit shots scored more often, but it was still true that the percentages favored control over power.

The mathematics of the game show that only one out of every five points in a match is apt to be earned — that is, hit cleanly through or past the other player. Four out of five are scored on errors — that is, on balls which the opponent has hit into the net or out of court. Without resorting to a slide rule, you can easily deduce that it doesn't pay to try to slug every ball past the other man. The best chance of winning is to make sure you put the ball into the court and let the other fellow commit the errors.

This is percentage tennis. It isn't necessarily defensive tennis. In fact, the most effective way to play these odds is by attacking. You have to move forward to the net at every opportunity, since this is the commanding position on the court. The defender is forced to make difficult, risky shots against you. If he is deft, he may be able to pass you or drive you back with a well-placed lob. But he is more likely to miss or make a weak return. And the weak return is the one you can safely put away for that fifth point, the earned one.

Even sluggers like Budge, Kramer and Pancho Gonzales don't try to make every shot an earned point. They use their power as the basis of an attack. Behind a hard-hit serve or drive they come to net, ready to volley a return that is a little too soft or high.

I had realized from the beginning that I lacked the natural power of these players. Now I realized that as a diabetic I couldn't afford to play their way. The style is too energetic. I had to make up for lack of power by finesse. In order to force my way to net, I would have to hit the ball with a fair amount of speed, but my main weapon would have to be control. I would have to be able to play the angles and hit the undefended positions on the court. I would have to outmaneuver the opposition and fool them with a variety of shots, delivered at a variety of speeds. *Controlled* speed was what I was after — some happy medium between the "pusher's" style of play and the powerhouse pattern. My kind of game would be a game of attack based on careful preparation and firm control of my strokes.

I had learned the strokes by watching the good players and pestering them for advice. It had become easy for me to imitate what they showed me. But as a diabetic doing some serious thinking about my future in the game, I began to wonder just how useful imitation was. On that subject, too, Kistner's medical training — as well as his interest in sport — gave me a sounding board.

"Watch this for a moment and tell me if you notice

anything," I said one Saturday afternoon at the university squash courts. I had taken advantage of a free half-hour to work out solo, banging shots against the wall, and Doc had stopped by to pick me up.

"That looks good," he said, after I had hit a few backhands. "You've got that Don McNeill backhand down pat."

I groaned.

"Isn't McNeill good enough for you any more?" Doc said. "I thought any tennis player would take that as a compliment."

"McNeill's backhand is great . . . for McNeill. For anybody else — if he wants to use it as a model. What I've been trying to do for the last half-hour is see if I can't cut it down to my size. Look." I brought my racket around in slow motion. "You know this big beautiful sweep he gives it — you've seen him. And then this full follow-through. Well, it's biologically wrong for me."

"Don't get fancy on me, Billy. I happen to know a little biology, don't forget. Of course, I never have dissected a backhand in the lab. I guess we just haven't come to that yet."

"Seriously, Doc. Put your overtrained medical mind to work on this for a moment, and see if you don't think it makes sense. Now, when I make this big motion with the racket, I'm actually burning more energy than I need just to hit the ball. I'm burning carbohydrates — right? And the faster I use up carbohydrates, the greater the risk of an insulin reaction."

"And of fatigue."

"And of fatigue. So —" I took my position with the racket again — "what I'm trying to do is this."

"You're shortening the stroke. Less backswing, less follow-through."

"That's it. The same basic pattern, only I'm trying to economize on it."

"Sounds perfectly reasonable to me."

In much the same way, I cut the backswing out of my serve, producing a stroke that made the purists wince. It violated the standard pattern of elaborate windup and cannonball delivery that had been taken for granted ever since the powerhouse style of tennis became popular, back in the early 1920s. The only thing in favor of the serve I kept developing all that spring was that it seemed to work. It was sharp and accurate, and even if it didn't split the ball open on contact or dig up the turf, it consistently forced the receiver to make a defensive return — which is all a serve is really supposed to accomplish. Behind it, I could take up the attack and force my way to the net.

That summer of 1940 I went east with a feeling of new confidence. As I lugged my bag and my armload of freshly strung rackets into the Seabright Lawn Tennis and Cricket Club, at Seabright, New Jersey, I felt a familiar rush of excitement. The locker room seemed more like home than the apartment I'd left in Cincinnati, the day before. Still, I had a moment of uncertainty about resuming my place in the circle.

I dropped my luggage and made that first, automatic

movement of a player arriving at a tournament — a look at the draw sheet.

"Who made up this draw?" somebody said over my shoulder. "Your mother? They've got all the pushovers in your bracket."

"They're all pushovers for me this year," I said, replying to the gambit.

"Oh? You playing in the women's this season, Talbert?" one of the older players called over, in an innocent tone of voice. "Now just don't ruin your chances by being overconfident. Some of these girls are mighty sharp."

Jimmy DeFay came in, carrying a champagne bottle in a cooler crooked in one arm, with a stem goblet in his other hand. "Hello, Talbert," he said. "Where did you get that necktie? It couldn't have come from Ashtabula or Columbus or wherever it is you go between seasons." He put the cooler down gently on the bench in front of his locker, twirled the bottle between his hands like a *sommelier*, pulled the cork, and — while everybody watched — elegantly poured himself a champagne-glassful of milk.

"Get your working clothes on, Talbert," he said, "and I'll play you a fast set of singles. Five dollars on it." He looked around the room. "Anybody care to stake me?"

I *was* home again. The usual locker room warfare was on, and I was right there in the trenches with the rest of the boys. Nothing was said about my diabetes or what had happened at Tampa, and I could see that no fuss was going to be made about it. To athletes, who take physical soundness for granted and have little experience with abnormal biology, what had happened to me was no more meaningful, really, than a pulled tendon or a bad touch of sun. It was assumed to be just one of those things that happen, now and then, to upset a player's form or put him on the sidelines for a spell.

There was no difference, either, in the attitude of the officials or the people at whose homes I was a guest on the circuit that summer. Diabetes was *my* problem. As long as I didn't make it theirs by failing to handle it success-fully, they'd treat me the way I wanted to be treated — simply as a tennis player.

I gave them no reason to think about the problem. Behind the progress I could see in my game was the progress I had made in learning to handle diabetes. I still kept a quick-energy ration on hand at the courts when I played — sugar, candy, orange juice — in case of unexpected trouble. But I didn't need as much as I used to, and I felt better all through my matches, because the new insulin and the new diet seemed to be working fine.

My tennis diet actually consisted of much more than the sugar ration. It started, every morning, with a break-fast containing a substantial amount of slow-burning protein — lean ham, eggs, milk. At noon, more protein in the form of lean meat or fish, plus vegetables. At that time, also, I introduced a slightly higher amount of carbohy-drate than before — bread, potatoes, perhaps a small portion of ice cream — to start building up my sugar reserve for an afternoon of tennis.

The low point of the day — in terms of energy — naturally came late in the afternoon, following a match.

Then, whether or not I had that vague "foreign feeling" that is the first hint of an insulin reaction, I took some orange juice.

Perhaps the most important innovation of all — possibly the most important meal of the day — was a late-night snack. This was something that, in my early experience as a diabetic, would have been considered risky. But, as I had reasoned with the doctor, a little extra food and perhaps a little too much sugar weren't quite as much of a danger as too little — especially during the night, when the sleeping mind couldn't cope with trouble if it did arise. Another small amount of carbohydrate and, especially, an amount of those slow-burning proteins would reduce the danger of an insulin reaction by giving the insulin something to work on overnight. A sandwich or crackers and a glass of milk became a bedtime ritual with me. Whether it meant rousing a reluctant room service in a resort hotel or asking a special favor in advance from my hostess at a country house, I knew it was an absolute must, and I couldn't let modesty or self-consciousness stand in its way. It was, after all, less embarrassing to need a glass of milk than an ambulance.

At each tournament, when I walked onto the court for my opening round of play, I wasn't just starting a match, I was pursuing a health campaign. I had studied the draw beforehand. If it indicated that later in the week I would be running into pushers, who might keep me on the court for a long time with their ping-pong tactics, I would have been building up an extra energy reserve against that crisis. I would also be spending less energy on practice during the week, and if I had an early opponent or two whom I knew I could beat, I wouldn't fool around with them. I'd try to make the easy matches short and businesslike.

This wasn't only sensible diabetic treatment; it was also sensible tennis, the kind of thing any player ought to do so that he could play his best when he needed to. I was playing much better than ever.

Back from the tennis wars in the fall, I found no gaiety at home like the pleasures of tournament life; no future in my job at Dunlap's to match the rewards of tennis; no satisfaction in my studies like the excitement of that season on the courts.

I was restless. My original college class had graduated in June; because of the time I had missed by dropping out, a few years before, to work as a bank messenger, and some time lost during the New Orleans incident that I never had made up, I would have almost a year to go before I finished college. Another year of trying to squeeze my studies in between jobs, of scrambling to meet the bills — when all the while I could be living it up on the tennis courts . . .

I stuck it out as long as I could. Another taste of winter-holiday tennis in the Sugar Bowl and at Tampa — this time with no trouble at all — only stimulated my appetite. The new LTA ratings came out in the Florida papers, and they confirmed what I felt about my game: I had been promoted five notches on the list.

In January I went home just long enough to tell my family that I was quitting college. No matter how important a degree might be, there was something else that seemed even more important now, and that was tennis. Then I headed back to Florida and the remaining tournaments on the winter circuit.

I was twenty-two years old, suntanned and court-weathered, feeling sounder than I could ever remember and as eager for life as I'd ever been in the days before I had even heard of insulin or seen a hypodermic needle. I was the sixteenth-ranking tennis player in the United States, and nothing mattered more to me than becoming the best.

I was a hungry tennis player.

Where I Belonged

I HUMMED happily to myself as I sped along the empty highway toward Palm Beach. The wheel of the big sedan felt comfortable in my hands after a couple of days' steady driving. This was the way to live — on your own and weighed down by nothing more than a couple of suitcases and a few freshly strung tennis rackets, no schedule to meet but a program of tournament matches.

The car was a stroke of luck that had come my way just as I was preparing to leave Cincinnati by bus, in order to keep the strain on my wallet as gentle as possible. Before I'd invested in a ticket, however, word had come from a Cincinnati dowager wintering in Florida, asking if I would drive her car down there for her, expenses paid. The car had proved to be a little stiff at first, having stood unused in the garage for months, and — as I'd noticed at the last moment before taking off — there was a certain element of risk in driving it. But what was the difference? The owner was in a hurry and so was I, eager to reach the palmy oases of the Florida courts. And here I was, almost at the finish line, without a bit of trouble en route.

No, I told myself, not the finish line — the starting point. Life was just about to begin.

The break with Cincinnati had been relatively pain-less. Things had been going better for Dad on his job in the last couple of months, so there had been no need to feel guilty about leaving. And he and my mother had given in to my decision with a minimum of protest. It was inevitable, they seemed to realize. Besides, the argument on my side was hard to contend with. What was I leaving behind, compared with the kind of life that lay ahead of me?

Absorbed in my own well-being, I didn't pay any attention to the siren until the police car drew alongside. I pulled over and waited.

There was no use pretending to be surprised. I was driving with last year's license plates, and I knew it. I was lucky to have got by as long as this.

At the musty stationhouse in town, I found out that the offense was a lot more serious than I had thought.

"A hundred dollars' fine," the judge said. He clamped his mouth tight around the words, as if to indicate he'd said all he was going to.

I winced. "Can I make a phone call?"

He nodded toward the phone and called the next case.

When I told the owner of the car about my plight, she was apologetic. She'd wire the money right away, she assured me, but it might take a couple of hours.

"I'll wait," the judge said amiably. "In the meantime, you can stay right here and enjoy our hospitality."

I was led through a doorway to the station's single large cell, already occupied by a couple of drunks and a woman with a disheveled look and a colorful vocabulary, which she was exercising steadily.

Feeling out of place in my well-pressed suit, I picked out an unoccupied bench and tried to make myself as inconspicuous as possible.

In a few minutes, the door opened again and a new client was shoved inside.

"Here's another boozer to keep y'all company."

The newcomer righted himself clumsily and staggered back to the cell door, making thick, unintelligible sounds of protest. Sweat was pouring down his face. The policeman waved him aside with a tired gesture, which roused me with a start.

"What's that you've got in your hand?" I said to the cop.

"This?" He held up a hypodermic syringe and a small bottle of a familiar-looking fluid. "I got it outa your buddy's pocket," he said, with a nod at my new cellmate. "Hey, whut's it to you, anyhow?"

"It looks like an insulin kit. I'll bet that guy isn't drunk at all."

The erratic movements, the pallid moistness of the skin, the rapid breathing — these were typical signs of an insulin reaction. The diabetic himself, if he was one, probably wasn't even aware what was wrong with him. That was the tricky thing about a reaction — it caught you by surprise. Unless you acted to ward it off at the earliest hint of any abnormal feeling, you might just stagger your way into a condition of shock.

The cop laughed humorlessly. "If there's one thing I

can rec'nize, it's a guy on the booze. This here's one," he concluded flatly.

"Wait a minute," I said. I was beginning to get anxious. "Did he have a wallet on him — any kind of identification?"

The cop opened a billfold and shuffled some of the papers in it.

"Look at that card," I said. "That'll prove it. This guy's a diabetic."

"A whut?"

"A diabetic. He's — " I gritted my teeth, biting on the word I hated. "He's sick."

The diabetic's identification card was a device all of us were urged by our doctors to carry for just such emergencies. Its importance had never seemed so vital to me as it did now.

"Look," I said, "it's an emergency. I mean it. Can you get him something sweet — a Coke or something? If we don't do something in a hurry, he's going to be in real trouble." I wasn't exaggerating the danger.

The cop, finally convinced, hurried down the hall and came back with a bottle of Coke. I had to hold it to the man's lips, not only because he couldn't hold it himself but because he seemed disinterested in help. He had no idea of what shape he was in.

It took only ten minutes or so for the crisis to pass. As it subsided, and with it the stir we had caused among the staff and the other inmates, my feeling of anxiousness began to drain away, leaving me with nothing but impatience and discomfort. When the man was finally told he could go, I felt relieved — not just for him, but also for myself. For those minutes of crisis, I had felt threatened. I had been forced to think of myself again as "one of them."

In an hour or so, the money for my fine arrived, and I went on my way. A couple of days of tennis at Palm Beach, and I was safe again. I was back where I belonged — among normal people, not among the "invalids."

A few weeks later, I was aboard the S.S. *President Roosevelt*, bound for Bermuda — a remote sort of paradise to most people, but just another stop on the winter circuit. I looked around at our troupe and thought how lucky we all were — Don McNeill, not long out of college but already used to rich and exciting experiences like this . . . Gardnar Mulloy, the tall, good-looking Floridian, a graduate of law school but so devoted to tennis that he couldn't give it up long enough to get started in practice. . . . Henry Prusoff, a big, dark bear of a man, a couple of years older than Mulloy but still more than anything else a tennis player. Gar and Hank were both married, and Dotty Prusoff and Madeleine Mulloy were part of our group, tasting the fun of circuit life along with the rest of us.

Bermuda was a new kind of adventure — another country, a landscape I'd never seen. I drank in all the small differences: the neat stucco houses with their tailored semitropical gardens, the air of British formality at the Coral Beach tennis club, the strangely quiet traffic of horse carriages and of bicycles ridden by grown-up men managing to keep an attitude of impeccable dignity as they pedaled along, dressed in short pants.

The second morning, I set out by bicycle to explore the town of Hamilton. It was a ride of about five miles from the house of my host, a man named Terry Mowbray, the proprietor of the large aquarium which was one of Bermuda's tourist attractions. The workout, I figured, would straighten out some of the shipboard kinks in my legs.

I pedaled along the shore roads, taking in the ocean view, and on into the traffic of downtown Hamilton. After a few blocks, I dismounted and tried to set my bike into a curbside parking rack. I couldn't seem to do it. The handlebars slipped out of my grasp and the bicycle clattered to the sidewalk. I tried to pick it up, but I just couldn't seem to get it off the ground. I was in reaction. I had miscalculated my diabetic needs. The morning's exercise had burned sugar. My morning insulin had used up the available food in my system, and now it was working unchecked.

None of this occurred to me at the time. I was aware of nothing but a vaguely unusual feeling, and a kind of instinctive hunger for something sweet. I walked dreamily down the street until I came to a grocery store. Without even realizing what I was doing, I went in and headed straight for an open carton of chocolate cookies, displayed in bulk next to the counter. While the clerk and a few customers watched in what must have been amazement, I scooped up a handful and began wolfing them down like a lost explorer stumbling onto a loaded dinner table.

The remedy took hold immediately. I took a shilling piece out of my pocket and handed it across the counter.

"I'm sorry," I said. "I wasn't trying to swipe your groceries. It was an emergency."

The clerk nodded civilly. "Really?" he said, without much conviction.

Until that moment, I had felt no embarrassment. The whole performance had seemed so normal to me, almost automatic. I was barely conscious of what had happened. But now I could see the expression of unease and distrust on the clerk's face. I started to explain about the diabetes, trying not to make a big clinical production out of it, but I realized that, at best, I was convincing him that I was just another one of those crazy Americans.

I hurried out, sat in the shade for a few minutes, and then pedaled on to the tennis club, where I had a tournament match scheduled that afternoon.

A few hours later, I left the locker room with Mulloy on my way to the courts.

"Stay away from liquor," he said suddenly, "if you want to get anywhere in this game."

That seemed like an odd way to strike up a conversation.

I was used to Mulloy's direct, almost brusque way of speaking, and I was aware that Gardnar himself was a teetotaler. He habitually passed up parties or left them early, tennis being such a serious occupation with him that he trained for it practically every waking minute of the day. But that was his business, and I didn't need the advice.

"I guess there are some guys on the circuit," I agreed,

"who collect hangovers instead of trophies. Of course," I added, "I don't see anything wrong with a drink now and then, as long as you don't overdo it."

"Eleven o'clock in the morning is overdoing it," Mulloy said sharply. "Madeleine and Dotty Prusoff saw you staggering down the street. You must've had a real early start."

I flushed. *Staggering* down the street? Could I have looked that bad off? I remembered the man in the Florida police station.

"If you mean what happened downtown this morning, I was absolutely sober, so help me."

Mulloy gave me a suspicious glance.

"I had some trouble with my diabetes," I added.

"I thought you took a needle for that." Mulloy, like a few of the other players, had occasionally seen me taking an insulin injection. Like most of them, he had never been exactly anxious to stand around and watch the operation or learn what it was all about.

We had come through the entryway between the stands. There was a clatter of applause as we reached the courts. Mulloy walked over to the umpire's platform at the court, where my match was scheduled to start in a few minutes.

"You'd better tell me about it," Gar went on, "in case something happens when I'm around."

"Sure," I said, "only don't worry. I can take care of myself."

Because Mulloy was an impersonal sort of guy, I didn't mind explaining it to him so much as I would have minded with others. He wasn't the kind to make a big thing of it. He wouldn't think I was asking for sympathy or special consideration, and it wouldn't occur to him to offer any. There was no room for sentimentality in Gar's businesslike approach to the game.

On those terms, and when the subject was forced on me, I wasn't so reluctant to mention my diabetes. It was when diabetes implied a weakness or a need for help on my part that I shrank from it. As a general fact of life, it was open to discussion, but as a personal problem, it was something private, not to be shared. Ordinarily, I saw no need for sharing it because, I felt, I had learned how to handle it by myself. It wasn't so tough, after all: You took your insulin faithfully; if you felt weak, you ate a piece of candy or drank a Coke or a glass of orange juice; if you didn't happen to have anything sweet on hand, in an emergency you could walk into a store and grab something. If that didn't do the trick, you went to the doctor.

Every day of activity seemed to crowd the diabetes into a smaller corner of my life, to make it less of an obstacle. I couldn't resist any opportunity to see just how far I could push it — and how much more I could enlarge the scope of my freedom.

One evening, later on in that spring of 1941, I was sitting in the lobby of a hotel in Asheville, North Carolina, thinking about nothing but the tennis match I would be playing next afternoon — the final round of the "Land of the Sky" tournament. So far, I had given my best performance of the tour, and even though tomorrow's results might be a foregone conclusion, I would have nothing to apologize for.

Gil Hall, who had been my opponent in the semi-finals that afternoon, tapped me on the shoulder. "Aren't you dressing for the party? If you'll hurry it up, I'll wait and give you a ride."

Hall, a New Jersey businessman most of the year, was, perhaps even more than Mulloy and Prusoff, an example of how hard it is to get the tennis life out of your system. Already in his forties, he still couldn't resist the impulse to get out on the circuit every so often, winter or summer. At the parties along the route, Gil was almost as much of a fixture as the champagne. Tonight's party, at a distinguished country house in the hills outside Asheville, was going to be one of the biggest — nothing short of a private Mardi Gras, judging by the talk around the clubhouse all week. It probably wouldn't be complete without old Gil, but I figured I'd better pass it up.

"I'm just going to sit here for a while and then turn in," I told him. "I'll wait to do my celebrating tomorrow."

Hall laughed. "You'd better celebrate beating *me*. Tomorrow you won't have any reason."

"You can't tell, Gil. I just might take Riggs this time."

Hall took my arm and started easing me up from the chair. "Be realistic, Billy," he said good-humoredly. "Bobby must have beaten you twenty-five straight times."

"Thirty-two," I said, "counting Jacksonville last month, and Houston, and a couple of other places in between."

"Then what are you doing here tonight — training for your thirty-third loss?"

I hesitated. "Is Riggs going to the party?" Whatever the reason, I still had that old hatred of being different.

"Probably. Everybody else is going."

"Okay," I said, getting up. "You talked me into it. Give me fifteen minutes to shave and dress." What did I have to lose?

The house was one of those vast Southern places in the Bourbon style. All along the portico, the tall windows were lighted up. Inside, an orchestra played from a stair landing the size of an ordinary living room. There must have been at least a hundred people there — dancing, chatting, eating from the elaborate buffet that extended down one whole side of a huge dining room, drinking the champagne that was carried through the house in endless relays by tray-bearing butlers.

I found myself snagged in a cross-current of conversation between a pair of New York bank executives whom I had met, the season before, at Westchester. They had come South, according to their annual custom, for golf and the sun. They were talking about the war.

"Oh, he'll have us in it, all right," one of them was saying. "Don't you doubt that for one moment. This Lend-Lease is only the beginning of it. He'll have our boys over there before long — Billy here, and the rest of them."

"I don't doubt we'll be in it one of these days. I don't think we can afford to stay out. We just can't sit back and let Europe go to hell, can we? Look what they're doing to London. I wonder if even old Churchill can save it."

"Old Churchill will do the job, you may count on

that," an Englishwoman named Angie something-or-other put in cheerily. I had been introduced to her on the way in — a tall, blonde, slightly aging tower of British strength, insisting to anyone who would listen that Winnie and stubborn spirit would save the day. "D'you hear him on the wireless the other evening?" She waved her fingers in a V-for-Victory sign.

At the buffet, a while later, sombody started an argument over whether or not Riggs had a chance of winning back his national championship from McNeill.

"Riggs was a fluke in the first place. With his game, he never should have won in '39."

"Fluke, hell. He's only been beating the best in the country for the last five years."

"Who is this Riggs person?" Angie asked. "Point him out to me."

I looked around the room for the small, compact figure. "I don't see him," I said.

"He didn't come," Gil Hall said. "He must have been thinking about having to play you tomorrow and it scared him."

"Never mind the wisecracks."

"In any case," Angie said, "don't you be frightened of *him*. Tomorrow, just you tell yourself, 'We shall fight him from the baseline, we shall fight him from the net.' " With an oratorical gesture, she wound up her paraphrase of the Prime Minister's already famous speech. " 'We shall never surrender!' "

"How can we lose?" I said.

Hours later, Angie came threading her way through a

roomful of dancing couples. "Here you are, you silly American boy." She put a glass into my hand. "I want to propose a toast. To your first victory over Mr. Riggs tomorrow. . . This afternoon."

"This afternoon? What time is it, anyway?"

"Four o'clock," somebody offered.

"Oh, you've got hours!" Angie said. "To hell with your silly Mr. Riggs and your silly tennis match. Let's join the conga line." She grabbed my arm, and we went flying into the swirling line of dancers.

For the finals of the Land of the Sky tennis tournament, the next afternoon, I had to change directly from my dinner clothes into my white flannels. I had got back from the party only a couple of hours before, with just about time for a long cold shower in between. That, plus my usual morning insulin and breakfast, was the extent of my training for my thirty-third match against the leading amateur tennis player in the United States.

Bobby Riggs was a player with no weaknesses — and no real strengths, either, except the all-important one: he got the ball into the court. He returned everything. His own shots were delivered, like the pitches of such baseball "junk artists" as Preacher Roe of the Dodgers and Eddie Lopat of the Yankees, with a baffling variety of speeds. They were always just about reachable, never quite where you expected them, and paced so that you seldom got a solid shot at them. The usual Riggs match might go on for hours: down-the-line drive met by cross-court shot, forecourt smash met by tantalizing passing shot, volley met by lob. Finally, in sheer exasperation, you drove the ball into the net or out of court, and imperturbable Bobby Riggs had beaten you again.

It wasn't that Riggs hadn't beaten far better players, time after time; even Don Budge had found him tough. It wasn't that I had no trouble with other good men. The fact is that I was still looking for that first major victory, a win over one of the country's top ten players. And Riggs had won the championship only a couple of years before and was on his way to another. But in the last few of that long string of losses I had been thinking that I could take him. One of these times I just had to.

One thing was sure. Even though he was a playful guy, who would sometimes fool around on the court, Riggs was not the kind of player who would beat himself. He was the percentage player par excellence, and there was no sense in trying to outlast him at his own game, especially since I figured to be short on stamina after the long night of partying. If I had any hope at all, it was to hit with a little more speed and authority than usual and try to get the points over quickly.

The match started according to form. Bobby, serving, took the first game with no trouble. I came back on my own serve to win the second. Another sequence of service and we stood at 2 all. Surprisingly, I felt perfectly fit. I found myself responding to every situation on the court as sharply as ever.

When Riggs came up on service for the third time, I started to push a little. On the first point, I tried a difficult crosscourt shot off my backhand. It caught Bobby going the wrong way and spun into the corner for a winner. I followed it with another backhand hard down the line into the opposite corner. Another point, and Riggs was behind on his own service.

There was a small clatter of applause, and Bobby smiled. He seemed relaxed and even somewhat listless, and before he had a chance to tighten up the pace, I hit a couple of more good winners and won the game. He pulled even at 4–4, and again at 5–5. But it was I who was hitting the good shots. Bobby was having trouble. As he took the balls from the ballboys and came to the line for his next service, I determined to keep him in trouble. I went in to the net behind my return of service and put away several good volleys.

I broke his serve again and held my own — with a loss of only three points in those two games. It was my set, 7–5, and I was feeling better and stronger with every point.

Keeping the pressure on, I ran up a lead of 5–1 in the second set before Riggs caught his balance. Then it became just like all the other times — all those thirty-two frustrating matches in the past. I rushed the net behind a perfect forehand return, and Riggs pattered all the way across the court, got his racket on the ball and sent up a perfect lob over my head. I hit it back, and he drop-shotted perfectly, just over the net. I served — deep to the backhand side — and Riggs fooled me with a soft cross-court placement shot. The score went to 5–4, and the tide was running Bobby's way now.

During the change of court, I took a small sip of orange juice just to be safe. I didn't really feel as if I needed it.

Riggs, on the other hand, looked tired. *Damn it,* I told myself, *all I need is one game, and he'll never be able to catch me! I just can't lose him this time!*

I took up my stance at the baseline. He'll expect me to play it safe now, I thought. I've got to cross him up.

I went for an ace on my first serve — and got it, the ball skidding sharply down the center line. Riggs tensed for the next shot, his hands clenching on the handle of his racket. I poured in another: it twisted off the wood of his racket for an error. Another error, on what should have been an easy volley for Riggs; then a couple of errors on my part as I became overanxious; finally, a long rally which ended when I took the net and brought off an overhead smash that even Bobby couldn't reach. It bounced high off the court and into the stands.

Until that moment, I'm sure the crowd had expected Riggs to take over at any time he chose and proceed to polish me off in his usual fashion. Now they must have sensed, as I had, that the ex-champ was in real trouble. I had him two sets to none, needing one more; and as it got under way, the crowd began applauding every point, whichever way it went.

Most of them were going my way. I felt loose and exhilarated, hitting every shot firmly and easily. With a big lead, I could afford to take chances, and the risks kept paying off — hard-hit first serves, sharp drives aimed straight for the corners, drop shots from a little farther back in the court than they could be safely played.

In that last set, Riggs was just another player, and I was on top of my game — far above it, in fact. Twice I broke his service; he couldn't seem to handle mine. With the score 5–2 against him, he put up a last flurry of resistance, trying to wrench the game back into his preferred pattern of long rallies. I refused to give up the offensive. He sliced a drop shot to my backhand. I raced in, picked it up, and dinked it back, diagonally, to his backhand. Retreating, by instinct, for the lob, I reached it and drove it down his backhand side. A lunge by Riggs, volleying back to my forehand. . . Again, I was waiting for it. I lobbed this time, forcing him back. Now I rushed to the net — and happily watched Bobby's return sail out of court.

I had beaten the country's Number 2 player, the former United States champion, and the most tenacious nemesis I had ever encountered. And I had beaten him without the loss of a set: 7–5, 6–4, 6–2. The gallery sent me off the court with a standing ovation.

That, as one tennis reporter wrote in his account of the tournament, was the biggest upset of the season. For me, in my fourth year of big-time tennis, it had an even sharper private meaning: it was a really important victory against the confines of diabetes. I had never dared to bend the rules so far — and so successfully.

I tried it again, a week later, when I drew Riggs once more in a tournament at Chattanooga. He swamped me. Late hours, I was forced to concede, were no sure-fire formula for winning at tennis. But neither were they fatal.

Over the rest of that year I played Bobby three or four

more times and never did manage to beat him again. He concluded his career as an amateur, after winning back the national championship and one or two other titles, with only the single loss marring his otherwise spotless record against me. That Asheville match seemed to have broken the ice, though. I went on to pick up several more victories over other players in the top rank.

One of the victims — like Riggs, a man who had escaped me for years — was Joe Hunt. I licked him in the National Clay Court Championships at Chicago, on a day when every shot off my backhand seemed to hit the line with magical accuracy, bringing up puffs of chalk from the court and groans of despair from my opponent.

The next day, exhilarated with that victory, I went up against Gardnar Mulloy. Gardnar was a slugger. He had the big serve and hard volley, but he also had a tendency to waste his power on risky shots. Normally on clay I could expect him to cause himself a lot of trouble that way.

This time, however, Mulloy was in fine touch. At the end of an hour I led, two sets to one, but the issue was far from settled. As we changed courts, Mulloy said, while swabbing himself with a towel, "This is only the beginning, Willy. Better drink some orange juice."

I nodded and poured myself a glassful from the pitcher at the table beneath the umpire's stand. Coming from Mulloy, the remark wasn't just a piece of gamesmanship, intended to worry an opponent or irritate him. Nor was it the kind of sympathy I dreaded. It was just a forthright warning that the pressure was on and that I'd better be prepared for it. Knowing the facts of my case, and also knowing how I felt about it, he would show me no special mercy. And why should he? As he knew from my explanation after the Bermuda incident, once I took the necessary precautions against insulin reaction, I was no different from any other player.

For almost another hour Mulloy ran me around the court. I retrieved shot after shot and kept fighting my own way back into an offensive position. Finally, he was just too much for me. I stumbled off the court, a loser in five long sets, not quite sure which way the locker room was until Mulloy guided me toward it.

Of the three or four more times I played Gardnar that season, I managed to beat him once. That was still another upset to add to my modest but lengthening string. Don Budge's old partner, Gene Mako, was another victim. And there were several near-misses that probably helped my status almost as much as the actual victories — a couple of slam-bang matches against Don McNeill, and a couple against Frankie Kovacs.

No matches, however, were fought more bitterly on both sides than the ones between me and young Ted Schroeder. The hostility that had originated in the Junior Davis Cup sessions, a couple of years before, was still warm, and I guess the attention Ted was getting as one of the rising lights of tennis didn't make me feel any more kindly toward him. It meant, for one thing, that he could exact demands on the tournament committees — the best of accommodations, the maximum of expense money — that they still weren't quite ready to deliver to some of the rest of us. Ted, for his part, didn't mind rubbing that fact in. It was every man for himself, he said, and the best deal for the best player.

That may have been no more than the simple truth, but when I took the court against Schroeder, I played as if trying to convince the committee that they'd favored the wrong man. And our volleys kept flying without letup when we met during changes of sides.

"How'd you manage to sneak your uncle in as linesman?" Ted would say. "He's certainly working for you on those calls."

"Same way you've been sneaking in that backhand drive of yours — pure luck. You've just about run out of it, though. You'll have to start working for your points, this set."

"I only work against *real* tennis players. This match is child's play."

All part of the standard patter that goes on constantly between tennis players — during matches, in locker rooms and clubhouses and even when they meet socially between seasons. All part of the psychological warfare of tennis — a game so personal and so dependent on timing and control that the slightest twitch of nerves can often change the whole course of a match. The difference was that, at the time, Ted and I meant it.

That extra element of rivalry only added spice to the flavor of the game. It was good to be in the competitive arena, dishing it out and taking it just like anybody else. And, by the end of that 1941 season, I was one of the elite in the very center of the arena — one of the country's top ten. I was low man in that group, but a member of it nonetheless, listed in big type when the rankings were announced. No matter how I might make out as a tennis player in the future, there was going to be one line reserved for me in all the future record books of the game.

Whatever scars diabetes may once have cut into my spirit felt healed over by now. Whatever sense of inadequacy I may have felt as a kid was gone. That old feeling of isolation, of being left out of things, was well behind me. Success in tennis had filled the empty places that trouble had left. I was a whole man.

Or so I felt at twenty-three, fresh from my first real triumphs in the big time and ready for more. It was like the picture of American life that you might get from reading nothing but the sports pages in that month of December, 1941, when the tennis ratings came out — true as far as it went, but not the complete picture.

Pick a Partner

I HAD come home in the fall, after Forest Hills and the series of California tournaments that followed. The annual jump to the West Coast provided a kind of tapering-off period, a last chance to settle scores or make an impression before the tennis troupe scattered for the year. After that, even the most single-minded tennis player had to give up and face petty realities like job or school. In this country, at least, there is nothing of any consequence left in competitive tennis until Christmastime, the Sugar Bowl and then the Florida circuit. And there were no foreign tennis centers to turn to between seasons, the courts in Australia and the Mediterranean having been shut down by the war.

I ended up in Los Angeles not only beaten (getting that final loss to Riggs out of my system) but just about broke. Reluctantly, I wired home and asked my father if he could advance me the price of a bus ticket. I shouldn't have asked. All I did was to put him on the spot.

Down to my last ten dollars, I grabbed a couple of rackets and went over to the Beverly Hills Tennis Club, the gathering place of many of Hollywood's tennis enthusiasts — Bruce Cabot, Lee Bowman, Errol Flynn, Gary

Cooper and others. As a group, they were among the most passionate devotees of the game I had ever seen — the kind who, I was sure, would have shoveled snow off the courts as I used to, if it had ever snowed in Beverly Hills. They played for blood — and for money. I had played there a few times, along with some of the other members of the tennis troupe, and knew there would be no trouble getting up a bet on a match — to say nothing of sets, games and even individual points. They bet on everything, with various combinations of odds and handicaps.

A couple of the tennis players, as well as actors, agents and other movie industry types, were on hand, so it wasn't hard to make up a couple of evenly matched doubles teams. A little too evenly matched, in fact. . . . It took me all day to parlay my ten dollars into the price of a Cincinnati bus ticket, and in the course of my financial efforts I wore out three different doubles partners. At the finish, I wasn't exactly fresh myself.

Dirty, rumpled, unshaven, and stiff from having sat up for two nights en route, I dragged my luggage into the apartment.

Dad glanced up from behind his newspaper. "Have a good trip?" he said, and went back to his reading.

Maybe it was his idea of a joke — really a form of evasion — making light of a situation so he wouldn't have to feel guilty about it. Obviously, there still wasn't any surplus of money in the family, although the air of imminent doom seemed to have lifted. At any rate, I was glad to be home again after the months of touring and of living — however luxuriously most of the time — out of a suitcase.

I didn't lose any time getting to work. The day after I landed, I went downtown to the Schaengold brothers' store, picked up my sales clerk's order book, and went behind the haberdashery counter. I had only a few months to bolster the family kitty and build up enough of a stake to get me started on the winter circuit.

Some of those winter tournaments were never played. The war that had seemed so remote suddenly struck home in a news bulletin that Doc Kistner and I heard one December afternoon in his living room.

Kistner's face froze into an expression of disbelief. "Billy, did you hear what that guy just said on the radio? The Japs bombed Hawaii!"

Like love and major league baseball, tournament tennis didn't come to a dead stop with Pearl Harbor. At its winter meeting soon afterwards, the tennis association did make moves to weather in for the duration, but word came down from Washington that organized sports were to be not only tolerated but even encouraged. As long as the public wanted to watch, the USLTA was told in effect, as long as you could find enough players who weren't tied up on GI duty and could get them to the tennis courts on their gas coupons or the crowded trains, you could keep on running tournaments.

Some of the clubs found these conditions too hard to meet and eventually decided to cancel their tournaments for the duration. But even before the circuit started to thin out, there was a change in the atmosphere of the game. It wasn't just the toning down of the tournament week festivities; there was a difference in the way the athletes thought and talked about themselves and tournament life.

Before, in what people were already starting to refer to fondly as "the old days," it was easy to think of yourself and your colleagues as tennis players and nothing else. In the special society of the clubhouses and the tournament courts, that had been enough to justify a man. There was hardly any talk about future plans, because no player really liked to imagine a time when anything more serious than rainy weather might keep him off the courts.

Now, on the other hand, tennis was becoming only a kind of interim activity. Everybody had plans, everybody had some place to go — air corps, artillery, a special training program, an ROTC commission. Old Gil Hall, who could remember singing "Over There" from the original sheet music at a World War I camp, was back in uniform already with the tankers at Fort Knox. And Jimmy DeFay had a comfortable spot all picked out for himself.

"I'll probably be in Washington for a while," he said. "Man whose family I stayed with at Southampton has just gone in as a colonel, and he wants to get a good tennis team together to match against the other services. How about you, Willy?"

"I don't know," I said. "I guess I'll hang onto my white pants until they hand me one of those GI suits."

"The draft?"

"If they'll take me."

"You don't mean to say that diabetes stuff gets you out of the war? Lucky so-and-so, you'll probably be playing Forest Hills while I'm getting bad bounces on some miserable gravel pit of a GI court!"

People I met at the tournaments — club members, fans — kept asking about my plans, a standard topic of conversation with young men in those days. Air Corps? Navy? Not liking explanations, I answered noncommittally, knowing that I really was out of it as things stood. The services weren't taking diabetics, as I had been told months before, when I registered for what was then optimistically being called the "peacetime draft." The policy was understandable: a man whose life depended from day to day on hypodermic injections at specified times must have seemed like a thin reed for the country's defense to lean on.

But things had changed in those months. This was war now, and according to the stories drifting back from the induction centers, they were taking everybody. "If you're warm, you're in." And when they had set the policy on diabetics, they were surely thinking in terms of invalids. The army doctors, I told myself, had never run into a free-wheeling, sports-playing diabetic — let alone one who was holding his own now with the very best players around.

In every tournament on the Eastern circuit, that summer, I was in the semifinals or finals, singles and doubles. In either event and sometimes in both, at every tournament, I found myself up against Ted Schroeder.

At twenty-one, Ted was cutting a wide swath through the Eastern courts. Sharp on his service, especially quick at the net, and armed with a full arsenal of skillful ground strokes, Schroeder was more than a complete tennis player. He was above all a ferocious competitor. Because he was subject to occasional lapses, it was not hard to win games from him, but it was tough to win a match. At the critical moment, he would pick up his game a few notches and pull through.

By the time we met in the Finals at Newport, Schroeder was all but crowned as the new American champion. The Forest Hills tournament, a couple of weeks away, was regarded as nothing much more than a formality, in which Schroeder would stop by to pick up the title that Bobby Riggs had abandoned.

Newport was having its last tournament fling for the duration. The resort was livelier than ever, but with a different kind of beat — part social fox-trot, part military march. Newport the summer salon was being crowded by Newport the war camp. The speeded-up activities at the naval base there had brought officers, gobs and civilian employes into the town. They crowded the hotels and restaurants, and they also swelled the gallery at the Casino courts. The tournament was a great local event, and the newcomers joined in the excitement. It was a large and unusually noisy crowd that watched Schroeder and me battle for the right to hold the Newport title until V-Day.

We both started well, in the grim, businesslike manner we always used against each other. The first two sets were full of prolonged points — rallies that kept springing back to life after what had seemed to be a winning shot. Each of us was putting out a little extra to reach shots that we might have conceded to any other man. Both sets went my way, 6–4, 6–3.

Ted came back ferociously in the next two sets and reversed the results exactly, winning 6–3, 6–4. And he kept on going, running up a lead of 4–2. I held my service in the next game, pulling up to 3–4 at the change of courts, with Schroeder coming up on service. I lingered for a moment, dabbing at my face with the towel, trying to figure out a new move.

Somehow, I had to break his serve in the next game — otherwise, I was sunk. I also had to break the pattern of long rallies that had already kept us on the court for two hours. By now I was feeling the wear of the match and of the matches that had preceded it.

There was only one thing to do in these circumstances — go all-out on the attack, move in to the net on Ted's service, behind my return. It was risky because it is the server, of course, and not the receiver, who is in the better position to attack. Schroeder would be coming to the net himself behind his serve, and that meant I would have to pinpoint every one of my returns to keep him from nailing it and putting the ball right through me as I rushed into the forecourt. But he would be serving into the wind, and that was in my favor.

It wasn't my usual style of play. Normally, I tried to return an opponent's serve deep and strong, but wouldn't attempt to force my way in to net until I was sure that I had made an opening for myself. The element of novelty might be all to the good, though. Schroeder wouldn't be expecting me to dare this kind of offense.

The very first serve came down the middle to my backhand. I drove it low — as I wanted it, as it had to be. Schroeder, moving in, had to take the volley below the level of the net — just what I was trying to force him to do. And because the wind was against him, he had to give the ball a little extra lift, to clear the net. As it came over, somewhat weak and too high, I was waiting for it. With a sharp backhand volley, I slashed it cross-court for a winner.

Schroeder looked at me helplessly, with a grimace of surprise, and went back to the baseline to serve. Once again I followed my return to the net and intercepted his volley. In a series of short, crisp points, I took the game. The score went to 4–4, then to 5–5, 6–6.

My serve now. I held firm, running off a quick string of points to take the lead, 7–6.

Once more a change of courts. I crouched well behind the service line on my side, watching Schroeder stride out to the server's position with his characteristic, slightly toed-in swagger. The pressure was on him now; a breakthrough would give me the match — exactly the kind of crisis that Ted seemed to thrive on. While ordinary players tightened up and folded in the stress of a match gone down to the wire, Schroeder brazened out the crucial points.

This time, he was serving with the wind at his back — a double advantage for him. I could concede him the game, figuring on holding my own serve again and then making my bid on his next turn to serve, when the wind would be against him once more. I could play it safe, hoping he might break under the strain and err. Or — I could go all-out, in spite of the risks, and try to end it right away. With fatigue and insulin chasing me, I decided I'd better take the gamble.

Using the same tactics I had applied earlier, I charged in behind my return of service. An exchange of volleys at close range, both of us at the net . . . a couple of errors . . . a couple of sharp placements . . . and Schroeder broke. The set was mine, 8–6, and so was the match and the big, ornate Newport Casino Invitation trophy. The *New York Times* next morning described my performance as "one of the finest offensive displays of the year." It was certainly one of my most satisfying victories — because it was against Schroeder, because it was against the champion-by-acclaim, and because it gave me the most distinguished title I had ever owned.

I went on to Boston feeling pleased with myself.

It was in Boston, just after I arrived for a tournament at the Longwood Cricket Club, that greetings arrived from my draft board. I was to report for an examination in the New York area, where I'd had my records transferred from Cincinnati, since the summons was sure to come during the Eastern season.

I repacked my bags and left the Longwood clubhouse to catch a taxi for Back Bay Station and the New York train.

As I stepped outside, a familiar voice hailed me. It was Gardnar Mulloy, fit and bronzed in the brand-new uniform of a Navy lieutenant, junior grade. With his sculptor's-model build draped in summer khaki and his All American face shaded by a natty officer's cap, he was a walking recruiting poster.

"You look like a million," I said, "but what are you doing up here? I thought you were off somewhere, learning how to tie knots."

"I'm past that stuff," Mulloy said. "I just finished a course at Annapolis and I've got a couple of weeks before reporting to my base at Jacksonville."

"You playing here?"

It was a superfluous question. Give Gar Mulloy a ten-minute coffee break, and he'd arrange to spend it playing tennis. If he was anywhere within reach of a tournament, it would never be played without him. He had just arrived, too late for the first round. "But," he explained, "they're letting me play two matches tomorrow to make up for it. What about you, Willy? I hear your number's been called. They aren't going to take you."

It was more of a statement than a question. "I don't know," I said. "Anyway, I'll have some time afterwards." I started into the cab. "I'll see you at Forest Hills."

"Wait a minute." He caught the door and held it open. "We ought to go into the doubles together. We could win it."

That year, being the fiftieth anniversary of the West Side Tennis Club, the national doubles championships, as well as the customary singles, were being played there instead of at Longwood. Mulloy's offer was a tempting one, and his appraisal of our chances might not be too far off. Mulloy himself had twice reached the finals of the doubles championships — once with Hank Prusoff, once with Wayne Sabin. I had been playing good doubles all year, including a semifinals contest at Rye which a reporter had called "one of the greatest doubles matches ever seen" on those Westchester County courts. One of my partners was a rangy, rather quiet kid from Philadelphia named Vic Seixas. Both at Seabright and at Southampton we had finished as runners-up to the team of Schroeder and Sidney Wood, and we had talked about entering the nationals together.

"I don't want to pull out on Seixas," I told Mulloy, "unless it's really all right with him. Why don't *you* put it up to him?"

"He's in the clubhouse now," Gar said. "Wait here."

A moment later, Mulloy came out. "I told him," he said. "I'll enter you as my partner."

I had no idea what an important part of my tennis career had been decided in that brief moment.

The examination at the induction center was brisk. Only a few questions, and then I was handed a card crisply stamped "4-F" — medical disability.

"You can go home, Talbert," the examining officer said. "For the duration." Like Mulloy, those Army doctors didn't waste words.

I made no lengthy explanations myself, to tennis fans or reporters. I had been rejected, the newspapers said in a line or two, "for medical reasons."

I went back to being a tennis player — no plans, and no strings on my freedom. I put on a jaunty air and wore it into the tree-shaded entrance of Forest Hills. Being left a civilian wasn't the worst thing that could happen to a man.

Underneath, though, I couldn't help feeling that I'd been brushed off as part of a category instead of being considered as an individual, and that was something that always grated me. I felt that they hadn't really taken my full measure. My pride in my own fitness had been touched; my confidence in being equal to any demand had been shaken. My membership among the "normal people" wasn't so secure, after all. When I went back on to the courts, I played like a man with something to prove.

That was Ted Schroeder's year at Forest Hills, just as everyone had expected. But his acquisition of the title was no mere formality. With the West Side grounds specially festooned in honor of its jubilee, and an air corps band on the scene to stir up the normally genteel atmosphere, the stage was worthy of a great performance. Schroeder and Frank Parker provided it. They battled to the limit before Ted pulled out the match and the championship with one of his standard fifth-set surges.

I had played my way down to the quarter-finals before bowing out, beaten by Francisco Segura, a college student from Ecuador with a face like an Inca sculpture, who had been charming the crowds and tormenting the favorites all season with his bow-legged walk, his fantastic, two-handed strokes, and his flair for comedy on the court.

The doubles was where I really came into my own. Mulloy had sized up our prospects perfectly. Not only did we win the national championship but we won it without much trouble. Ironically, our very first victims, in the opening round, were Vic Seixas, my intended partner, and the man he teamed with in my place, the Czech Ladislav Hecht. The finals, against Schroeder and Wood, were tough going for the first two sets; then they became a rout.

As the crowd stood to applaud, the band broke out in a lively march, and the final score — 9–7, 7–5, 6–1 — went up on the post beside the court. I stood looking at it for a dazed moment. In a gesture of exuberance, I ran over to Mulloy, grabbed his hand and pumped it excitedly.

He grinned with satisfaction, but withdrew his arm gingerly. "Take it easy," he said. "I've got another tournament to play next week."

We went to the net for the standard gesture of truce with our opponents and the presentation of the trophy, and then I left the court, shaking my head in awe at my serious-minded partner.

That victory was only the beginning of a lasting partnership, a whole new phase of my tennis career, and a unique chapter in the history of the game. Both Gardnar and I had other things than history in mind at the moment, however. Gar ate his customary well-balanced dinner and spent the evening quietly resting up from the week's exertions. At the time of the greatest triumph either of us had ever enjoyed, he was already in training for his next match.

As for the other half of the United States champion doubles team, I went on to Manhattan and the Stork Club to round out the experience with a night-long celebration.

The White Flannel Uniform

THE war turned things upside down. For years, as a youngster fenced in by diabetes, I had yearned for the freedom that normal people had. Now it was being on the loose that made me different. The normal thing was to be tied down. It was a time of regimentation, a time for giving up and doing without. Schroeder, the champ, left the circuit for the service. Mulloy went overseas as an LST skipper, to the kind of beaches with no tennis courts attached. Doc Kistner, having finished his med school studies in Cincinnati, postponed a professional career to put in his hitch with the Army Medical Corps.

At first I tried to get in step with the times. Although disqualified from normal duty, I thought I could make myself useful, say, as an athletic instructor at a training camp. But as far as diabetics were concerned, the services told me they just weren't having any.

The closest I could seem to get was a defense job, as a civilian employe of the Navy, working out of an office in Cincinnati and later in Indianapolis. It was paperwork, dealing with inventories of plants which the Navy Department was taking over for war production. I chafed under the office routine, especially when the weather turned warm and the calls started to come in from Rye, Seabright and Newport. I had to turn them down. That season I confined my tennis to a few week-end tournaments in the Middle West and to Forest Hills, where I spent my vacation playing the nationals.

I crawled out from under the IN and OUT baskets full of Government requisitions (multiple copies of each) and went to work for an electronics company. That job, at least, let me off the tether from time to time on business trips, including one long Eastern mission that coincided happily with the tournament season.

I went home from the Eastern circuit that year as the second-ranking tennis player in the country. I had reached the finals in both singles and doubles at Forest Hills. People in restaurants or on the streets in cities where I considered myself a stranger stopped me to ask if I wasn't Billy Talbert, the tennis player. Sometimes, when I admitted it, they asked why a fellow like me, "healthy enough to run around a tennis court, chasing a ball," wasn't in uniform like their own boys. I didn't like making excuses, and none would have been adequate.

In my own field, among tennis people, I didn't have to justify myself. Being a star of the game was enough. Everybody seemed more than happy to have one around. It was a seller's market. Not only was I one of the elite, but I was also in circulation. Other players were out of the country or else available only intermittently, whenever they could pry a week or so of furlough time out of their commanding officers in order to get to a tournament.

I didn't even need my job any more. There was a whole calendarful of invitations to tournaments and exhibitions — from the big Eastern clubs where by now I felt practically like a member, from clubs on the Southern circuit, from places like River Oaks, Texas, and Neenah, Wisconsin, the playgrounds of millionaire sportsmen. And I went on the best of terms: the best hotel or a cottage to myself on the club grounds; transportation in some club member's private plane. Budge and Riggs never had it better.

I never really got back on my job. It was like the college days all over again — a choice between dreary routine and pure fun. I wound up by giving in to the kind of life I really wanted.

For anybody who prefers to think of himself as a free spirit, the life of a touring tennis player is really ideal. You are on the move, meeting people under the happiest of circumstances, and then passing on before the relationship has been put to any great strain. Wherever you go, you are part of the gaiety of tournament week. And when the week is over and the hosts are ready to settle back into the workaday grind, you go on to the next crowd and the next tournament, taking the holiday with you. You have the freest of life wherever you are. Independence is something you come to take for granted.

When in New York, I was in time for the fun of the Long Island shore, with an occasional evening of café life in Manhattan. In the South, I was part of the resort crowd. In California, I had a standing invitation into Hollywood's tennis circle.

Since my first trip to the West Coast, back in 1941, my contacts with the Hollywood crowd had broadened beyond the games at the tennis club in Beverly Hills. I had sailed on Errol Flynn's yacht, talking tennis and women with him while he sipped a glass of what seemed to be his favorite drink (although I never could really believe it, even when I saw it) — Flynn, the perfect figure of a swashbuckler, had a passion for green crème de menthe.

Almost every day there was a match, as intense as a Wimbledon final, at somebody's private court — Jack Warner's, perhaps, or Charlie Chaplin's. Warner, the producer, had an appetite for the game like that of a kid making his first trip on the circuit. As for Chaplin, he may have been a great comedian on the screen but at the court, whether he was playing or watching, he took life as seriously as a Eugene O'Neill tragedy.

The matches at the Beverly Hills club, too, were still going as strong as ever. There was one continuous match, a running feud in doubles. In it, Frank Shields, the former Davis Cup player, and Pat DiCicco, the Hollywood man-of-the-world (Pat never acknowledged any other occupation), played against Bruce Cabot and me. Shields and I would bet each other a few dollars; Cabot and DiCicco played for a few hundred, preceding each match with a kind of ceremonial hassle in which they tried to wangle advantages out of each other. That, to them, was as important a part of the game as serving or receiving.

Pat would insist on, say, first serve for his side, plus a handicap of two games to the set. Cabot would counter with a demand for choice of court — with the wind or against — and a handicap of one point for every remaining game. But DiCicco seldom let himself be outmaneuvered, at least on the money end of the game. A zestful individual with a tangy vocabulary, he had a few words to cover the situation, as he did most situations: "Cabot," he said, collecting the stake as we walked off the court, "never try to outhustle a hustler."

Hoagy Carmichael was another of the Hollywood tennis regulars. Like Charlie Chaplin, he switched from comedy to drama at the mere sight of a tennis racket. To melodrama, in fact. With Hoagy on the court, you could be sure you were in for as much fireworks as forehand. One muffed shot would send him into a tearing rage.

Afterwards, though, in the clubhouse or at one of the players' homes, Hoagy would revert to type. He'd wander over to the piano and start running through his large stock of songs he'd never had published — and never would — singing the risqué lyrics croakily to his own accompaniment. Somebody would make a few phone calls, and pretty soon the place was filled with people, and the game had turned into a party.

On my way back to Cincinnati from one California trip, I stopped off at St. Louis for two reasons. The World Series was being played there that year, and I had never lost my boyhood appetite for a ball game. The second reason was a pretty St. Louis girl named Dorothy, whom I'd met, earlier in the summer, at a tournament back East, where she was visiting. I had sent her a wire from Los Angeles, saying I'd call her when I got into town.

As I stepped off the airplane ramp at St. Louis, I was surprised to see Dorothy waiting there, waving to me from the crowd that lined the fence beyond the runways. Pleased as I was, I was also dismayed. I had counted on slipping in and catching the ball game before letting her know I'd arrived.

Trying to conceal my disappointment, I gave her a cheery hello, telling myself that it was probably just as well this way — I'd have gone out and stood in line at Sportsman's Park, and then maybe I wouldn't have got in.

"Hurry up," she said, taking my arm and steering me toward her car. "We don't have much time."

"Time for what?" I said. "Where are we going — if I'm allowed to ask."

"You don't really have to go if you don't want to," she said — she fished in her handbag and held out a pair of tickets — "but I have a couple of box seats for the World Series."

I looked at her delightedly. "Dorothy," I said, "will you marry me?"

She laughed. "Not until after the series."

That was part of the luxury of being free — to be careless and breezy about the things other people took seriously. The mood lasted. Not too long after the World

Series, we were married. But it didn't work on such casual terms. We separated. We were divorced. Marriage wasn't free, wasn't fun and, unlike tennis life, it didn't come easy.

In tennis, almost everything seemed to come easy as you approached the top.

One evening in New York, toward the end of 1944, I was chatting with William du Pont, Jr., the pre-eminent sportsman of that distinguished family. I had come to know him, several years before, through Eleanor Tennant, the tennis coach, whom I used to chauffeur to tournaments during my early, penny-pinching days on the circuit, in return for my own passage. "Teach," as Miss Tennant is known to all tennis players, had taken me, along with her brilliant protégé Alice Marble, to play on du Pont's private courts at Bellevue, his vast, beautiful Delaware estate. Since then, I had become one of the four or five regulars whom du Pont invited down for a week end of tennis whenever we were in the area.

The conversation, that evening in New York, shifted from tennis to sports in general and then to the business end of sports — public relations, the handling of crowds, the management of properties. Du Pont, a lean, gracious man then in his early fifties, sucked on his pipe thoughtfully and said, "Billy, you seem to know something about the way these things operate."

"I ought to know a little," I said. After all, I had grown up with a behind-the-scenes view of sport, and I had had a taste of business, both in my college studies and on the job.

"What would you think about coming to work for me?"
I was available.

There was more of an atmosphere of sport than of business in my job as personal assistant to Mr. du Pont. I lived at Bellevue and entered into a full, rich, country-gentleman's kind of existence — outdoors much of the time, on the move a great deal.

My boss set a pretty stiff pace: he liked to get up at four or five in the morning to drive down to Maryland for a couple of hours of fox-hunting, or to put in some time with his stable of race horses before settling down to his day in the world of business. Promptly at 9 A.M., he was at his office in his bank at Wilmington.

Early rising had never bothered me, even when I had been up late the night before; ever since I was a boy, I had always been impatient to tear into a new day. My insulin schedule made the habit permanent.

I liked walking into the pungent gloom of the stables at dawn, and leaning against the morning chill to watch the horses go through their early paces at Bellevue's private track. I liked the trips — to the du Pont cattle farm in Maryland, to the stud farm in Virginia where the du Pont horses were bred, to the public track at Delaware Park which Mr. du Pont had designed and built, and to other tracks from New York to California where his Foxcatcher Stable entries were running.

Aside from the rigorous schedule he maintained at Bellevue, du Pont was a lenient employer. Every so often, he'd take off on some long trip by himself, leaving me with no more demanding chores than to "look in at Delaware and make sure that everything is in shape for the opening," or "see that the boys have everything they need at the stables."

In a week or so, I might get a call from him in California.

"Billy," he'd say, "I'm going to be out here for a few weeks yet. Are there any tournaments you can play to keep yourself occupied?"

"I imagine I can find a couple," I'd tell him.

"Go ahead, then. And good luck."

If I had really been concerned with the job and less absorbed in tennis, I might have been troubled by his increasing generosity.

Even when du Pont was in the East, I was often free to go wherever an important tournament was being played. And Willie du Pont would have been the last man to object to the tennis exhibitions I played, from time to time, as my small contribution to patriotic causes.

They had started when I got a call from a Chicago tennis patron. He and some other friends of the game, in cooperation with the USO, were trying to arrange a couple of tennis exhibitions at service camps. Pancho Segura, the tough little Ecuadorian, had agreed to play. What about me for the other spot?

I tossed a couple of pairs of flannel shorts and a few rackets together for what I thought was going to be a couple of days of tennis. It turned into a series of tours in which Segura and I played each other dozens of times before audiences in uniform — GIs, sailors, marines, WACS, WAVES. Many of them had never even seen a tennis match before, and some, as they told me afterwards themselves, had never expected to sit through one. Pancho and I knew we had our work cut out for us, keeping them interested. It was a matter of pride — in ourselves and in the game we loved. Somehow, I think we both felt, we had to make it seem worth while for a couple of guys to spend their time "running around a court, chasing a ball," while other men our age were in uniform.

By the time we reached the playing area at some GI camp, both of us were often bushed, sometimes having already played a couple of matches at other camps the same day. But we always gave the game whatever we had left in us.

As tennis players we were evenly matched, almost to the point of stalemate, Pancho himself ranking right alongside me in the national ratings. That made for exciting tennis. Furthermore, we had the benefit of Segura's other talents: as a comic actor, Pancho — at his full height of 5' 6" or so — stood head and shoulders above anybody else in the game.

"Pancho!" he would shout at himself after missing a volley or driving a forehand out of court. With a horrified expression worthy of a man who has just seen his house go up in flames, he'd clap his hand to his forehead and stalk around the court. Sometimes, to vary the act, he'd raise his racket to the heavens, muttering wild oaths in his native Spanish. He might have been reciting a restaurant menu, for all anybody knew, but it sounded like a man in torment, asking what he'd done to deserve such a catastrophe. The GIs loved it.

"Lord Talbert," Pancho would say afterwards, as we climbed wearily into the car that was taking us on to our next stop, "we make a few more tennis fans today, I think."

Before I could reply, he'd be asleep, his head lolling back against the cushions. Altogether, he must have slept through a couple of thousand miles of American landscape.

At night, when we reached our hotel — in Chicago, New York, or whatever city we were using as our base of operations — I'd shake Segura into consciousness long enough to get him installed in his room. He'd look around approvingly at the accommodations I had arranged, smile sleepily and say, "Billy, I certainly give you the right name when I call you Lord Talbert. Lord Talbert, you really know how to live!"

My Year

WHEN I arrived at the West Side Tennis Club, in Forest Hills, for the 1945 national championships, there was a telegram from my father waiting for me. ALL THE BEST OF LUCK, it said. THIS IS YOUR YEAR.

The wire was a family tradition. Each year he had been sending me the same message, even when this terse couple of lines added up to more than he'd had to say to me when I'd last seen him at home. This year the message could be read not just as a bit of fatherly sentiment but also as a reasonable forecast of my prospects in the tournament. This year, I was the favorite. Like Ted Schroeder, a few years before, I was now the logical choice to take over the title of tennis champion of the United States.

So far, it had indeed been my year. At twenty-seven, in the pink of condition, I had brought my game to its peak. Controlled speed — that happy medium I'd been seeking between the powerhouse style of play and the pusher's technique — was its characteristic. I could put my first service where I wanted it — into the backhand corner of the receiver's court, or down the unprotected middle — and with enough severity to put my opponent on the defensive right from the start. My ground strokes were not only consistent, but they traveled deep, finding the corners and the lines. My volley showed "touch"; it was not just a return but a shot that I could drop or punch into an opening across the net.

Feeling confident that I had the basic stuff, I had engaged a professional, Dick Skeen, to help me polish my weapons for the big push. We had spent hours in practice on the courts at Bellevue. The move had paid off handsomely. Thanks to Mr. du Pont's easy attitude, I had found time to enter nine tournaments that summer, and I had won them all. Forest Hills, the tennis experts conceded, ought to be the tenth, and I wanted — as desperately as I had wanted anything in years — to make them right. By now I had won just about every important trophy in American tennis — Newport, Seabright, the Eastern Grass Court, the National Clay Court, the National Doubles. Every one but the really big one, the Men's Singles Championship of the United States.

There is nothing spectacular in the few acres of lawn, parking space, grandstands and playing surface that make up the site of the national tennis championships. The short, leafy approach to the West Side clubhouse barely muffles the sound of auto traffic, barely screens the nearby apartment houses, delicatessens, movie theaters and used car lots. During a tense exchange on the court, when the crowd is silent, you can almost hear the rumble of the Queens subway under the boulevard, just a block away.

Yet, when a tennis player leaves the weathered brown 1920s-Tudor pile of a building that is the clubhouse, walks through the dining porch onto the terrace where a few people sit over their tall drinks, and starts down the neatly edged path toward the courts, he is as remote from the world of traffic and commerce as if he were on a Caribbean island whose only interests are sport and sun. He is in the very capital of the world of tennis, and he is a member of its privileged class.

If he is more than just one of the players — if he holds the special position of favorite — this tiny domain seems even more his own. As he steps onto the terrace, a brace of rackets under his arm, and starts down the walk toward the farthest courts — the pair of immaculately cured lawns in the stadium that are reserved for feature matches — he can sense the eyes following him, the crowd beginning to fall in behind him, leaving the lesser matches on the field courts to assemble in the stadium for the bigger event.

Each day, for me, the national championship seemed more and more inevitable. I made my entrance on the court; my opponent took his position at the far side of the net; an hour or so later, I returned to the clubhouse, while the results of another triumph were posted. Straight through the quarter finals, I advanced without losing a set.

On the day before Labor Day, I went out to the stadium to play Pancho Segura in the semifinals. Gardnar Mulloy, back from overseas and playing the nationals again after a two-year absence, gave me a friendly swat across the seat of the shorts. "Save a little for the doubles," he said.

Mulloy had already been knocked out of the singles, but, playing as a team again, we were already within sight of our second doubles championship. That same afternoon, following my match against Segura, we were to play the doubles finals against an upstart team of young servicemen, Air Cadet Bob Falkenburg and Seaman First Class Jack Tuero.

I gave Gar one of those don't-worry-about-a-thing signs, and stepped onto the court.

After innumerable GI camp exhibitions, over a couple of seasons, plus frequent meetings in regular tournaments, Segura and I had no surprises left for each other. It was always simply a question of whether my control or his sheer ferocity would win out. Pancho had been playing excellent tennis; on a given day he could be as tough an opponent as just about anybody in the game. But this season I had the upper hand. In the last few weeks, I had met him in the finals of two or three of the Eastern tournaments and had come out on top each time.

This time, Pancho started off as if out for vengeance, but I pulled out the first set, 7–5. I took the second more easily, 6–3. Then, just as I was about to close out the match, luck pulled the string.

In the course of a last-ditch rally, Pancho drove a ball wide to my backhand. I ran for it, stepping into the stroke with my right foot. Instead of sliding just a bit on the grass, as usual, my foot jammed, and the other leg — the left one — buckled. I could almost hear something snap. As the point ended, I held up my hand, to stop play, and rubbed my knee for a moment. There was a

murmur in the crowd. I walked about briefly, then sig-
nalled Pancho to go ahead. In a few strokes I finished
the set, 6–4, and had my place in the finals.

I might have got by all right after that, except that my
appetite for action got the better of me. I had the habit
of living hard and playing hard, and I hated to acknowledge that there were any limits to what I could do. The
doubles was coming up, and both for Mulloy's sake
and my own, I couldn't see passing it by.

But all through the match against Falkenberg and
Tuero, my leg was troubling me — getting worse and
worse, in fact. In trying to favor it, I strained it even
more severely. The match dragged, and I was becoming
practically immobile. Mulloy was doing all the work.

"Just hang on," Gar said, "and we'll get by."

I nodded, wincing with the effort as I walked to my
position at the net.

The match became interminable. Mulloy and I, our
normal pattern of play disrupted by my injury, couldn't
seem to get hold of ourselves. Every time we'd run up a
game or two, our young opponents would come surging
right back.

By the time we'd won a set, 12–10, dropped one 8–10,
and stalemated a third at 10–10, the sun had gone down,
the balls were barely visible, and the crowd had thinned
out. I sighed with relief when the officials suspended play
and put the match over until the next day.

"I'll see you in the morning," I told Mulloy abruptly,
hobbling off the court. As soon as I'd dressed, I caught
a taxi and headed for a hospital.

"It's a pulled tendon," the doctor told me. "You'd better stay off it for a week or so."

"Week!" I said. "Doc, I've got to get it fixed up to-night."

The doctor shook his head. "It's nothing I can fix. You've just got to wait for it to heal."

"Okay," I said, "don't fix it. Just tape it or something so I can play tennis."

I spent the night at the hospital, taking shots and packs to ease the pain. In the morning, I went back to the clubhouse, and when I took the court that afternoon to play Sergeant Frank Parker for the championship of the United States I looked like a throwback to the 1920's. Instead of the usual shorts, I was wearing a pair of long white flannel trousers, concealing a bulky bandage that encased my leg from ankle to thigh.

Parker, the defending champion, was a fine, seasoned tennis player who had labored for years in the shadow of Budge and Riggs, and had finally come into his own when they quit the scene. Like Riggs, Parker was more of a mechanic than an artist. He had no big strokes. Unlike Riggs, Parker was a deadpan performer, all business. It was Parker who had beaten me at Forest Hills the year before. Even on one leg, I was anxious for the chance to turn the tables.

Once again, confronted with a percentage player, I could not afford to play him at his own game. The strain on my injured leg, added to the normal insulin problem, ruled out even the remotest chance of outlasting him at

long rallies. I would have to try to end the points quickly
by going for the winning shot.

There was one weakness in Parker's game so glaring
that it was almost legendary. For years he had been
struggling to correct a faulty forehand, trying such a
variety of grips and swings that a running gag had
developed along the circuit. When Parker made his entrance in the East each season, the question would go
around the locker rooms: "What does this year's model
look like?" That forehand, naturally, was the point of
attack for most of his opponents.

I disagreed. It seemed to me that Parker's forehand,
even though the least steady of his ground strokes, was
more of an offensive shot than his backhand. It was what's
known in the trade as a "going" forehand; it came at you
with some push, a fair amount of speed; it was harder to
get set for. With his backhand, at least you knew where
to move for it. That was the target I preferred.

I had seldom played better tennis than I did in the
first set of that return match. My service went crackling
in for aces, time after time. My backhand worked beautifully. Every time that backhand of Parker's came at me
I was in position for it. The trouble was that Parker just
wouldn't give ground. The set went to deuce; we tied
again and again, and I just couldn't keep it up. My
leg, encased in its heavy swathing of bandages, began to
feel like wood. I began to have trouble getting up to the
net in time to take advantage of a weak return. A string
of errors finally undid me, and I dropped the set, 14–12.

After that, it was no contest. Parker, playing nearly

errorless tennis, ran out the match, 6–1, 6–2. There was nothing phony about his victory. It was one of the most exemplary performances of percentage tennis: he hit everything into the court, gave nothing away.

For me, the day wasn't a total loss. After resting for a while in the locker room, I went back into the court and stumbled through not one but two more matches. Mulloy managed to pull us through the doubles — we took the suspended third set, 12–10, and the fourth, 6–2 — to give us the title for the second time. Finally, I teamed with Margaret Osborne to win the mixed doubles championship as well.

It was two years before my knee recovered from the strain.

There was substantial consolation in the day's two victories. Margaret and I had won the title the previous two years, and this third consecutive triumph was unique in the history of the event. As for the men's doubles, the two championships which Mulloy and I now had won were as much as any team in the past had been able to achieve. And, we figured, we still had a few more cracks at the trophy ahead of us.

But for the second year in a row, now, I had been thwarted in my bid to become the individual tennis champion of the United States. I was never to come that close again to the thing I had wanted most for years — not knowing how much I could want other things that I had let go by.

Reunion and Recognition

In the special view of tennis players, World War II was the period between the 1939 Challenge Round and the 1945 national championships. Even as the Forest Hills tournament got under way, MacArthur's troops were landing in Japan to carry out the surrender terms. Tennis, like every other kind of activity, began to emerge from wartime restraints. There was an atmosphere of release.

Tournaments that had been suspended were renewed; players who had been out of circulation came home — except for a few who, like Joe Hunt, had given their lives to the war, and a few others who had been sidetracked by it. But all of the top-rankers, every one who had had a taste of tennis life at its best, came back for more.

Mulloy and Parker, Kramer and Schroeder were all in action. Gil Hall, old enough after his second war to qualify for the seniors' championship, came around for an occasional crack at a trophy against the younger players.

Jimmy DeFay was back, too, looking for the old kicks of tournament life and running into disappointment. The doors weren't open as wide as he'd expected; if he wanted to play, he had to settle for something less than the best of terms on accommodations and living expenses.

It wasn't, as Jimmy said, that the circuit had gone to hell "while my GI back was turned." The truth was that, as a young player, he had been just good enough, never brilliant; charm had made up for what his game lacked. But what was charming in the youngster was starting to seem brittle and routine in the man, and there were just too many other good tennis players around — to say nothing of the brilliant ones.

The increased competition only freshened my appetite. I had something to prove again, to myself and to the tennis public. Some of the best men had been out of the lists at the time I was winning my laurels, and I couldn't really be satisfied until I had defended them in the tougher postwar competition.

When Ted Schroeder and I were matched again, my eagerness boiled up into belligerence. Schroeder stopped the match at one point to ask the officials for permission to put on spiked shoes — a device to provide better footing on slippery turf, but also one of the standard ploys to interrupt the rhythm of an opponent's winning game. I objected.

Ted became angry. He was trying to get back into the game after a couple of seasons off the court, he pointed out, and this match was important to his comeback. "I've *got* to have spikes," he insisted. "My whole future may depend on it."

"You've got no future," I said. "You'll wind up as a pro at some public court."

Both of us could barely wait to get the match over with and get at each other hand to hand. We rushed for the locker room afterwards with the same thought in mind. Without a word, we dropped our rackets and went for each other with fists up. It was the payoff, the climax to our years of simmering hostility. Probably we'd have shoved each other around like a couple of schoolboys, without any serious damage, but we never even got that far before cooler, more adult heads and hands prevailed.

Doc Kistner, married now, out of uniform, and pursuing his medical career in Boston, had come down to watch the tournament, and sensing trouble from the stands, had come dashing into the locker room right behind us. He got between us and, with the help of a couple of players, managed to separate Ted an me.

We stood glaring at each other for a moment, then finally broke down, grinned at each other sheepishly and shook hands.

"For a guy as cool and deadpan as you are," Ted said, "You've got one hell of a temper."

"For a guy I've been calling a bum for so many years," I said, "you're one hell of a tennis player."

It was a relief to get this petty rivalry — a holdover from kid days, its origins and reasons all but forgotten — out of my system. *Talbert*, I told myself, *you're getting too old for that kind of stuff.*

I certainly wasn't a kid any longer. I was a seasoned athlete, already in my prime, one of the veterans of the circuit, an established star. Even on one sound leg and in a field crowded with top-level players, I managed to win the ranking of Number 6 in the country. Over the next two seasons, I climbed up again to Number 3. I had no reason to doubt myself now, no reason to feel I hadn't earned the position I had held when other players were out of the field.

If I needed any proof that I had won the position I wanted in the game of tennis, it came to me one spring day in 1946, when I was riding the train from New York, back to Wilmington and my job with Mr. du Pont at Bellevue. I tossed my hat up onto the rack, sat down and unfolded the newspaper I had picked up at Pennsylvania Station. On the sports pages was a story announcing the selection of the United States' first postwar Davis Cup team — Frederick R. Schroeder, Jr., Frank A. Parker, Gardnar Mulloy and William F. Talbert. (Kramer and Tom Brown were added later.) Those few lines of type represented the realization of a wish — it had seemed too remote, too unlikely to call an ambition — which I had entertained as a tennis neophyte and which the war had all but buried. When the international campaign began, I would be one of the elect wearing the national emblem, standing in the grassy limelight as the anthems were played. Assuming we got safely through the elimination rounds, there would be a trip, longer and more exciting than any I had ever taken — to a brand-new place. If I kept playing up to standard in the months ahead, I would be making the long jaunt to Australia to recapture the big trophy lost to this country ever since 1939.

I leaned back in my chair in the parlor car with a deep feeling of fulfillment. This, after all, was the sum of what I had wanted from the beginning: recognition — the acknowledgment that, even when the competition was at its toughest, I could hold my own with the best of the "normal" people. Now I had that, I thought, it meant that diabetes had been completely eliminated as an influence on my life. It was no bar at all, it stood in the way of absolutely nothing that a man could reach for.

Only I wasn't satisfied to leave it at that. It was as if I had to keep proving that it was true, over and over again.

"I don't understand you," Jack Kramer told me one day, after a match. Jake was having the big season everybody had expected of him, rising to his position as one of the greatest players in tennis history. With his big game of serve and volley working beautifully, he had beaten me that day, but as usual I had given him a tough couple of hours on the court.

"What don't you understand?" I said, stowing my gear in the locker.

With a heave, Jake stripped the drenched shirt off his lean shoulders. "The way you breeze through this game," he said. 'Look at me — always in training, always worried about getting enough sleep, eating the right food, keeping in shape. And you, for God's sake, you never go to bed, never miss a party — "

"I'm not in this game for the free liquor, Jake. I just like knowing that I'm wanted. I like being with people when they're having fun."

"You've got a bum knee," he went on, "and you still play every event in the tournament — singles, doubles, mixed. You must be crazy."

"What the hell, Jake, live it up while you can."

He grabbed a towel, headed toward the showers, and stopped. "You know, Willy, if you really trained for this game, you'd win everything in sight. You'd never lose a match."

I shook my head. "The truth is, I wouldn't do as well as I do now. If I did push-ups every morning and tucked myself in at 11 every night, I couldn't play tennis at all. I'd be tight as a drum for every match. I'd never get a wink of sleep, lying there trying to figure out how to outguess the other guy in the next day's match." I didn't say it, but to myself I added, *And maybe fretting about all the risks of diabetes that I had overcome by keeping too busy to let them enter my mind.*

"Anyway, Jake, I want to win everything *and* live it up, too."

The truth is that, having come this far, having got what I wanted, I was becoming restless and uneasy, and I didn't want time to think. Whenever I found myself looking ahead, certain stirrings about the future came to mind. My thirties weren't so far ahead of me, and with them the athlete's inevitable downhill slide. I wasn't sure where I would go then. Off the tennis courts, what was I? A guy with a job that had started as a wonderful opportunity, sincerely offered by a generous employer. I couldn't say that I'd done much with the opportunity. What remained of it was the freedom to play a lot of tennis. Which put me right back where I started. I was operating in a closed circle. Comfortable, for now, but closed.

In my private life . . . Well, I had already made a failure of marriage. The result of that failure, too, was more freedom. It had cut me loose from the one really close personal relationship I had attempted since I was a kid heading out to a ball game or a day's fishing with my father. Freedom to do what?

In a mood of nostalgia and vague unrest, I impulsively packed a suitcase and caught an airplane flight to Florida, where my father and mother were living now. During the last couple of years, Dad had settled into a job there — an unspectacular one, to say the least, but I gathered from letters and from occasional brief visits that it satisfied him.

At lunch with my parents at their small apartment in Coral Gables I could sense an atmosphere of peace in the household, far different from the tension and uncertainty of my college days, when we had been only three isolated individuals, living separate lives in the same house.

Afterwards, Dad and I went out for a walk along the beach. I scuffed through the sand, enjoying the warmth of the sun and the mild flutter of the sea wind against my face as I tugged at my thoughts, hardly conscious of my father walking alongside me.

"Something's bothering you," he said suddenly. "Do you want to tell me about it?"

I turned, startled. In another family this might have been a routine remark, but in our relationship it was an extraordinary event. After years of little more than the kind of polite conversation exchanged by strangers, of inner thoughts and feelings being kept tightly private, my father was inviting me to confide in him.

It wasn't easy to respond; the habit of reserve had been with me too long. At first I could only listen while he confided in *me*. Small things, mostly, the kind of day-by-day matters that we should have got around to long before — his job, the new friends he and my mother had made among their neighbors in Florida. Then he became reminiscent; he began to remember the days when I was first learning how to swing a racket. He admitted how scared he had been that I'd suffer an insulin reaction from the exertion and be frightened off. He went on to my college days, and how much he'd hated to see me quit school.

"But," he said with a smile, "you were a stubborn son of a gun — like me, I guess. I really couldn't blame you. College couldn't have been much fun, the way things were. Hell, Bill, any way you decided to play it, there was no point in worrying about you. Whatever you wanted, I knew you'd work for it." He added quietly — a little sadly, it seemed — "You could always take care of yourself, Bill."

There was nothing to say for a while, and then we sat down on a rise overlooking the beach — face to face, as we hadn't been in years. I found myself straining for some confidence to offer him in return.

"What would you think about me turning pro?" I said. It was a subject we had discussed once, years before, when I was seriously considering the idea but finding no

takers. He'd been opposed, then. I wasn't really considering it very seriously now, but it was one of a number
of thoughts that had crossed my mind lately.

"Maybe I ought to do it now," I went on, "while my
price is high. Another few years, and maybe nobody will
want me."

He lit a cigarette and drew on it slowly before saying
anything. "What's the future in it? Right now, tennis is
still fun for you. Make it your bread and butter, and
you'll lose the fun. Probably not much bread and butter
in it, either, as far as I can see." He picked up a pebble
and flung it into the surf, getting that easy, natural
pitcher's motion into the throw.

"I'm not trying to make up your mind for you, Bill,
but I see you better off as an amateur. Any day. You're
meeting fine people. On even terms. A gentleman among
gentlemen. As a pro, you'd just be a hired hand."

He flicked his cigarette after the pebble, and added
carefully, "Not that a man your age shouldn't be thinking about the future."

"I've got plenty of tennis left in me," I said, as much
for myself as for him.

"Sure. I hope you never give it up. Only someday the
forehands are going to start landing a little shorter, the
net will get higher, and you'll be just another guy. If
you want to go on living this kind of life, you're going
to have to start paying for it yourself." He broke off and
asked me suddenly, "You haven't been having any
trouble with the diabetes, have you? That isn't what's
been bothering you?"

"Hell, no," I assured him hastily. "No trouble at all."

I got up and brushed the sand off my trousers. "What made you ask that, anyway?"

"I don't know, I just wondered. Sometimes it seems to me as if you're still running from it after all these years. As if it's chasing you and you're afraid it'll catch up."

We walked back toward the house — me and a gray-haired, blue-eyed man, still muscular and weather-seasoned, though starting to show his age now. It made me feel suddenly older, too.

"I know you've been going pretty hard, Bill. Which is okay — I mean fun's fun, and I hope you always do have one hell of a good time. Only you ought to watch yourself a little. Not because of the diabetes, maybe, but just because everybody has to."

I put my hand on his shoulder, rather tentatively. "Don't worry, Dad," I said. "I've left the diabetes way behind. Let's go see if we can talk Mom into letting me take you two out to dinner."

All the way home on the plane flight north, bits of that conversation kept sticking to my mind.

You could always take care of yourself, Bill. The way he had said that — with respect, but also with a tinge of regret . . . It was true, but maybe it was the very thing that had stood between us. I had been proud of my self-sufficiency — it was much more than that, really. Hadn't I proved, in crisis after crisis, that — diabetic or not — I could take care not only of myself but of him and my mother, as well?

And what a blow to his pride that must have been. How could I have expected him to be pleased and grateful for something that I myself resented — somebody else's help? All I had done, in those years, was to remind him of his own failure. It was only now, when once again he was taking care of himself and my mother, that he could face himself. And now he could face me.

Independence. I used to bask in it, like sunlight at the beach, not knowing I was being burned.

Well, so it hurt a little. There were things that felt worse, like spending your life in the shade. Damned if I'd go crawling for cover. I wouldn't know how.

Or would I? The job at Bellevue . . . That wasn't exactly being on my own. Not when I wasn't doing it justice. Willie du Pont had been kind enough to string along with me, but I couldn't kid myself any longer. I wasn't making myself as useful to him as I might have, and he knew it. I must have disappointed him, only he was too kind to say anything. On my side, I wasn't building a career, I wasn't making any kind of future for myself. I was a tennis player. That was what I really cared about. The Davis Cup playoffs were about to start. Another national doubles championship was coming up, and Mulloy and I had special reasons for wanting to win it this time.

When I arrived at Wilmington I gave Mr. du Pont my thanks and told him I would be winding up my affairs at Bellevue to go back to the business of full-time mughunting on the tennis courts. He was as cordial as ever and wished me luck, but he didn't try to talk me out of leaving.

The Prize

UNITED STATES
LAWN TENNIS CHAMPIONSHIP
CHALLENGE TROPHY
NATIONAL CHAMPIONSHIP
DOUBLES

A PAIR of matching silverplated cups bearing this inscription was on display at the Longwood Cricket Club in August 1946, just as they had been for most of the last twenty-seven years. They were typically ungainly pieces of sporting silverware, too deep to make decent punchbowls, too shallow to be used as umbrella stands, too roomy to fill with flowers. Nevertheless, they were among the most attractive prizes in the whole showcase of tennis awards.

The irresistible glamor of the doubles trophy lay in the list of winners that followed the inscription, covering most of the surface — and in the fact that, after all this time, the cups were still here, up for grabs, instead of locked away in the living rooms or libraries of some of the earlier heroes who might have taken possession of them.

Starting with "1919 — Norman E. Brookes and Gerald L. Patterson," that list added up to a tennis Hall of Fame, ranging over the whole history of the game since the golden age of Postwar I.

"Big Bill" Tilden's name was there, right after "Little Bill" Johnston's. The roster of tennis immortals went on, including Vincent Richards, George Lott, Lester Stoefen, Ellsworth Vines, Wilmer Allison, John Van Ryn, Don Budge, Gene Mako. It was with no small feeling of pride that I could read two of the most recent entries:

1942 $\begin{cases} \text{Lt. (jg) Gardnar Mulloy and} \\ \text{William Talbert} \end{cases}$

1945 $\begin{cases} \text{Lt. Gardnar Mulloy and} \\ \text{William Talbert} \end{cases}$

A third time would mean that the trophies were ours for keeps. Other doubles teams in the past had had the same chance to take permanent possession of the cups. No one had ever done it. That was part of their legend, and part of their special allure. Tilden and Richards, Richards and Norris Williams, Lott and Johnny Doeg, Lott and Stoefen, Allison and Van Ryn, Budge and Mako . . . all these great teams had won the United States doubles championship twice. No one had ever won it three times.

The possibility that the doubles cup might finally be retired gave the 1946 national doubles an air of extra drama. But it wasn't simply the excitement of a chase. There was also conflict, because we weren't the only ones in the field who had a chance to take the trophies home. Jack Kramer and Ted Schroeder had won the title in 1940 and 1941, and they were back as the favorites.

On the day the tournament opened at Longwood, Jake caught me stealing a covetous look at the trophies as I was passing through the clubhouse. "You aren't making any plans for those things, are you, Willy?" he said. "Ted and I are shipping them to California at the end of the week."

"You'll have to borrow them from us if you want them," I said. "Gardnar and I are throwing a party after the tournament. He's filling his with milk. Mine will have beer."

The kidding didn't mean a thing. All four of us wanted the doubles cup the way thieves want money.

Ever since that near-miss against Allison and Van Ryn during my first tour of the Eastern circuit, I had been carving out an increasingly comfortable niche for myself as a doubles player. I felt at home on a singles court; the last few years' rankings showed that. But doubles was really my game. I had learned my tactics early, and I had the control to carry them out. Mulloy had the power it takes to make good tactics pay off.

A good doubles team goes onto the court with two over-all aims in mind. One is to get to the net quickly. The other is to force the opposition to hit up. In championship doubles well over half of all winning points are scored at the net, and most of those volleys are made on shots which the other side has lifted a little too high. High enough, that is, for the volleyer to put away.

There is a pattern of play by which this two-part aim can be pursued with great effectiveness. It is neither secret nor complex. The only trouble is that it requires patience and runs counter to all the savage instincts of the average man with a weapon in his hand, a ball within reach, and hundreds of square feet of grass or clay to aim it at.

To begin with, on the serve you must forgo the hard, flat cannonball in favor of a relatively slow twist service, aimed carefully and deep to the receiver's backhand. This gives you more time to get to the net behind your serve, generally three precious steps' worth of time. Because it is easier to control it also reduces the chance of a fault on that first serve, the cardinal sin in doubles. A fault forces you to come in with an easier, safer second service, for which the receiver can safely move forward a step or two. He may then be able to make his return an attacking shot instead of a defensive one, beat you to the net and nullify the advantage that goes with the service.

With this awful prospect in mind, even devastating servers like Budge and Kramer spike their big guns when it comes to doubles, and rely on the quieter twist service. They use the cannonball only as a once-in-a-while shot, to keep the opposition off-balance or to gamble at that strategic moment when the odds are high and all rules are meant to be broken (including the rules that follow).

Once he reaches the net, the server forms an offensive front with his partner. Both are ready to volley the return. Although there may seem to be an opening down one of the alleys, they will aim their first volley down the middle. The reason is a simple matter of geometry. At the middle the net is six inches lower than at the sides, and the ball has the full length of the court to travel without going out. This means the volley can be hit deep and low. It keeps the opposition back from the net and forces them to dig the ball up from the court and hit it up.

When the opposition serves, the wise doubles player will never try to score with his return. He may lob or else try to return the ball to the feet of the onrushing server, to force him into a weak return or, again, force him to hit up.

As the two teams inevitably converge at the net, the volleys keep going low down the middle, until finally one man or another has been pulled definitely out of position. Only then, as the high return comes over the net, will the wise doubles player sometimes permit himself to shoot for the alley. And even then, as Budge, one of the most expert of all volleyers, puts it, he'll hate himself for doing it.

This is the point where power really counts in doubles. After the court has been set up by a series of well-controlled shots, the muscleman of the team moves across the net to take the weak return and knock it off for a winner with an overhead smash or a hard, climactic volley.

I had seen Allison and Van Ryn do it that way — Van
Ryn, the playmaker, setting the trap, and Allison, the
powerhouse, moving across for the kill. That is the ideal
combination for doubles: a playmaker and a powerhouse
— a Lott and a Stoefen, a Mako and a Budge, a Schroeder and a Kramer.

Mulloy and I, power and control, worked that way together, and we had worked well from the beginning.
We had those two legs on the trophy to prove it.

The third one, it was obvious from the beginning of
that 1946 tournament, was going to be no easy job, either
for us or for the Californians. There were at least two
other topflight entries in the field. Frank Parker, the
reigning singles champion, was teamed with the up-and-
coming Bob Falkenburg, a tall, strong kid who was starting to attract almost as much attention on the sports
pages as his beautiful sister Jinx had on the magazine
covers. Don McNeill, the ex-champ, was entered with
Frank Guernsey, a small, clever player who had established himself as a genuine doubles artist before the war.

But even lower down in the field, before we encountered
any of these other favorites, Mulloy and I ran into trouble. The lingering effects of last season's knee injury were
with me, limiting my mobility; and our eagerness to win
made us tight. The old precision we had enjoyed as a
team escaped us.

In the third round, against a team of unknowns from
Belgium, Gardnar and I found ourselves within two
points of being eliminated before we managed to pull
ourselves together and win in five sets. The next day we

were extended to four sets by a team of American also-rans.

The pattern persisted into our semifinals match. Mulloy and I were both playing better now — the touch was coming back; I was forcing myself to move just a little more quickly, run just a little harder than I thought my knee would allow.

Yet, somehow, we were behind, two sets to none. Our opponents, Parker and Falkenburg, were playing expertly together, trading us volley for volley — and they kept getting the best of the deal.

We stretched ourselves further — we had to — and won the next two sets. Now each point became a test of nerves as well as skill. Neither side would concede a thing. Every apparent putaway was chased after, winner after apparent winner was put back in play by heroic saves. The crowd, which usually expresses its feelings at a tennis match (especially in Boston) by an occasional burst of genteel applause, was actually screaming with excitement.

In the tenth game of the fifth set, Parker and Falkenburg needed just one point to beat us. We fought them off. A moment later, they were once again within a stroke of victory. Spectators were standing on their seats and cheering as if it were the Yale game. They were still standing, still yelling, when Gardnar and I, after a series of back-to-the-wall stands and nerve-racking exchanges, finally managed to put across the winning point and stumbled toward the clubhouse.

All week long, the tension had been so great — we had

been kept so persistently in danger — that I had hardly had a chance to take liberties with my training. I couldn't have stayed awake past eleven o'clock at night if I'd wanted to; I watched my diet like a diabetic just introduced to insulin and scales, knowing that the next time I went on the court I'd probably need every bit of energy I could muster; and during play I took that precautionary ration of sugar at the first surge of any abnormal feeling.

Yet I was exhausted. I sat in the locker room for a long time, summoning enough ambition to reach the showers. I lingered in the steamy shower room and dressed slowly. I wanted to see the second semifinals match — Kramer–Schroeder versus McNeill–Guernsey — but there was no rush. Don and Frank, I figured, were good enough to keep the Californians on the court for quite a stretch before yielding to the inevitable. And judging by the explosions of applause that kept reaching me from the stands, it seemed that I must be right.

"How's it going out there?" I asked a player who ducked in for a moment.

"Terrific!" he said. "McNeill and Guernsey are absolutely murdering them!"

I hurriedly pulled on a jacket and dashed for my seat in the player's section of the stands. I was barely in time for the finish. In one of the most devastating form reversals of the year, Kramer and Schroeder were humiliated, 7–5, 6–3, 6–2. The last two sets had been a total rout. Schroeder, crushed by the outcome, immediately set about drowning his disappointment. Jake was so disgusted that he took the first plane home to California.

"Well," I said to Gardnar, with some satisfaction, "that leaves it to us." At the very least, nobody *but* us could take the trophy home that year.

But McNeill and Guernsey, it became obvious the next afternoon, when we met in the finals, were just as eager to keep the cup out of our hands as they'd been to block the Californians from it. Guernsey was the surprise of the tournament, although perhaps his performance shouldn't have startled anyone, considering the touch he'd shown in his prewar appearances and also in winning the national indoor title with McNeill the past winter. He still had the touch. His shots, though not powerful, were terribly deceptive. Time after time, he directed the course of play, maneuvering the ball until the opening came, then flicking chalk off the lines with beautifully angled volleys. McNeill, meanwhile, kept firing the heavy artillery, blasting any ball that came into his sights.

We kept pace. Mulloy was serving beautifully — that first delivery setting the receiver back on his heels almost every time. The score seesawed back and forth. They won, 6–3, and we came back at 6–4. Theirs, 6–2, then ours, 6–3.

In the fifth and final set, we fell behind 3–5, but managed to stave off defeat. At 6–7, with Mulloy coming up on service, I told myself: *Here's one we can count on, anyway.* I relaxed a little, saving myself for the effort to break through them in the next game. Only, suddenly we were behind — 40–love. We saved ourselves by winning five straight points.

A few changes of court later, and we were behind 10–11 — again with Mulloy serving. And again we were on the edge of disaster before a string of winners saved us.

At 13–14, my serve came up. I paused to take a swig of orange juice — better to be sure, I told myself.

My serve wasn't working right. The score edged up to 30–40. If we lost this one, it was all over.

I walked briskly back to the baseline, brought my racket up in my peculiar, quick, backswingless motion. The ball went deep to Guernsey's backhand. He played a beautiful long cross-court shot out of reach of Mulloy at the net. I was sure I couldn't get to it, yet I knew I just had to. At the last moment, I brought my racket around sharply.

If I had taken a normal backswing, probably the ball would have been past me. But the merest fraction of a second, saved by my foreshortened stroke, made the difference. The racket connected, and the ball shot back across court, past Guernsey and — I thought — into the alley for a point. I was dismayed when I saw Guernsey and McNeill rush toward each other jubilantly, their hands outstretched in congratulations.

Gardnar and I looked around in confusion. There was a rumble of disbelief from the stands. There had been no "out" call from the linesman. A moment later, my first impression was confirmed. "Deuce!" the umpire called, in a firm, clear voice. My return *had* been good, and we

were still in the match. I went back to the baseline and
made good on my serve. Fourteen-all.

The score went to 15–15, 16–16, 17–17 and 18–18. No
set in a national doubles final had ever gone that long.
McNeill served. The score became deuce, our advantage,
back to deuce, and then McNeill erred and we went on
to win the game.

For the first time, now, we held the upper hand — the
score 19–18 in our favor, only one game needed to win,
and Mulloy, whose service had been the most effective
on the court, was stepping up again.

We took the first two points. I walked back to Mulloy.
"All right," I said, "let's get this over with." I took up my
position on the backhand side, a few yards back from the
net.

Mulloy served — a fine one. The return went back to
him, short. He picked it up on a half-volley. Guernsey
volleyed back, down the middle. I moved, cut it off and
rapped it sharply, right between Guernsey and McNeill.
We were one point from the title.

Mulloy planted himself carefully at the baseline, wiped
his racket hand against his flannels and delivered a perfect high-bounding twist into the backhand corner.
The return was cross-court. Mulloy, moving up fast,
reached it on the volley this time, punched it low and
deep. McNeill dug it up. Another exchange, and then a
return came soft to my backhand. I angled it sharply
into the opening on McNeill's side of the court, and
through for the winner. The crowd let out a shout in
unison. Mulloy and I were champions for the third time.

You can read it in the final inscription on the big cup that now stands on the mantelpiece in our library.

Three weeks after Longwood, Mulloy and I won the clinching doubles point for the United States in the Davis Cup playoff against Sweden. Now, along with the other members of the United States team, I had a shot at the second of the season's big prizes. In November we would be heading for Sydney, to challenge Australia for the international trophy.

I looked forward to the next few months with nothing but impatience, but when the team was assembled for the trip the time seemed to have flown by and I was almost sorry. Something more important than tennis had happened to me in the meantime. I had met a girl named Nancy Pike.

Nancy

I HAD just come off the courts at a tennis club in suburban
New York when a group of friends waved me over to join
them on the clubhouse terrace for a drink. With them was
a slender girl with dark eyes, jet hair and a small, finely
molded face. Not a detail escaped me as I drew a chair
to the table and sat down, my eyes on her. She smiled —
a total illumination.

"Bill Talbert, Nancy Pike," somebody said helpfully.

"It's about time somebody introduced us," she said.

"My sentiments exactly."

She laughed. "You don't know what I mean. It's a private joke."

"All right. Let me in on it."

"I only meant it was funny — all these years after I
discovered you."

"*You* discovered me?"

She nodded, with a mischievous look. "Years ago.
We were at Easthampton that summer, and I went to
the tennis with a girl friend of mine. I think it must have
been your first time on the circuit — you couldn't have
been more than eighteen or nineteen yourself."

"Did I meet you? No, I would have remembered."

She shook her head. "We were just watching. We couldn't decide whether you really had any future as a tennis player, but we made up our minds that, of all the players at Easthampton, you definitely had the best-looking legs."

Everybody laughed, and I had to join them.

"Stand up," I said, "and give me a chance to return the compliment. If that's what it is."

"Some other time," she said, and went back to her coffee.

Coffee was her drink. Even at cocktail time, while everybody else built up the customary before-dinner glow with Martinis, she sipped from her coffee cup, and seemed to be having as fine a time as anybody. That was all I had a chance to find out — the coffee and the quickness of her laughter.

I looked for a chance to find out more, and it happened just a few days later. I went to a tournament dance and saw her as soon as I walked in. She was dancing, and I cut in.

"You've got me beat, I'm happy to say," I told her. She was puzzled.

"The legs," I said. "Very lovely."

She blushed, but not without laughing.

She was tall, I noticed, and moved gracefully. I also found out that she lived in New York with her family, worked as an editor for the fashion magazine *Vogue*, and took her job seriously. That became something of an issue between us during the following weeks. Around midnight, when I was ready to move on from wherever

we'd spent the early evening (as I thought of it) to some
place where the music was mellower and the lights dim-
mer, Nancy was thinking about the page layouts waiting
for her at her desk in the morning.

"You'd better take me home, Willy. I've got a big day
ahead of me."

"A nightcap," I said. "I know a place just up the street
with a fine piano — guy plays all the great show tunes."

She shook her head. "I'm just not up to this pace, I
guess. I don't know how you do it, night after night."

"Skip it," I said. "I'll take you home."

I could go on by myself. I always could.

This time, though, I found I didn't really enjoy it.
Sitting by myself at the bar, listening to the piano and
waiting out the small hours, I felt lonely. I felt the need
for someone, and it bothered me to realize that.

When November rolled around, Nancy saw me off on the
plane for San Francisco, where I was to join my teammates for the trip. "I'm counting on a drink from that
monstrosity of a cup," she said.

"It'll be champagne," I warned her. "As far as I know,
the Davis Cup has never been filled with coffee."

"I'll live a little. You just bring it back, and I'll
gladly drink champagne. And, Willy . . ." The smile was
replaced by an earnest look. "Take care of yourself."

From the moment we landed at Sydney, I started
watching for mail from New York.

Australia was something none of us was quite prepared
for. Mulloy, Kramer, Schroeder, Parker, Tom Brown and

I . . . as ranking tennis players, we were all used to being lionized on the tournament circuit. By now, I was accustomed to talking to sports reporters and having the photographers crouching around as I accepted some trophy or other. But all of that was nothing compared to the fierce glare of publicity that was turned on us as soon as we stepped out of the huge flying boat and into the warmth of Australia's upside-down summer.

There was an intensity of feeling about tennis, the international competition and the men engaged in it that you could hardly believe. It was more than a game — it seemed to be the great public issue. People were all heated up about it, as they rarely are in the States about any sports event short of the World Series or a heavyweight title fight.

We were met by a crowd at the dock and again at our hotel. There were receptions, lunches, dinners, attended by government officials ranging from the Prime Minister on down. We were followed along the streets when we left our hotel; we gave autographs. The first day we went out to practice, I thought we must have gone to the wrong courts. There were more people in the stands and ranged along the fences than I'd often seen at a Forest Hills tournament.

As far as the reporters were concerned, we didn't just give interviews — we had to hold press conferences, with whole batches of reporters at once. And the local journalists weren't satisfied with the standard predictions of "tough match, but we plan to give them a hell of a fight." They were not only concerned with the daily state of every

player's health and tennis strokes, they were also interested in our private lives as if we were visiting movie
celebrities.

"What about your divorce, Billy? Could you tell us just
a bit about that?"

"I'd rather skip it, if you don't mind."

"Any plans to remarry?"

"No," I said. I felt uncomfortable. Accustomed as I
was, by now, to public statements, I wasn't at all accustomed to talking about myself.

"Well, now, you weren't in service during the war. You
had some sort of exemption, I presume?"

There it was — the question above all that I disliked
having to answer. I gave them the explanation that had
been sufficient for the newspapers back home when the
draft board turned me down: "Medical reasons."

"Yes, I understand that, but just what sort? I mean,
would you mind being a little more specific?"

I tried to keep it simple. "I had diabetes," I said
lightly.

"Fully recovered now, I suppose?"

"I say," another reporter put in, "isn't that rather extraordinary? I mean to say, one doesn't *recover* from diabetes, to the best of my knowledge. And I had the impression that diabetics aren't permitted to take exercise."

There was a stir among the reporters, followed by a
whole series of questions about me and diabetes — just
how often I had to take my insulin injections, what other
restrictions I had to observe, how much of a risk it was,
how I'd got started on my unusual course as an athlete.

It was all in the papers the next day, along with a picture of me in action: "Billy Talbert, who conducts his career in tennis with a hypodermic needle as well as a racket. The American Davis Cup star is a diabetic, playing the game under doctor's supervision since the age of fourteen."

Even making allowances for the exaggeration and the tinge of melodrama that colored all the stories — it was part of the reporter's job to make things exciting, I told myself — still I didn't like the treatment. Couldn't they have mentioned the diabetes without making such a big thing of it, and concentrated on the tennis? Well, I tried to comfort myself, at least I told them everything I had to say on the subject. Now maybe I'm finished with it.

It didn't work that way at all. A day or two later, when we reached Melbourne, the site of the Challenge Round, I found a note addressed to me under the letterhead of a local organization dedicated to the training and care of diabetics. As a "well-known" athlete, it said, I was in a position to be of "inspiration and inestimable help to fellow sufferers of diabetes." Could I spare a couple of hours, some time in the near future, to play a brief tennis exhibition for a group of diabetic children and perhaps chat with them afterwards for a while?

I didn't care for that term "fellow sufferers." I wasn't a "sufferer" of anything; my idea was to lick it and leave it behind, to get as far away from it as possible. There were comparable organizations back home. I had always given them a wide berth.

If I had been completely my own agent, I would have done the same down in Melbourne. I had an excuse. The tennis program was demanding. There wasn't much time left before the Davis Cup matches, and the results of our practice sessions would have considerable bearing on the final selection of players for the international play-off.

Yet, when a phone call came, the next morning, as a followup to the note in my hotel mailbox, I realized that these considerations weren't the only ones. I wasn't just acting for Bill Talbert, private citizen and tennis player. Like Budge, Mako and Riggs in that first Davis Cup match I'd witnessed at Germantown, before the war, I was a representative of the U.S.A. That little emblem on the pocket of my blazer, identifying me as member of the American Davis Cup team, was a responsibility as well as an honor. It made you a little bigger than yourself.

"I'll be glad to do it," I said over the phone. "What day do you want me?"

A couple of mornings later, I drove out to one of Melbourne's handsome parks. With me was Gardnar Mulloy, who had agreed to come along as my opposition. Several dozen youngsters, some as young as seven or eight, others in their late teens, were assembled around the hard-surfaced public court. They were all diabetics, the group's director told me, and in the week or so since the Americans landed, they had come to know the name of Billy Talbert as well as they knew the names of the Australian team. A few of the children, he said, had played a little tennis themselves. He added hastily, "Under the most careful supervision, of course." I nodded, wondering what it would have been like if this kind of organization and its group activities had been available to me when I was a young diabetic. Over the years, the old convictions about diabetic treatment had been breaking down. In my day, I had been considered foolhardy for even daring to swing a tennis racket. There were some doctors, I knew, who still felt very much that way. Yet there were also many who had come around to endorsing the kind of program I had undertaken. Now diabetics were even being encouraged "to play a little tennis."

I could feel the dozens of eyes on me as I took the court with my rackets under my arm. I waved a hello to the group, acknowledging the director's introduction. In spite of myself, I felt an immediate contact with them.

For the kids' benefit, I called over to Mulloy, who had taken his position across the net: "I'm warning you, Gardnar, I've had my insulin, I've had my breakfast, and I'm ready for anything this morning."

I singled out a boy in the crowd, "Did you take your insulin this morning?"

"Yes, sir," he murmured.

"I've bean tyking mine for thirty-seven months," another boy offered proudly in a beautiful Down Under accent.

"Good. You keep it up," I said. "Mr. Mulloy, here, isn't a member of the club, like you and me, but he's a fine fellow just the same. Maybe we'll make him an *honorary* member."

There was a cheer of assent from the gang.

We played a set, pausing every now and then to explain some aspect of the game for the younger kids. Even though we were taking things easy, our audience seemed to be as wrapped up in the proceedings as if there were a trophy at stake. They cheered constantly and with unreserved partisanship. I was their boy.

"You ought to bring this crowd along with you next time you play a tournament," Mulloy said during a change of court. "An outsider doesn't stand a chance around here."

I grinned. "You know who'd better win this match. If it isn't me, you may never get out of here alive."

When we returned to the hotel, in time for lunch and the afternoon practice session, I realized that, whatever reservations I may have started with, I'd enjoyed myself. It was like that time at Children's Hospital in Cincinnati, after my crisis on the Southern circuit. No matter how reluctant I might be to admit it, I had felt a sense of identification with those young diabetics.

Yet it was nothing I couldn't gladly put aside for the tennis — we were to play one of the Australian tournaments before the Davis Cup matches themselves. Curiously, in that tournament and in our practice sessions, I realized that I was getting at least as much of a play from the crowd as my more celebrated teammates, Kramer and Schroeder, and perhaps even more. I had a sizable rooting section of my own, which kept growing larger as the newspapers continued their daily reports on the United States team and the Challenge Round prospects.

The stories, to my dismay, kept identifying me as a diabetic.

And as the stories continued, there were more letters in my hotel mailbox, more phone calls. There were requests for more exhibitions, visits with diabetic kids, speeches before diabetes organizations. There were also personal requests for advice and help.

I played one or two more exhibitions and made one or two speeches. I answered as many letters and calls as I could. Mostly they were from inexperienced diabetics or their parents, just wanting a sympathetic ear or a few words of reassurance from somebody who had been through the mill. A few of them really did need help — the help of a good doctor.

"Talk to your doctor." That was really the best advice I could give in most cases. It was also the simplest. I couldn't afford to get too deeply involved. I hadn't come ten thousand miles to open a traveling clinic for diabetics who hadn't learned to take care of themselves. I'd come to play tennis.

I never did get to play the big one. With the climax of our trip coming up, Walter Pate, the nonplaying captain, assembled the team in his hotel room. The playing team had to be selected and submitted to the Davis Cup officials; no more than four men could be named, and only those four would be eligible to play in the Challenge Round matches.

Pate, chosen by the United States Lawn Tennis Association to guide the fortunes of the American team, was a Wall Street lawyer who loved tennis, though he had

ever gone through the tough international grind himself. He had deferred to the judgment of the players
themselves on every major decision so far, and now,
when it came to the choice of the team, he put it up to
us again for a vote.

The unhappy facts stared me in the face. In the work-
outs, my knee trouble was still evident; my game hadn't
really come around. There were four men on the squad
who could do more good than I.

"Well," I said reluctantly, "if it were up to me, I'd
have to pick Kramer, Schroeder, Mulloy and Parker."

There was no dissent. I looked on from the sidelines
while my teammates took back the Davis Cup without
the loss of a match.

The return home was a triumphal procession. Between
Sydney and New York, where the cup was delivered to
the USLTA, it was filled time after time with champagne
— twenty-eight quarts to the load, by actual count. Round
after round of toasts was drunk to us conquering heroes
in white flannel shorts.

Nancy drank her glassful, at the climactic celebration
when we reached New York.

"I'm not sure I'm really entitled to this," I said. "That
was one hell of a long trip to take just for the practice."

"Don't be silly," she said. "I'm sure Kramer and Schroeder wouldn't have won if the rest of you hadn't been
there to keep them sharp. Anyway, you've brought the
cup back — that's the main thing."

"Is it?"

"No," she said quietly.

"The main thing," I said, "is that I'm home. Whe
you are."

We touched glasses and drank.

"Hate champagne," I said. "I've seen this bowl fill
so many times now, I don't ever want to taste the stu
again."

"I'd never miss it," she agreed.

"Should have filled it with coffee, after all."

"Thank you," Nancy said. She rummaged in her han
bag. "I just remembered. I brought something for yo
in case you didn't see it while you were in Australia

She fished out a folded piece of newsprint — a pa
torn out of *Time* magazine, a few weeks previous, ju
before the Challenge Round. It wasn't, curiously, fro
the sports section but from the news pages of the ma
azine. There was a picture of me in practice at the Ko
yong Tennis Club courts in Melbourne, with a crow
pressing its faces up to the fence behind me. I winc
as I read the brief story that accompanied it:

> Diabetes was making U.S. Tennist Billy Talbert a
> special sort of hero in Australia. Amazed that he had
> been taking daily insulin since he was 10, admiring
> Australians showered him with fan letters, flocked to
> watch him practice . . .

I folded the page absently and stuck it into my wall
It was the end of being Billy Talbert, tennis player, li
other tennis players. Here at home, too, my diabetes w
no longer a private thing.

XVIII
Setback

JST as in Australia, the letters began to arrive — from ll over the country, addressed to me in care of *Time* ıagazine, the United States Davis Cup team, the United tates Lawn Tennis Association, and local diabetes or-anizations, which forwarded them through tennis chan-els. Many of the letters were heart-warming, some just lain heartbreaking.

DEAR MR. TALBERT,

Two years ago this July 14th our son was taken to the hospital in a coma and it was a terrible shock when they told us it was diabetes.

He has been such a brave boy about taking his shots and keeping up his diet but it has been hard to make him understand why he could not do certain things like other youngsters.

All of us were so cheered up when his teacher brought him the article about you. Now we are living in hope he will not be disappointed and that it is possible to lead a normal life . . .

DEAR BILLY,

My favorite sport is football. About 2 mo. ago they discovered I had Diabetes. I have to take insulin like you. I take 50 units every day. My mother showed me where you play tennis but she says football is too rough for me now. Do you think so?

I forgot to tell you I am 12 yr. old . . .

DEAR SIR,

I am writing you regarding my husband, a diabetic like yourself. He has kept this fact a secret from his employer, being afraid of the consequences.

However, I feel it would be wiser to let him know. At least the "secret" would be out and there would be no need of being afraid all the time! Please tell us what we should do. . . .

All these private feelings, thrust into my hands lik valuable gifts from total strangers . . . "We are afraid . . "I am worried . . ." "My wife and I are heartsick." Emtion — my own or other people's — made me uncomfor able; I didn't know what to do with it. All I could see to offer was a kind of formula: A good doctor and cheerful attitude . . . thorough knowledge of your ow case . . . common sense and reasonable care in followin a few simple regulations.

The formula was accurate enough; it was based on n own experience. But it seemed remote, as if the subje no longer had much to do with me. It was for *oth* diabetics. For my own part, I was just going through t motions of diabetic care.

I took my insulin every morning and my milk an sandwich before bed. In between, however, I kept stretc ing the limits farther and farther, as if determined to fi out just how much I could get away with. Or perha

s my father had put it when we talked on the beach in
'lorida, to find out how far from diabetes I could
un.

It was a program of carelessness, but a deliberate care-
essness — my own peculiar form of independence, no
onger an objective but a compulsion. At first it had been
 means to an end; now it had become an end in itself.
 had started, years before, by looking for some relief
:om the confinement of diabetes; now I was in headlong
ight from it.

Where the diabetic, traditionally, was supposed to
:ay almost inert, I *had* to be continuously on the go.
Vhere the diabetic was taught moderation, I *had* to
idulge myself. Diabetics were supposed to be cautious,
nd I liked nothing better than to take off in the direc-
ion of any impulse that stirred me. An extra few sets of
ennis after a tournament match, a midnight swim at a
each half an evening's drive away — that was the kind
f action I doted on. A tournament-week party the night
efore the finals or a café evening right after — I liked
he pretty girls, I was always ready to go. Faster and
aster. Any place, any time. Anything to keep myself from
aving time to think about where I was going, or why.
)r how to stop.

Once it was ambition that had driven me. I had wanted
o be a tennis star, in spite of all the medical records that
aid I couldn't. Now I had got there, and I couldn't seem
o face the idea that there was someplace to go beyond
:. Beyond tennis and beyond the kind of freedom I had.
o, running hard, I marked time.

At the drop of a tournament committee invitation,
traveled anywhere for the tennis. And I didn't pace my
self at it, the way other players did. As Kramer said,
kept entering every event on the books.

When I returned from a tournament trip now, it was t
New York. Of all the places I'd seen, it was the one
loved best, the place I felt I belonged. A hotel was hom
enough for my kind of life. As soon as I lighted in th
city, anyway, and dropped off my luggage and change
clothes, I'd be on the move again, making the late-hou
rounds I loved.

On my way home from one trip, I found myself be
tween trains for a couple of hours in a Midwestern city
It was early in the morning and time for my daily insuli
injection. There wasn't much of a crowd in the statio
at that hour, so I thought I could take my shot unob
trusively in the men's washroom.

I had just prepared the hypodermic when a han
clamped down roughly on my shoulder. I turned an
found myself in the grip of an unfriendly-looking police
man. He squinted at me with an expression of contemp
and loathing.

"You ain't gonna get away with that kind of stuf
buddy," he said. "Not in this town."

He grabbed the syringe out of my hand. I was to
astonished to argue at first.

"I'll take this," he said. "Now get your stuff togethe
and come with me." He started to shove me, protesting
ahead of him out the door. "Damn hopheads think any
thing goes around here, huh? Well, you'll find out."

"This is insulin!" I said. "I'm not —"

"I don't care what kind of stuff you're on, buddy, and don't care what doctor you're gonna tell me prescribed t for you."

It was useless. As far as the cop was concerned, I was a dope addict, nabbed in the act. I had to let myself be ustled down the street, trying to maintain some composure in spite of the stares of early-morning passers-by who stopped to watch us as we marched the couple of blocks to the precinct station.

The desk sergeant there was more reasonable, but still no pushover.

"Diabetic, eh?" he said, with a tinge of suspicion.

"That's right," I said. I pointed to the syringe full of milky fluid which the policeman had put on the desk as evidence. "I don't know what you think this is, but it's insulin."

The sergeant picked up the hypodermic. "You know, 've heard that story before. And I've seen syringes like his filled with heroin and milk."

"All you've got to do," I said, keeping my voice calm, "is check the stuff. Analyze it, if you think it's heroin."

"We will. Don't worry, we will."

He looked me over carefully. "All right," he said inally, "let's see your diabetic's card."

My heart dropped a foot or two as I reached for my wallet. I knew there was no diabetic's identification in it. knew where the card was, all right. It was in the night able drawer of my hotel room, back in New York. For ome time now, I had managed to "forget" to keep it with me, as if trying to lose the identity it gave me

As I fumbled in my wallet, however, feeling the perspiration start under my collar, I found something else
"Here," I said. "Read this." I handed over the magazine
clipping that Nancy had given me, months before.

The sergeant glanced at the picture, then at me. I
tennis shorts, on an Australian court, it occurred to me
I probably didn't look much like the guy in a business
suit standing in this police station.

Without a word, the sergeant picked up the phone and
called the sports department of the local newspaper. "You
ever hear of a guy named Billy Talbert? Tennis player. . .
That's right. He supposed to be sick or something? Dia
betes — something like that? . . . Yeah. . . . No, nothin
special, just wondered if you ever heard of him . .
Thanks."

In a little while, after some more questions, I was
turned loose. As I left the station, I couldn't help remem
bering the diabetic I'd met, some years before, in a town
jail in Florida, and I understood, as I had never really
understood before, just how he must have felt, being
locked up as just another "guy on the booze." At the time
I had been concerned for him, anxious to help. But until
now it had never occurred to me to think, *That could have
been me.*

In New York, I was seeing a lot of Nancy Pike — lunch
dinner, long evenings afterwards. And it was neve
enough for me. But the evening always seemed to wind
up in an argument, and always the same one. Why did

he have to get home so early (early, for me, being any
me before 2 or 3 A.M.)? What was so damned important
bout her job, anyway? What was wrong with my want-
ig one more drink in one more bar? A few Scotches in
n evening — did that make me a drunk? Had I ever
nown the slightest sign that I couldn't handle it?

Nancy endured my challenge in patient, though
rieved silence. But the next day at lunch, she said, "How
an you be so sweet now, after being so nasty last
ight? Really, I didn't say any of the things you accused
ne of saying. Two drinks and you become downright
ade!"

It wasn't the drinks. I was pretty sure I knew what it
·as, and I went to a doctor to confirm it. I was due for
check-up anyway, and with the move to New York I
eeded a new doctor. Some friends referred me to a man
·ith an office not too far from my hotel — not only an
xcellent physician, they told me, but a tennis enthusiast
)o.

I had had an insulin reaction, I told him. I could be
retty sure that was the trouble, because I had played a
·t of tennis and eaten lightly during the day; and my
·ehavior, as Nancy described it, fitted the pattern. Too
uch insulin — or more accurately, in most cases, not
nough food at the right time — has different effects on
ifferent diabetics. Some become relaxed, even lethargic;
thers become tense. Some turn gay, others sulk. My
attern seemed to be "rudeness."

The doctor nodded. He was a short, massive man with
n owlish, sunburned face (the tennis, no doubt) and a

direct, friendly manner. "Well," he said, "the amount ⦙
insulin you're taking checks out all right. You're n⦙
fiddling around with that?"

"No."

"Then you know the answer as well as I do."

"Eat a little more, especially at dinner."

"That's right. You're eating a snack at bedtime ever
night?"

"Every night."

"Good. That's important — hell, you know that as we
as I do." He glanced over the results of the tests he ha⦙
given me. "In general, I'd say there's nothing wrong wi⦙
you. A trace of sugar in the urine right now, which is ⦙
to the good, especially for a man exercising a lot. Kee⦙
it that way and you won't have trouble with insul⦙
reaction." He tossed the file aside. "You say you feel ⦙
right otherwise — no thirst, no loss of weight, no fatigu⦙
You're having a good time — which is what a fello⦙
your age ought to be doing. You're in better physic⦙
shape, God knows, than 99 per cent of the men who wa⦙
right past this office every day of the week. Go on, get o⦙
of here before I have you thrown out for impersonati⦙
a patient."

I laughed. I could see we were going to get along fin⦙
Not even Dr. Walt, the man who had started me ⦙
tennis, had taken such an openhanded approach towa⦙
diabetes, an approach so congenial with my own.

He stood up from behind his desk and held out h⦙
hand. "I'll be looking for you in the tournaments th⦙
summer."

"I'll be there," I said, picking up my hat. "How much
o I owe you for the check-up?"

"Skip it," he said. "If you ever turn pro and start
naking money from tennis, then maybe I will, too.
Until then — "

"Doc," I said, reddening a little angrily, "off the courts
've always paid my own way. I don't mean to change
ow."

Off the courts, I was working at whatever came along,
rovided it didn't tie me down. I sold advertising for
ome special publications connected with sports events:
he work left me entirely on my own, assured me of
izable commissions for relatively short periods of work,
nd afterwards there would be no string on my services.
very now and then, when I was about to take a trip,
ome acquaintance in business would engage me to
egotiate a sale or a purchase of some kind. I was a free-
ance par excellence, with no obligations, no schedule to
ollow, no hours to keep.

As the consultation with the doctor reassured me, there
vas no reason a diabetic couldn't live this free-wheeling
ind of life if he wanted to. A slight insulin reaction was
asy enough to remedy if you acted promptly.

What I hadn't told the doctor was that I hadn't had
ust *an* insulin reaction — it was happening to me regu-
arly, almost every evening.

Not that I was conscious of it while it was happening.
would have known if I had paid attention to the
aguely "foreign" feeling that preceded it — that subtle
int which in the past, during tennis matches, had always

sent me reaching automatically for sugar. I was ignorin
the signal, as if unwilling to acknowledge it.

After taking Nancy home, in an atmosphere of strai
I would stubbornly go on for my nightcap before return
ing to the hotel. There, out of habit, I would have m
usual milk and sandwich sent up to the room — and tha
habitual gesture would automatically save me from an
serious trouble. That last act of the day — the final ratio
of protein and carbohydrate — would readjust the bal
ance automatically. The danger would pass without m
ever having noticed it.

It was only the next day that I would find out tha
I'd been in trouble again.

Nancy didn't know what the trouble was. She ha
been aware of my diabetes even before the newspape
stories from Australia. Once or twice she had raise
some question about it, but I always brushed the subjec
aside as unimportant. We had never really discusse
diabetes, especially not in personal terms, not in relatio
to me.

Still, she was aware that something was wrong, an
that somehow it might have some connection with dia
betes. In the morning, after one of our grim good night
she would phone my hotel from her office.

"Willy? Are you all right?"

"Sure I'm all right," I said cheerily. "You don't think
went out on a lonesome bat or something after I left you?

"N-no. Just wondered. You were in such a foul mood.

"I was? Nan, I'm sorry."

"It's kind of hard for a girl to keep taking, Willy."

"I know, I know. Honestly, Nancy, I'm terribly sorry."

A few evenings later, we argued again.

I had got up early, spent a busy morning in the city, eaten a very light lunch. In the afternoon, I had played some tennis with an old fellow campaigner, Bobby Riggs, who happened to be passing through town. In Bobby's standard pattern, it was a long-drawn-out affair. That evening I met Nancy for dinner about eight, and then we started on the usual rounds with some friends.

Around 1 A.M., the party broke up. Nancy and I stood outside the Stork Club, waiting for a cab.

"Well, Cinderella," I said, "it's past midnight, and I don't see any pumpkins cruising the street." I nodded to the doorman and climbed into the cab after her. "Turn east and keep going," I told the driver. "Stop when you get to a good place. Any place."

"Willy, don't," Nancy said. "Even you look bushed You hardly ate any dinner."

"I never felt better."

She sighed and fell quiet. Suddenly she turned to me. "Willy, tell me. What are you trying to prove? That you're different from other diabetics? Maybe you are — I don't know and I don't care. Are you trying to convince me that you can do anything anybody else can do? Or don't you care about me? Maybe you're just trying to convince yourself."

"I know what I can do and what I can't do."

"You try to do too much. You live twice as hard as any normal man."

"I don't give a damn about — "

"If you give a damn about *me*, then you'll stop this childish argument that we always get into, and act reasonably. Honestly, you make me feel like a heel, and for no reason at all. It's late; I'm tired; and any sensible girl with a job would feel the same way."

"If you want to go home, just say so."

"Willy, don't say it like that. Look, for your own good —"

"Why don't you let me decide what's for my own good?"

"Well then, do it, for Heaven's sake! Take care of yourself!"

"I damn well will!" I said, really furious now. "I'm sick and tired . . ." My voice trailed off . . . "Tired . . this nursemaid act."

"You know I've never said anything like that before," she said defensively. "I've always put it on a purely selfish basis — *I* can't take this kind of life, *I* have other things to do with my life besides sitting around in these East Side joints, making myself sick on coffee while you try to outlast everybody else in the place. But if you won't do it for me, then do it for yourself."

I didn't answer. I couldn't seem to focus my words. But I knew what I meant: *I'll do what I please! And I don't need you or anybody else taking care of me!*

"If you're trying to say you're tired of me," Nancy said really angry now, herself, "then I think it's time we stopped seeing each other. Let's just forget the whole thing."

"Forget . . ." I couldn't have cared less. I fumbled for a

handkerchief and mopped my face, dripping with perspiration.

I kept the cab after Nancy got out, walking straight into her family's house without a word or a backward glance. It was about 3 A.M. when I returned to the hotel — or so the elevator boy told me afterwards. Room Service received no call that night for my usual milk and sandwich.

In the morning, Nancy fought off the impulse to make her usual phone call. She was determined not to make one more gesture of truce, swallow one more of my apologies.

Toward noon, though, she began to feel uneasy.

Maybe something really *was* wrong, this time. She decided she'd call the hotel and just make sure I'd been out that morning.

She found that I hadn't left the hotel but there was no answer in my room. Nancy became alarmed. She asked the desk clerk to have someone look in on me.

There was a long wait, and finally another voice, this one very official-sounding, cut into the line and said, "May I ask who is calling for Mr. Talbert, please?"

Nancy explained.

"Oh, Miss Pike." The voice sounded relieved. "We were just trying to reach you. We found your name and address among Mr. Talbert's papers. Could you come to the hotel at once, please?"

A few minutes later, Nancy was taken to my hotel room. I lay there in bed, unconscious, in a state of deep shock. All attempts to rouse me had failed.

It was like the scene in Tampa, years before, when my first youthful flight toward freedom had been cut short by a diabetic attack that plunged me into the depths of coma. This time, the cause was the opposite; instead of insufficient insulin, the trouble was insufficient food. The long day's exertions had made severe demands, which I had failed to answer. I hadn't eaten enough during the day. I was already in a serious insulin reaction when I reached the hotel — too far gone even to remember my all-important bedtime snack. Without that buffer to protect me, I had lapsed deeper into reaction at the most hazardous time of all — while I was asleep, unaware of trouble, unable to do anything about it. Now I lay deep in its throes.

The ambulance was slow in arriving. While waiting for it, Nancy began frantically to rack her memory for some piece of information about me and diabetes that might tell her what to do. The only thing that came to her mind was my habit of taking something sweet during a tough tennis match. In desperation, she sent for a bar of candy from the newsstand in the hotel lobby, and began trying to force it into my mouth. It was exactly the right remedy, but there was no use. My teeth were clamped stubbornly shut, as if I had embraced unconsciousness — determined to resist help.

Nancy watched as I was taken on a stretcher, inert and unknowing, and rushed to the hospital.

Twenty-four hours went by before I came to. I blinked, trying to figure out what I was doing in this hospital bed, why my doctor was standing by the bed. I started up, then groaned as a pain shot through my head. I felt stiff all over.

"What hit me?" I said. "A Mack truck?"

The doctor shook his head. "Something you forgot to eat, I'm willing to bet."

"I had dinner," I said. "And then . . ." I gave up. The effort of trying to remember was too much.

"Relax. This was a bad one. And you've no excuse for it, my friend. You know better."

By the time I reached the hospital, he told me, I was so deep in shock that it had taken hours before huge amounts of a sugar solution, injected intravenously, had shown any effect. But now I was safely past the insulin crisis.

Gradually, some of the events of a couple of evenings before came back to me. I winced, thinking of how I had steered myself directly into the pitfall.

Nancy! Hazily I could recall an argument in the taxi. I must have offended her again. And, after that, not to have called her all day! She must think I really meant it this time.

I rang for a nurse. "Can I get a telephone plugged in here?" I asked. "Right away?"

"I don't see why not," she said with a knowing smile. "Especially if it's to phone Miss Pike. She's been calling about you every few hours."

So Nancy knew. When I found out just how much she knew, and at what close range she had learned, I was grateful, but I was also embarrassed by the trouble I must have caused her, by the thought of myself in a stupor, unable to help myself. Nancy tried to make it easy for me. No recriminations, no I-told-you-so's, and she made light of the grim details of waiting beside me in the hotel room.

"Of course," she said, "you know you've ruined my reputation. At least as far as my parents are concerned."

As the wait for the ambulance dragged on, Nancy had called her mother to explain that she might be late getting home.

Mrs. Pike was distressed when Nancy told her where she was. "I hope, dear," she said, "that you're leaving Mr. Talbert's door open."

I laughed when Nancy told me about it. "I plotted the whole thing," I said. "Now you've got to take me home and introduce me to your parents as the guy who compromised their daughter. I'll have to explain to them that even wolves don't bite when they're unconscious."

The melodrama was over. We were playing life again the way I preferred it — lightly.

I couldn't just sweep the whole experience under the rug, however. Three days in the hospital gave me long stretches of time in which I couldn't avoid thinking, and during those hours I kept coming up against my own future.

It just wasn't enough to be free. I had to do something with my freedom, otherwise it became a kind of slavery in itself. You wound up like this — helpless, depending on somebody else to pull you out of trouble.

I moved out of the hotel and took an apartment. A fresh start. I wanted to leave what had happened behind me. I'd get busy and begin making the rounds, seeing people. Somewhere there was a spot for a tennis player with a pretty good business head.

A few weeks after I'd left the hospital with nothing more than a headache for a souvenir, I ran into a man I knew on a Manhattan street corner. He was a South American whom I had met at a tennis tournament during one of his frequent visits to the States.

"Where are you headed, Alberto?" I asked him.

He looked at his watch. "Right now, lunch. Tomorrow, home."

I always got a kick out of that brisk, literal manner of his. "I catch the sleeper plane for Buenos Aires. You busy, Willy?"

"Not especially."

"Why you don't come along?"

"To lunch or to Argentina?"

He shrugged. "Either way, fine time."

I flipped a coin — and, in the same motion, tossed aside my serious intentions. It came up Argentina. Well, it was too good an opportunity to pass up. I'd never been to South America before, and the people I had intended to see in New York would still be here when I got back.

The next night, with a couple of suitcases and an armload of rackets, I climbed aboard the plane to Buenos Aires, bound for a tour of the South American tennis circuit.

I felt fine and eager. The experience of a few weeks before hadn't dulled my appetite for tennis or for the excitement of new places. But my first night in the big, luxurious Alvear Palace Hotel in Buenos Aires, after I'd finished my glass of milk and a *galleta*, I placed a note on the table beside my bed. It was carefully typed in Spanish with the help of a member of the hotel staff, and addressed to the chambermaid. It read:

> Please wake me. If I do not get up at once, please give me something sweet to drink and then call a doctor. I am a diabetic and may be having an insulin reaction.

I read the few brief, businesslike sentences to myself. The meaning was as strange to me as the language, as foreign as the broad Argentine boulevards below my hotel window. I was scared.

Yanqui Goes Home

I CARRIED the note with me all through the tour, like a bottle of pills left over from a bout of the flu: you keep telling yourself you don't really need them any more, but you don't dare throw them away.

Each night I propped the note on the night table in my hotel room in Buenos Aires. I had another written in Portuguese, when I went to São Paulo and then on to Rio de Janeiro. Each time I had to fight off the temptation to tear it up, in anger and disgust with myself. Yet that would have been foolish, and in a way it seemed more cowardly than leaving it. I was old enough to start facing the truth about myself, and if this was part of it, then I'd better start learning to live with the fact. After all the years of flight, all the times I had congratulated myself on what I thought was escape, I was caged like all the others. I was no better off, no stronger than all those diabetics who simply gave in — all the worried, frightened people who wrote me letters. I *was* just another one of them, after all.

That's what the note seemed to mean. Yet I couldn't really swallow that. Afraid? Maybe. A little. But why not? Why shouldn't I shrink from the thought of repeating that scene at the hotel in New York, of causing trouble for the people who were treating me so royally everywhere I went?

My rank in the United States had assured me a welcome at any club in South America; Alberto's connections in tennis society down there had opened the doors even wider. The whole route was paved with red carpet.

And scared or not, I hadn't missed out on any of the fun. Fear wasn't crowding me. It hadn't kept me out of the surf at the broad white Copacabana Beach. And it wouldn't keep me off the courts tomorrow at the *club de tenis*. It would remind me to take my insulin in the morning and my bedtime snack at night, and it left me a whole day's living in between. Tomorrow I would be playing tennis, giving the game just as much as I always did, and getting just as much out of it.

It was true. On the courts, the next day, I felt nothing but the exhilaration of a perfect tennis day — bright, warm and still. I was hitting everything sharply and easily. My opponent, a lean, quick boy with a mustache, was something of a local favorite, with a few good wins against the native competition, but he didn't have a chance. Gasps of surprise went up from the white-shirted crowd, and now and then an *"Olé!"* as I nicked the lines and brought off volley after volley. In an hour the match was over — 6–1, 6–1, 6–1. Feeling sorry for the kid, I put my arm around his shoulders and walked him off the court with a few words of encouragement.

Fresh and reassured, I came out of the locker room and joined a group on the clubhouse terrace — Alberto and his wife had come up from Buenos Aires; they were with a few people I'd already met, and a few new ones.

"Fine game, Willy," Alberto said. "You play like that, you should be champion of the United States."

"Mr. Talbert has good day," a prosperous-looking gentleman across the table said with a deprecating shrug. "He is very lucky *yanqui*."

A late afternoon breeze began to stir the palms. In a while, the southern dusk would begin to thicken; the sky would strike a few sparks of stars; and eventually we would move on to some place with guitar music and the perfume of expensive women.

I'm a very lucky *yanqui*, I thought.

"Tomorrow you don't have so easy time when you play Vieira. You think you beat him like this?"

"I think so," I said, not realizing at first what he meant. Vieira was the Brazilian champion and could be trouble, but I wasn't worried.

"I'll make a bet, Mr. Talbert. Five to one you will not beat Vieira as you beat this man today."

He began to count out five hundred dollars in cruzeiros.

"Five to one that he doesn't get more than three games off me? Is that what you're saying?"

It would be a foolhardy dare, as Alberto hastily pointed out. I couldn't be sure of holding Grandma Moses to three games, let alone an experienced international tennis player. But the odds were irresistible, I was in the mood for challenge, and with five hundred dollars I could afford to stretch my trip an extra couple of weeks.

"*Ben!*" I said. "You're on!"

The next afternoon, brushing aside Alberto's last-min-

ute efforts to call off the bet, I played Vieira. I beat him
6–0, 6–0, 6–0.

That night at the hotel, I tore the note into small
pieces and dropped them into the wastebasket. It had
served its purpose. I knew there was no more to be afraid
of than there had ever been — and that was only myself.

But I didn't prolong my South American tour. There
was only one more thing I really wanted to do before
going back to New York: I had promised to visit with a
group of diabetic children here, as I'd done in Australia.
I went, this time, with no reluctance and no mental
reservations.

There were about a dozen of them, gathered in a
churchyard, under the shade of a gnarled old tree. No
tennis exhibition, this time. We just sat in the quiet of
the stucco-walled yard and talked about diabetes —
through an interpreter. Yet it was surprising how we
understood, the kids and I, without the translation. The
most important words in their vocabulary — *insulina,
reação, açúcar* — sounded familiar to diabetics in almost
any language. There was a curious bond here, an immediate response that reduced the thousands of miles between countries to no distance at all, and made differences in manners and customs seem unimportant. The
grave little bows with which they greeted me seemed
strange, and their ancient church, with a bell that clanged
in an arched tower, was like nothing I could remember
from my boyhood in Cincinnati. But we had something
very important in common.

As I left, shaking hands with each of them in turn,
they promised to take their insulin, eat well, and write

me letters in New York. And one small, dark-eyed girl assured me that she was going to be a tennis player when she grew up.

"*Ben!*" I said. "Tell her," I instructed the interpreter, "that I'll see her at Forest Hills."

After that, I was ready to go home.

In New York I let myself into the apartment, dropped my luggage and called Nancy. Afterwards, I started on the weeks' accumulation of mail.

DEAR MR. TALBERT,

Ordinarily I would not dream of writing a letter like this but I must discuss this with someone and my parents just do not understand. Mr. Talbert, I have been a diabetic for more than a year, since I was eighteen. I made up my mind to "take it in stride" as my father says. But I have had some terrible experiences and I am frightened.

If I could talk to you sometime perhaps you could tell me what to do. As you know, it is so much easier to talk to one of "us" . . .

It was written in a neat girlish hand, addressed from a nearby suburb and primly signed "Miss Ruth Harris." Miss Harris sounded surprised when I phoned her in the morning and invited her to have lunch with me when she came into the city.

I might have been surprised at myself, but for the first time I had no doubts about what I could say or how I could help. To begin with, I could say that I knew how it felt to be afraid.

Grab the Brass Ring

IT took the doctor to put it into words for me.

"What's so special about being afraid?" he said, rock-ing back in his desk chair and fixing me with a chal-lenging glance. "Everybody lives with a touch of it, if he's got any sense at all. Everybody learns to get over it or work around it, if he wants to get anything out of life. It doesn't make you any different from everybody else."

He had a way of scolding you so entertainingly, with such gruff good humor, that you didn't mind it. You came away, finally, feeling that it had been a fair fight and the better man had won.

"I don't mean the physical part of it so much," I said. "Even a really bad insulin reaction, like the one I had — I know it's nothing fatal. I know I shouldn't have let it happen to me, anyway." He nodded. "But it's the idea of being in a situation that you might not to be able to handle by yourself. It makes you . . . well, dependent."

"You," he said flatly, "are just about the most inde-pendent character I have ever met, diabetic or other-wise. A little less of that wouldn't do you any harm."

"All right, Doc, let's not talk about me, then. Let's

talk about diabetics in general. How can you get around
the fact — "

"I've got a better idea," he broke in. "Let's not talk
about you *or* other diabetics. Let's talk about people,
which is what we are really talking about, anyway."

He heaved himself forward in the chair and whipped
off the owlish eyeglasses. "Look, my friend," he said with
an imperative gesture, "you say 'diabetic' as if it meant
some special category of human being. Well, it doesn't.
Having diabetes doesn't change what a man is. I have
patients come in here who are real heels, and I can tell
you they were heels to start with. Getting diabetes didn't
make them that way, and it didn't make them any
better, God help me — and their poor wives and hus-
bands. And I have some who are real great guys. Not
because they have diabetes, either. They were just as nice
before."

He rocked back and forth for a moment, taking aim
for the final blow.

"A man is first of all a person," he said, "and only
second a diabetic. Now, the only question is, which way
is he going to spend his life? How is he going to live —
as a person or as a diabetic?"

I didn't have to be told how to enjoy life. I'd been
brought up knowing that. But it had taken me all these
years — and perhaps a touch of that universal fear — to
understand what I was. I had been running from an
image of myself that I had created. The diabetic and the
"normal" person — it was a distinction *I* had made.
There was nothing wrong, no shame, in being "one of

them" if you were willing to recognize that they were all people.

As a diabetic, Ruth Harris had been convinced that her parents couldn't understand her problem, but as four people we talked about it over the lunch table. Diabetes wasn't even the real problem; it was people.

Ruth, a vivacious, attractive girl of about twenty, and obviously the apple of her father's eye, had been a happy, active and popular teen-ager at the time she became diabetic, a little more than a year before. She was a good swimmer, loved to dance.

"The boys," Mr. Harris said, with a mixture of pride and jealousy — "well, they were camped so thick on our doorstep I'd practically have to fight my way into the house when I got off the train nights. I couldn't blame them, Talbert. I've got the best-looking daughter in town. Now . . ." He shook his head and turned to Ruth accusingly. "You can't expect the boys to keep calling if you keep turning down dates. Am I right, Eleanor?"

Mrs. Harris nodded sadly. "Ruth has hardly been out of the house in months."

"I told you, Mother, I just don't feel like it," Ruth said.

I knew why she didn't feel like it. She had already told me, a week or so before, when the two of us had talked alone. The first time she'd gone on a date as a diabetic, a couple of months after leaving the hospital, she'd had a terrible time. She hadn't really felt ready for it; she had worried for days in advance about having an insulin reaction. But she knew how determined her father was that nothing about his daughter should be changed by diabetes, and she didn't want to disappoint him.

Of course, the thing she was afraid of did happen — a reaction, and a bad one.

"It was horrible," she had told me. I thought she was going to cry, but she stifled the tears. "It was a senior dance — last year, when I was in high school — and everybody thought I was having an epileptic fit, and I couldn't do anything about it. It must have been so repulsive, and I didn't know what was happening until afterwards. I was just so helpless. The boy I was with — well, he didn't call me after that, of course."

"Didn't you tell your parents about it?"

She thought for a moment. "Not really. Not everything. I knew Daddy would be embarrassed, the way I was. I don't know, Mr. Talbert . . . I just felt as if I had done something awful. And I can't stand the thought of going some place where it might happen again." She fingered her coffee cup nervously. "You know how it is."

"Sure," I said. "It's happened to me."

I helped Ruth tell her parents the painful story, that day we all met for lunch. They were shocked; Ruth was obviously relieved to get it off her mind.

"Look," I said, "I'm no doctor, Mr. Harris. I don't know the answer to Ruth's problem. I'm willing to bet it can be worked out without much trouble — but only if you start by admitting the problem exists. Why don't you talk to her doctor, all three of you, and make sure first of all that she's getting an adequate diet for dancing and swimming and any of the things she likes to do?"

That would be the next step — for Daddy and Mother to get personally involved, to start learning the ins and outs of their daughter's case, instead of just trying to pretend she was the same untroubled little girl she'd always been. That had left her to cope with it on her own. And there was just so much, when you came right down to it, that a person could handle by himself. Any person. . . .

I had a letter from the Harrises late that summer. With it came a snapshot, taken at a lake in Connecticut. It showed Ruth laughing up at the camera from the water alongside a diving pier. The picture, Mrs. Harris wrote, was taken by "one of the boys staying at the lake who is very interested in Ruth."

The letter reached me at a place I hadn't expected to be during that summer of 1947 — in Boston, the site of the national doubles tournament. At the beginning of the season I had told Gardnar Mulloy he'd better find himself a new partner because I wouldn't have time for the circuit that year. I hoped to be doing something more with my life than playing tennis.

When the national doubles got under way, Mulloy and Frank Parker were one of the top-seeded teams. But by that time I had joined the field myself. As a partner I picked up Billy Sidwell, a visiting member of the Australian Davis Cup team. It was a union of outsiders. I had bowed out and Sidwell had been left out, Jack Bromwich and Colin Long having been paired as the Australian doubles team.

For a couple of fifth wheels, we did a pretty good job and certainly an impartial one, beating not only Parker and Mulloy but also Bromwich and Long. We finished as runners-up to Kramer–Schroeder, who finally won that third national doubles title they had been after.

As I packed my gear at Longwood, preparing to move on to Forest Hills with the rest of the gang, Gardnar Mulloy gave me a knowing look. "Well," he said, "I see you're still a tennis player."

I could feel the needle — my second of the day.

It is an established fact that a good amateur tennis player can earn money at the game without actually turning professional — established on the word of players themselves. Some of them, after formally giving up their amateur standing, have rushed confessions into print, like Hollywood actresses getting up from the psycho-analyst's couch. As they point out, some tournament committees, anxious to corral a top-ranking player, have ways of getting around the USLTA regulations, just as colleges get around the rules on recruiting football players. The USLTA allows a maximum of fifteen dollars a day (it used to be less) in room, board, laundry and other expenses; in addition a player may be paid travel costs to and from the tournament. But as Jack Kramer once wrote about his own experiences on the circuit, it would have taken more than that to keep him playing tournaments, and he got it — "in cash on the barrel-head."

This may be true, but it doesn't explain amateur tennis or the men who play the game. It isn't money that keeps a man a tennis player, that makes it so hard for a guy approaching thirty or past it to break away from the circuit, even after he's made up his mind to do it. In fact, it's in spite of the profit motive that tennis players die so hard.

On the basis of two decades' experience on the circuit, I can say with some authority that amateur tennis is no place to look for a big income. Although the high payoffs may exist, they are relatively rare, even for the men at the top of the rankings. And if every single club in the country decided to flout the LTA rules — a contradiction in terms to begin with, since the clubs in effect *are* the LTA, and help *make* the rules — you still couldn't reach the high-tax bracket with a tennis racket. There aren't that many big tournaments, and there isn't that much money even in the biggest ones.

What the game does offer is the one thing that probably *beats* money: a chance to live well without it.

As a kid just breaking into big-time tennis, I had gone to Bermuda. I didn't go for the money. Years later, as a veteran taking what I thought would be my last fling at the game, I went to South America — but not to get rich. There was no money in either trip.

But who wouldn't have wanted to go, just for the excitement of going places, and in a style you certainly hadn't been brought up to expect? I toured the circuit because there the life was lushest, the girls prettiest, and I loved being out there on the court in front of the crowd.

To live the kind of life tennis gave me, I would have had to earn the kind of salary that few men ever dream of earning. I was getting it all for free. There was no better way of living that I could think of for a young guy having no personal attachments and wanting none, a guy with no plans.

That had been me. But not any longer. . . .

As the spring of 1948 dragged on toward the opening of the Eastern circuit, the thought of leaving New York had no appeal to me. It would mean being away from Nancy, and that was something I resisted more and more.

What I really wanted was to ask Nancy to marry me, but I couldn't. Not when the risk of making a flop of marriage again seemed so great. It wouldn't work unless I was equipped for it with something more useful than a tennis racket.

Yet I also resisted any kind of career that would force me to hang up my racket altogether, a job that would keep me in New York and make marriage possible but only at the expense of cutting me off from tennis altogether. And there didn't seem to be any other kind of job. The more I talked to people who might have some use for me in their companies, the more everything sounded like my wartime experience all over again. I could see myself buried alive in some carpeted tomb of an office, unable to escape long enough ever to get to a tournament, unable to afford the circuit's style of living on my own. And I was convinced that exercising regularly was not just a matter of fun but vital to my health.

One afternoon, as I returned from making the rounds and started to let myself into my apartment, I heard music inside. I frowned in annoyance, thinking that I must have left the radio on that morning when I left. I opened the door, dropped my hat and started across the room.

"Greetings, Willy-boy," said a familiar voice. Jimmy DeFay waved to me from the couch, where he was stretched out comfortably. "Make yourself a drink."

I grinned, genuinely glad to see him. "How did you get in?"

"Oh," he said vaguely, "I've got ways."

"If you could talk the doorman of this building into letting you in, then you can talk your way into anything." I poured myself a small dollop of Scotch. "Come to think of it, you always could."

"My greatest talent. Tennis is just something to fall back on, in case I should ever catch laryngitis or something. Here, give me a refill, will you?"

I freshened his glass and handed it back. It hadn't taken him long to find out where I kept the liquor. "You in town on business?" I said.

He shook his head. "As far as business goes, let's say I've retired — temporarily."

"How come? When you left the circuit last summer I thought you were on your way to make a mint in the shipping business. San Francisco. Wasn't that it?"

"It didn't pan out. My boss turned out to be a skinflint, first class."

Jimmy's boss was a man we'd met at a tournament in California. "He seemed like a nice guy," I said.

"You only saw one side of him — the tennis side. Oh, he was decent enough when we were out there playing his tournament. But get him out of the clubhouse and into the office. . . You want to know something? After I went to work for him, whenever I'd meet him at the club, all I ever got from him was a dirty look."

"You must have been doing pretty well with the company if you could afford to join that club."

"I wasn't a member. I signed in as the boss's guest."

I gave him a look somewhere between astonishment and admiration.

"Well," Jimmy said, "how else did he think I was going to play any tennis? Why, I couldn't even afford a decent car on the salary he was paying me. I tried to borrow his Caddy one week end to drive down to Los Angeles. I thought that might make him realize what pitiful shape he was keeping us wage slaves in. Know what the old Scrooge told me?"

I couldn't hold back the laughter any more. "I can guess," I sputtered.

Jimmy grinned. "Right. So that's why I decided to retire from the shipping business and take a crack at New York." He sat up and poured himself another drink. "At least back here in the East they have a proper appreciation of tennis players. Mind if I bunk in with you for a few days while I look around?"

"Make yourself at home," I said. I noticed he was wearing one of my shirts.

Being Jimmy, he could at least see the ludicrous side of what he'd done in San Francisco. But underneath, he really did believe he had it all coming to him — the car whenever he wanted it, free run of the tennis club. That's the way it had always been on the circuit, hadn't it?

One more tour, one more season, and who could tell — I might be spoiled for any other kind of life myself. September — the end of the Eastern tour, the time of the nationals at Forest Hills — would also be my thirtieth birthday. It could be the point of no return.

"You didn't have your mind on the game this afternoon," Nancy said. It was a spring evening, about a week later. We had driven out to Long Island, where I played a friendly game of doubles on some friends' private court before returning to the city for dinner.

"I guess not." I studied the menu without reading it.

She glanced around as if looking for somebody. "Aren't we waiting for Jimmy?"

"DeFay?" While in New York he had been spending most of his evenings with Nancy and me. "I guess I forgot to tell you. He's left."

Jimmy had found New York somewhat less appreciative of tennis players than he'd hoped, so he had called Boston, finally. A man from Longwood said he had a spot for him if he was interested in learning the banking business. Jimmy had taken the train that morning.

"Poor guy," Nancy said. "He's kidding himself, isn't he?"

I nodded. "He'll be back, I'm afraid. He'll keep leaving and coming back until he's used up all his chances."

"You make it sound awfully grim."

"It is grim. Let's forget it and have dinner." I put on a brisk air and gave the waiter our orders.

"Now," I said, to Nancy, "for the rest of the evening, tennis is absolutely taboo. All right? If I even say the word or mention a player, I have to pay a forfeit."

"Like what?"

"Oh, something I value. You get up and leave, or something."

"Thank you, Willy. That's the sweetest thing you've said all day."

"That's what I should have been talking about instead of — "

"Careful. You'll ruin everything."

I laughed. "You just saved my life."

The rest of the evening was fun. I didn't have to pay the forfeit.

As I helped Nancy with her coat afterwards and started toward the door, a hand reached out from one of the tables, and a tall, graying man stood up. "Billy, how've you been?"

"Fine, Tom." I turned to Nancy. "This is Mr. Johnson . . . Miss Pike." I knew Johnson, like so many people, from some place on the tennis court. At the moment I couldn't remember where.

"I haven't seen you since the nationals," he said, giving me the clue. He was a member of the West Side Tennis Club in Forest Hills. "What are you doing with yourself these days?"

"Looking for a job," I said.

"I've got one for you."

"I'll take it."

Johnson's ruddy face stiffened in surprise, then crumpled into a wide smile. He began to chuckle. "For a moment I thought maybe we were really going to do business."

"I'm ready if you are." I was serious. There were just so many chances, and I couldn't be sure how many I'd used up already.

"All right," Johnson said. "Be at my office first thing in the morning." I took his card and slipped it into my pocket.

In the cab Nancy turned to me with a look af amazement.

"Who," she said, "was calling who's bluff? If I understand what went on in that high-powered transaction, you just went to work for Mr. Johnson."

"That's the way I understand it." I felt as if a huge weight had just been lifted from my shoulders.

"What kind of job is it? What does he do?"

"I haven't the ghost of an idea," I said honestly. "Something in Wall Street. That's as much as I know." I took the card out of my pocket and turned on the dome light in the cab. "Security Banknote Company," I read. "Sounds solid enough, doesn't it?"

"It sounds like a full-time career, too. What about tennis?"

"Nancy," I said, almost persuading myself that I meant it, "I don't care. If it has to be one thing or the other, then I've just got to forget about the tennis."

"You'll never be able to, Willy. Not if you want to be happy."

"I'd better start learning, then. I've sat on the fence long enough — too long — waiting for something impossible to come by. If I don't jump now, I may never be able to do it. I'll wind up just like DeFay and all the other guys who never outgrew the circuit."

Much as Nancy loved tennis, I couldn't picture her as a circuit wife, spending hours on the clubhouse terrace with the others, in conversations revolving endlessly around yesterday's linesman's call and the condition of the courts. For me and for Nancy both, there was more to life than wind and bad bounces.

There was no place on the circuit for what I was sure I wanted and what I knew Nancy would want — children and family life. Especially if you wanted your children to grow up feeling sure and well taken care of, without the kind of crises that had divided my own family. I wanted to be able to face my kids with no barrier of shame. And Nancy . . . crisis was no part of her experience. As the daughter of a successful Wall Street commodity broker, she'd grown up knowing security, and I had no right to spoil it.

Sure I would mind giving up tennis. It was hard to imagine being completely cut off from the circuit and

tournament life. But that was better than giving up all
the rest of what life had to offer. If those were the choices,
then I had made the right one.

"Do you mind if I take you home a little early?" I asked
Nancy in the cab. "I want to make sure of a good start
tomorrow."

My usual running start on a day was a little too brisk
for Wall Street. I had been waiting outside the door of
Johnson's office for half an hour before he arrived. He
shook my hand and led me inside.

"What I've been looking for," he said, "is a man who
can do a selling job. I've seen enough of you around the
tennis club to think you can do it."

"I've had some experience," I said.

"I knew that." He moved a few things on his desk.
"How much do you know about our company?"

"Not a thing."

"No reason you should. Fortunately, people in the financial field do know about us. Foreign countries, too."
He pointed to a display of framed documents that
lined the office walls — samples of foreign currencies,
stock and bond certificates.

"All those are our work," Johnson said with some pride.
"We printed them. That's what we are, basically — printers. In a very special field, with special requirements.
Currencies, securities, any kind of financial document
representing an organization's promise to make good on
its word. A company votes a new stock issue; we draw
up and design and print the paper. *If* we can convince

the company we can do the job as well as we think we can, and better than our competition."

Johnson took a cigarette from a box on his desk and offered me one. I shook my head.

"Now *there*," he said, "is where our salesmen come in. Which means you, if you're still interested."

"I'm with you," I said.

The phone rang. Johnson answered it, cupped his hand over the mouthpiece and said, "One of our men. Stay where you are, Billy."

I judged by the phone conversation that it wasn't easy to convince a company, no matter how well known Security Banknote might be. Johnson seemed disturbed. But what I heard couldn't have sounded luckier for me.

"A tough one," Johnson said, putting down the phone and turning back to me. "You'll find out that a board of directors is just like any customer. You've got to be able to see them in order to sell them. Looks as if the competition may have an inside track on this deal."

I tried to sound casual. "Maybe I can help," I said. "I know a man on the board of the company you were just talking about. I'm sure I can at least get into his office."

It was a corporation in which, I knew, one of the du Ponts had an important interest, and I was on friendly terms with several of the men in that large and distinguished family as a result of my connection with William du Pont, Jr.

Johnson pursed his lips approvingly. "Go ahead and try it."

I picked up the phone and called Wilmington. In a few minutes I had an appointment for Johnson and me later in the week.

Tom glanced at his watch and slapped me on the back. "Half hour on the job and you're on your way to earning your first commission. Not bad." He hitched his chair forward. "Maybe you and I had better get a little business of our own settled."

I took a deep breath. I had come in ready to accept almost any reasonable terms. But luck had put me on the offensive, in a position that I hadn't expected. Now it was like the point in a tennis match where you had the choice between laying back and playing it safe or taking the gamble, going all-out to press your advantage. In a situation like this on the court, I knew what I'd do: I'd go all-out.

"Tom," I said carefully, "if we make this sale, you can chalk it up to tennis. I got to know the du Ponts through tennis. I think I can safely say I'd never have been able to make that phone call otherwise."

Johnson nodded, somewhat puzzledly.

"A lot of people you have to deal with in this business are tennis people," I went on. "Fans, club members, friends of the game. I probably know quite a few of them already, from playing tournaments around the country. If I can keep getting around among these people, I think I can do a better job for you."

"You mean you intend to keep playing tennis."

"I mean I think it's important for me to keep playing tennis. I don't mean going on the circuit. I've had enough of that, and it's a full-time job in itself. I mean getting to a few of the big tournaments. Keeping myself in touch with the game."

Johnson swung around in his chair, saying nothing for a moment.

"How do we know you won't be giving your attention to tennis instead of the job? I don't mean you'd do it deliberately," he added. "But where's the incentive? If it came down to a choice between a match and a contract . . . well, you could sit back on your guarantee and let the contract go. After all, Billy, when we hire you, we've got an investment in you. We've got to consider the risk."

"Suppose I take the risk."

"How?"

"Whatever guarantee you usually give your men, suppose I take a smaller one."

Johnson thought that over.

"And," I added quickly, "a fatter commission."

Johnson stared at me, shook his head and laughed. "Billy," he said, "I should have known I was in for a tough match when I took you on." He stood up and offered me his hand. "It's a deal. I think we're both going to be glad we made it."

As soon as I got down to the street I headed for a phone booth and dialed my doctor's office.

"Doc," I said, "I know you're busy, but there's something important I've got to check with you. I'll make it fast."

"Come on up to the office and I'll squeeze you in."

"I'm not having any trouble," I said, afraid I might have given him the wrong idea. "I just wanted to talk to you about getting married."

"It's the girl's father you're supposed to ask, not your doctor."

"No jokes," I said. "I'm serious."

"I'm not in this business for laughs, either, my friend. You're old enough to make up your own mind."

"What about the diabetes?" It was something I had read about, talked about with doctors before, but it counted now — too much to take any chances. I didn't want anything to go wrong this time.

"You know the story on that, Bill. Diabetes is a responsibility, just like any other. If you're man enough to take care of it, what's the problem? Children? Well, you know the score on that, too. It's chancy. There's a certain hereditary factor there — we're not really sure just *how* much it counts."

I waited. "Is that all?"

"Hell no!" he said. "Marriage is as serious a step as a man can take. It's *loaded* with responsibilities. Are you willing to take them on? Do you love the girl? Do you want to spend your life with her? Those are the questions you ought to be asking yourself, my friend. And if you think I can answer them for you, you're wasting your time. Come talk to me sometime when you've got an *easy* problem."

I understood what he was trying to tell me. "Thanks, Doc," I said. "If I'm as lucky as I've been so far today, I'll be an engaged man the next time I see you."

I hurried uptown to meet Nancy.

Life and Diabetes

NANCY and I were married in the fall of 1948 — four months after I landed that first contract in Wilmington, two months after Gardnar Mulloy and I won our fourth national doubles championship, and a few weeks after we won our first doubles point in a Davis Cup Challenge Round, part of a 5–0 sweep over the Australians. Nancy was in the stands at both those tennis events, as she has been many times in the years since. She has also been in my corner through many rounds in the campaign to live successfully with diabetes. And I am not the only diabetic who has gained a lot by her being there.

A year or so after we were married, Nancy was giving me a hand with the day's mail. "Listen to this one, Willy." It was a letter from a young woman, writing, she explained, about her fiancé:

> Stuart has been a diabetic for a number of years and has always taken excellent care of the problem. However, a few months ago he happened to have an insulin reaction at his office. His employer thought he was drunk and fired him. I persuaded Stuart to go back and explain the truth of the matter. His employer apologized but said that in view of the "risks" he could not re-hire him.

Since then Stuart has applied for a number of other positions but he insists on mentioning his diabetes when he is being interviewed. As a result he has not been able to land anything, even though he is a conscientious and competent man in his field.

Nancy looked up. "That's just awful."

"It happens, though," I said. "You'd be surprised how many companies still don't know the score on diabetics."

"Do you get many letters like that, Willy?"

"Every so often. Guys getting fired, or turned down. Guys afraid to even apply for a job. Afraid they'll lose it that way sooner or later. Women, too. They get out of school and can't face life on their own."

"What are you going to tell this girl?"

I took the letter from her and glanced through it. "Pretty much the same thing I've told some of the others. Have her friend — what's his name? Stuart? — come in and talk to me. I'll try to size him up, see if the trouble is what it seems to be. Sometimes it isn't the employer but the diabetic. Maybe he's overselling the hazards of diabetes instead of what he's got to offer as an employe. Anyway, maybe it'll help him to talk about it."

"There ought to be something to do about the employers, though — the people who won't give them jobs. Somebody ought to educate them."

I nodded. "I've been working on that part of it with the diabetes organizations. When I find out about something like this, we get up a letter to the company, pointing out the facts about diabetes in general. At least we may keep the next man from being fired, or help somebody else get a job who deserves it."

"I hope so," Nancy said. She went back to opening letters.

A few weeks later, I was at a business meeting that included the president of one of the country's largest industrial firms. As the group left the conference table, he called me aside.

"Between the two of you Talberts," he said with a friendly smile, "our company may get straightened out yet."

I had just concluded negotiations with him for a security issue — so much for one of the Talberts. I was aware that he and Nancy had known each other for years, too, but I didn't understand what she had to do with his company.

"I had a call from your bride the other day," he explained, "and I found out something about our organization that I hadn't known. She asked if our personnel department had any policy on hiring diabetics. I didn't know, but naturally I had to find out. It seems we didn't exactly welcome them with open arms."

"No reason you should, any more than you welcome a *non*diabetic who applies for a job. Or," I added firmly, "any less."

"I know, I know." He held up his hand defensively. "I've been given the complete orientation course. About the only thing our personnel boys could really say to explain the policy was that once or twice we'd had diabetics get sick in the office. Reactions, I think you call them. Know what Nancy told me? 'Why, perfectly healthy women faint in offices, don't they?' "

"It's a good point," I said.

"Don't worry," he assured me. "I've sent a memo around setting out some of the points Nancy explained to me. I think you can consider us an enlightened company from now on, as far as diabetics are concerned."

Even with many companies becoming enlightened about diabetes, the job problem is still troublesome. But as with many problems, the root of the trouble is often attitude rather than health — the diabetic's attitude, not the employer's. Diabetes may be only incidental, or a convenient explanation for something much harder to deal with. Jobs in a given field may be tight for everybody; or another applicant may be better qualified for the position. But if you want to look for a crutch, for a reason to feel unfairly treated and sorry for yourself, you can almost always find one; diabetes, unfortunately, is an easy one to pick if you happen to have it — and if you've acquired the unhappy habit of using it that way.

The trouble isn't always quite as serious as it seems at first, and there are worse things that can happen to you than diabetes, as a fellow member of the club once pointed out to me.

This was a middle-aged man who wrote that he had a chance to get a job as a mail carrier. He liked the idea of getting outdoors, but being a diabetic he was concerned about how well he would be able to handle the exercise. I cautioned him that I wasn't a doctor and that he ought to consult his own. All I could say was that exercise had been no great problem to me, once the right formula of diet and insulin had been worked out for me.

About six months later I had a call from him.

"I happened to be in town and wanted to let you know," he told me, "that everything worked out the way you said. I went to the doc and he beefed-up my diet and changed the insulin. I took the job and I'm walking the route five days a week." He was pretty proud of himself.

"How's it going?"

"Pretty good."

"No insulin reactions?"

"Nope." He thought it over for a moment. "Something worse."

"What's that?"

"Flat feet." He laughed. "Try and fix *that* with a lump of sugar."

In the everyday life of the diabetic there are more questions than any doctor's prescription and anyone else's experience can quite cover.

What if your company wants to send you on a long business trip? Suppose you've taken your insulin, say, at 8 A.M. in New York, then fly to Los Angeles. Don't you have to get up at five the next morning to take your next shot safely on schedule? And what about meal schedules?

What if a girl is overweight — how can she diet without upsetting her whole diabetic equation?

Suppose you're having dinner at your prospective mother-in-law's and she keeps trying to force you to eat an extra helping of her richest dessert?

Diabetics sometimes ask these questions painfully, having been trained to regard them as matters not just of etiquette or business but almost of life and death. The answers, I've found, come much more easily when you approach them, in my doctor's words, "as a person, not just as a diabetic." That is, with a sense of how much freedom you have, how much you can work out for yourself, and how much you have in common with other people, instead of with a sense of the restrictions and of your "difference."

Even mothers-in-law, being people themselves, are not impervious to a simple, straightforward explanation when one really has to be made. (Whether it really does is something I'll get to in a moment.)

On the subject of travel, I can offer some reassurances out of my own experience. Once, in my kid days on the tennis circuit, I drove forty-eight hours without even stopping for sleep — a routine I managed with no ill-effects, although I wouldn't recommend it as a habit to anybody, diabetic or not.

The most furious traveling I have ever done in my life was done not merely in spite of diabetes but in *behalf* of diabetes education — as part of a campaign sponsored by the American Diabetes Association. In ten days I covered thirteen different cities from New York to Los Angeles, Memphis to Seattle, appearing on television and radio programs and playing tennis exhibitions in each place. I started with a dozen programs during the first three days alone, wound up with a late afternoon performance on the West Coast, and was back in my office the next morning.

Although I wouldn't urge this kind of schedule, either, as a steady thing, and wouldn't volunteer for it myself on that basis, travel isn't such an overwhelming problem to a diabetic willing to exert some common sense on it. On a long airplane flight, for instance, when it is evident that breakfast is going to be delayed long past my usual hour by the change in time zones, I arrange for the stewardess to bring me some orange juice in advance, in order to tide me over. I get up early for an insulin shot if the change in time zones requires it; but not too early, because I know that a delay of even an hour in my morning injection isn't anything to get excited about.

The important thing is that many of the diabetic's fretful questions needn't arise in the first place; many of the explanations to other people aren't really necessary. An extra piece of pie isn't the crisis it seems, or that it once may actually have been in the earlier history of diabetes. Insulin, especially long-lasting insulin, has loosened the tether, widened the margin for error and the diabetic's range of freedom. The opportunities for living are there for the diabetic who isn't afraid to seize them.

How many calories or food units you had at lunch, how many in a Scotch and soda — some doctors still consider this kind of arithmetic a basic part of diabetic care. Others point out that the numbers game can be played too hard. Counting or weighing food portions robs a meal of its pleasure; fretting over a drink can spoil a party; fussing over diabetes can become a way of life if you let it.

Actually, as doctors themselves admit, it's usually a phony way of life, built on deception and often ridden with guilt. Even the most disciplined diabetic, being only human, is bound to slip or cheat a little, once in a while. He eats an extra helping of potatoes; he can't resist the peach melba at dinner or the doughnut during the office coffee break. If the diabetic has been trained to do the arithmetic, he rushes home to test his urine and finds he has a small percentage of sugar. He feels guilty — he has violated the rules and the sugar is his punishment. A couple of days before his next appointment with the doctor, he starves himself to get the sugar-count down. Perhaps he phonies the figures on the daily records which some doctors ask their patients to keep. The doctor examines him, looks over the records, finds nothing wrong. And the patient leaves to begin the secret "sinning" all over again . . . but never really enjoying it.

The sad part of all this is that in most cases, probably, the patient is feeling guilty for nothing, is fretting about sins that don't exist. Many authorities on diabetes will tell you, now, that there is no harm in the presence of some sugar in the urine as long as the diabetic is taking his insulin faithfully, as prescribed. Much better, in fact, to err on the side of overindulgence than on the side of starvation. This is because a little extra sugar is the diabetic's defense against insulin reaction; and reaction, since it occurs with relative suddenness and its symptoms are often hard for the patient to spot, is more of a risk than the original problem — diabetic coma, which comes on only very gradually, with plenty of warning.

Not all doctors agree with this viewpoint; there are schools of thought on diabetes as there are on every human problem. There are also great differences, of course, in individual cases, and they may require different methods of treatment. The one sure rule for every case is that, to begin with, you must have a doctor you believe in, whatever his particular kind of program may be. The measure of his program, and of the confidence he has earned, is how much he frees his patient from the *symptoms* of diabetes — the weight loss, thirst, fatigue, at one extreme; the susceptibility to insulin reaction, on the other — and how well he enables the diabetic to lead a normal kind of life.

Once a woman phoned me, in tears, telling me that her eleven-year-old daughter was suffering terribly from diabetes, and asking me for advice. It sounded so urgent that I told her to come and see me right away and bring the child.

What I saw was pitiful. The girl looked emaciated, tired and scared.

I asked the mother why she hadn't changed doctors in view of the child's poor response. She said the doctor was a friend of the family and she didn't want to hurt his feelings.

"Which is more important," I said, "his feelings or your daughter's life?"

Some months later, I had a letter — as usual, snapshot enclosed. Mother and daughter both doing fine. They had consulted a specialist, and the girl was on her way to a normal kind of living.

For me the incident was one more reminder of the parents' responsibility in the treatment and training of a diabetic child. A boy or girl of five or ten is too young to understand the details of diabetes and its methods of treatment. The parents have to serve as proxy, learning the case thoroughly, absorbing information that can be passed on to the child as he grows up to it. And it isn't only the facts but (at least as important) the attitudes that the child will take over from the parent. All the more vital, then, for the grownups' attitude to be a cheerful, reasonable one.

Those two terms do not conflict with each other. Keeping diabetes under control, I have found with my doctor's help, is largely a matter of giving reasonable attention to the right things. And there are fewer of them than some diabetics may realize.

In my own program there is no weighing of food, no juggling of calories, no daily record of urine tests, to be kept like a bookkeeper's accounts. The only rules are broad and painless:

1) Insulin, every day. No changing the amount except on doctor's orders. Some diabetics get the idea they can make a practice of overeating if they take an extra shot, or can lose weight by taking a smaller dose. This can lead to trouble. If you're really going hungry or putting on too much weight, let the doctor change the insulin for you.

2) Extra sugar at the first sign of insulin reaction. During a certain time of the day, the insulin you've taken will reach its peak of activity. If you know what that period is (mine is late afternoon), you'll be alert for that "foreign feeling" at the time you're most vulnerable.

3) A well-balanced diet. No gobbling down a whole

box of candy, no soda-fountain binges. Which is no great hardship, nothing that doesn't also make sense for the average nondiabetic. There's no ban, anyway, against a dish of ice cream, a piece of pie or a soda now and then, if I crave it.

There is no longer any need, my doctor insists, to starve the diabetic or to load his life down with food charts and elaborately regulated menus. A healthful diet, adequate for the activities of job, hobbies, household duties — this is the base. The right kind, amount and schedule of insulin will insure that the food is properly and beneficially used in the diabetic's system.

"What I am interested in," he says, "and what you should be concerned with, is not arithmetic — how much of something you ate or didn't eat, or how many hours you played tennis, or whether your sugar is a fraction up or down. The question is: *How do you feel? What are you getting out of life?* If you feel bad, then we have to do some figuring to put you back on the track. If you feel good, then you're doing what you're supposed to, and there's no need to worry about it."

Some doctors, of course, feel that this is too liberal an attitude. They may work from different viewpoints, emphasize other aspects of treatment. Their methods may be perfectly effective. That is something the diabetic can judge by the way he feels.

For myself, I know that one or the other must be the master — I or it, the person or the diabetes. If living is important, if my own plans and desires count for something, then it is the person that must be the important thing, not the food values or the percentage of sugar in the urine.

Having diabetes, it sometimes seems to me, is much like bringing up a child: it must learn to live with you, not you with it. You are the one who has to run the family.

Other diabetics learned this long before I did. Before sports had stopped being a taboo in the life of the diabetic, these people were leading busy and creative lives in other fields. H. G. Wells in literature, Puccini in music, Cézanne in painting, Clemenceau in international affairs, Fiorello La Guardia in our own political life — all diabetics.

Now more and more diabetics are discovering that their range of opportunity covers sports, too. A boy I talked to a couple of years ago, at the request of a worried father who had just brought him home from his first lesson in taking insulin shots, is a star on the football and swimming teams at his prep school. From the mother of an Indiana teen-ager named Tom Stewart — not only diabetic but also crippled in one arm as the result of an accident — I periodically receive press clippings reporting Tom's latest victories on the tennis courts.

About ten years ago in New Orleans, I stopped to visit a tennis player named Hamilton Richardson, at sixteen one of the outstanding juniors in the country. Ham, I had been told, had just gone through the experience of learning that he had diabetes. He was dubious about continuing his tournament career, but seemed encouraged to hear about some of my own experiences with the problem. Richardson's recent career is a familiar story to tennis fans: Number 1 player in the United States at twenty-three, member of Davis Cup teams, Rhodes scholar.

In our discussions of diabetes, Ham and I often disagreed — he felt that I underrated the value of keeping records and took too many liberties with my program in general — just as we were later to find ourselves unable to see eye to eye at a crucial moment in tennis.

Under the kind of program I follow or under any other, no diabetic can expect to sail through life completely free of trouble — which can be said of any nondiabetic as well. Even the best-regulated diabetes, like the best-brought-up of children, becomes unruly at times. You have to be watchful for the "red lights" — the foreign feeling, the other signs of occasional danger. And even after nearly three decades of experience, my alarm system isn't foolproof. Sometimes, like anybody else, I'm too absorbed in living to watch as closely as I should.

At Southampton, during the 1949 season, I was in the finals of the singles against Pancho Gonzales, the tall, dark and willful California prodigy, who was then the national champion and has since become the world's professional champion. Nancy, looking lovely in summery maternity clothes, had come out to watch the match — one of her last chances to play the role of tennis wife before motherhood took over. Gardnar Mulloy was with her in the stands.

As a somewhat aging part-time tennis player facing

one of the most powerful hitters in the history of the game, I decided my best chance of upsetting the young champ would be to slow him down by changing pace, feeding him shots at a variety of speeds to break the natural rhythm of his strokes.

It worked beautifully for one set. The next two went to Gonzales. In the fourth, my game collapsed altogether. I double-faulted, lost my own service at love, hit shots wildly out of court, missed others as if I were playing with a ping-pong paddle instead of a tennis racket. The score went to 3–0 against me, and the spectators began to leave their seats.

When I paused at the official's stand during the change of court, Mulloy came dashing onto the grass. He put a glass of water thickened with sugar into my hand.

"Drink this, Willy," he commanded.

I downed it automatically. It was the answer. Mulloy had realized that I wasn't just being beaten; I was totally without control — a diabetic in insulin reaction.

In a reversal of form that baffled Gonzales and brought the audience back to the seats, I ran through ten out of the next eleven games and went on to win the match and the Southampton trophy.

There was another occasion in my life when Gar Mulloy made an unexpected appearance from the sidelines, as a friend rather than as a tennis partner. It was a sad occasion for both of us, one day in 1952.

A telephone call reached me at my office in New York. From Coral Gables, Florida, the secretary told me.

My parents, I thought . . . it had been a while since I'd been down to visit them. Maybe I could get away one of these week ends for a trip.

But it was Gar Mulloy's voice at the other end of the line — a different-sounding Mulloy, strangely reserved and hesitant.

"Willy," he said, "I have some bad news. I'm sorry."

"What's the trouble, Gar? Where are you, anyway?"

"I'm at your folks' house. I came out to spend the afternoon with them." There was a long pause; then Gar said, "Your dad, Willy. . . ."

My father and Mulloy had been sitting out on the lawn talking when Dad suffered a sudden severe stroke. Gar had carried him into the house to await the doctor, but it was no use. Gar was holding him when he died.

I put the telephone down and cried for the man who had taught me never to give in to tears. Since I had stopped being a small boy, still learning that lesson under his teaching, I had forgotten it just once. That was a couple of years before, when Nancy's doctor told me that our son Pike was born; and then I had wept for joy. Now it was for all the times, years before, when we should have let ourselves give in to our feelings — Dad and I both — and didn't know how.

Over the Hill

THE tennis partnership of Mulloy and Talbert lasted long after we had won our fourth national doubles championship. But in 1950, even though we just missed a fifth title (an Australian team beat us in the finals), the USLTA decided that we had outlived our usefulness as a Davis Cup combination. Mulloy played (with Schroeder as his partner), but I was benched, as the United States defended the trophy at Forest Hills — and lost it.

That was the first of a string of disappointments in Davis Cup competition, not just for me personally, but also for American tennis in general. The big silver punchbowl went Down Under and seemed likely to remain there indefinitely, as the Australians began to reap the fruits of a program to encourage tennis as the national sport and to develop young tennis players. Jack Kramer, who had made a tremendous impression on the Aussies, was the model they picked for their youngsters. An endless sequence of teen-age prodigies began to appear out of the Australian courts, equipped with Jake's "big game." Serve and volley — the Australians had these big weapons, plus the ground strokes to back them up. They quickly assumed a dominant position in the international tennis scene.

On our side there seemed to be no young talent capable of bringing back the trophy and restoring the prestige of American tennis. There was one youngster, however, named Tony Trabert, in whom I felt a particular interest — a sense of identification, in fact, because of the similarity of our names and backgrounds. Like me, he had come from Cincinnati to try his luck on the circuit, and under pretty much the same shoestring conditions. His luck hadn't been good, but in this eighteen-year-old, with the muscular build of a football player and the talents of a natural athlete, there seemed to be at least the raw material of a champion waiting to be developed. Unfortunately, in this country there was no organized program to do that kind of job.

"A kid like this shouldn't just be turned loose on the circuit," I said, thinking aloud for my own benefit while talking to Nancy. It was a winter evening, and we were riffling through a batch of travel folders in the library of our apartment. "Somebody ought to be working with him every day. Somebody who's been around in the game. He's got flaws that need to be smoothed out, and he needs to learn some tactics to go with all that muscle."

"Somebody like you?" She held up a bright folder. "Here's a lovely-looking one, Willy. Antibes, on the Riviera. Will we have time for Antibes? Maybe on our way up from Rome."

"I could. I ought to."

"Take me to Antibes, or coach Tony?" She put the folders back in the desk drawer. "You're leaving for

Europe in a few weeks. Unless you're planning to send me alone — which you might as well forget about, right now."

"Don't worry. I've been counting on this vacation as much as you have." I hesitated. "Nancy, I've been thinking. Where would I be now if people hadn't done things for me? Tennis people, some of them total strangers. All the way from the couple back in Chillicothe — I told you about them once — who gave me a place to stay when I went to my first tournament away from home . . . guys who lent me a racket when I couldn't afford to buy one . . . I could never have become a tennis player on my own. I'd never have made it. I'd never have met you, either."

"You want us to take Tony to Europe," Nancy said.

I nodded. "I owe such a lot to tennis. It's time I started paying some of it back."

She considered this.

"Judging by the amount of gear we're packing, you're planning to spend a lot of this vacation catching up on your tennis, anyway. At least it'll save us the trouble of finding you an opponent."

Every morning for the next five months, in foreign places from Sweden to Italy, Trabert and I got up early to work out on the local courts while Nancy scouted the local landmarks for the afternoon's sightseeing. En route, we played the European tournaments — for Tony a process of tempering in the fire of international competition. It was a rugged schedule; probably no other pair of tourists has ever done Europe under such strenuous conditions, and probably none has come through in better physical shape.

By the time we returned to New York, it was clear not only that Trabert had come into his own but that so had an effective new doubles team. Tony was to earn the rank of Number 3 player in the United States that year — a spectacular climb from the Number 24 spot he had held only two seasons earlier. Meanwhile, in Europe and at home, Tony and I won fifteen straight doubles tournaments without a single loss. As the time for the Davis Cup Challenge Round approached, however, the team was broken up at the request of the tennis association's Davis Cup Selection Committee.

"Only a temporary move," one of the officials assured me. "We want Tony to get used to playing with other partners so we'll have more than one possible combination in case of emergency."

The other combinations didn't work out. Mulloy and I teamed up again and beat them easily in the summer tournaments. I waited for the committee to put the team of Trabert and Talbert back together again.

Just before the departure for Australia, Frank Shields, the nonplaying captain that year, phoned me at my office and asked me to meet him at the Racquet Club.

He greeted me apologetically. "Willy, I have a favor to ask you. "We're only taking a small squad to Australia this time. Would you mind dropping out?"

"Who are you planning to use in the doubles?"

"I don't know."

"Tony and I are the best team."

"Maybe you are, right now. But we're thinking beyond this year."

"Then all that business about another combination in case of emergency — that was just double-talk?"

"Don't get sore, Willy."

"I'm not sore," I said. "I've got other things to get excited about than a tennis match."

It wasn't until later, when I was at home after a day full of other things than tennis, that I realized what the decision meant, what the day meant in the calendar of my life as a tennis player: At thirty-three I was too old. I was the past generation, being told that I'd had my turn and that it was time to make room for the future.

Not that I felt old, even by athletes' standards. Oh sure, I may have slowed down a shade, like a veteran ballplayer who has "lost half a step getting down to first base." But I knew the tricks that made up for that half step, and more. I was in fine shape. I could hit the ball just about as sharply as ever. I could stay with a five-set match.

But maybe there was something else I had lost, something irretrievable: I wasn't hungry any more.

Or at least that was the way it looked to the men who made the decisions, and that amounted to the same thing. As far as they were concerned, I was a guy who played tennis for the fun. A little too much fun, some of them felt, I was sure. Too many tournament parties, too free-and-easy an attitude toward the kind of discipline that other players subjected themselves to.

Well, I had my own way of living, my own reasons for resisting extra discipline, and I was too old to start apologizing for it.

They were right, in a way. Tennis was still a fierce kind of excitement; a match was still something to be won, an opponent someone to be beaten. But it had stopped being the all-consuming purpose, the most important thing in life. I was Bill Talbert the tennis player only when I stepped onto a court, and that wasn't so very much of the time any more. In my own mind, I was mainly the man whose name was lettered on a Wall Street business card and a Manhattan mailbox — the Talbert family's breadwinner, Nancy's husband, Pike's Daddy, and his brand-new kid brother Peter's, too.

As far as tennis was concerned, I had gone the route. I would keep playing tennis because I enjoyed it, not because there were any new heights of the game for me to scale. I would win matches and perhaps an occasional tournament. I might be called on sometime to play an early-round match against some lesser country in the Davis Cup eliminations — if there was no young player around to handle the job. But when it came to the big plans, where American tennis strength was being measured and American tennis prestige was at stake, I was out of the picture.

On Top Down Under

I STAYED out for two years. It was a period when the prospect of ever overtaking the Australians, which had once seemed grim, began to look even worse. Australian players came to Forest Hills and Longwood, and took our national championships home with them. The Davis Cup stayed in its showcase at the headquarters of the Australian Lawn Tennis Association in Melbourne.

A couple of months before the 1953 Challenge Round was to begin, I had a phone call from Lawrence Baker, a Wall Street lawyer who was then chairman of the USLTA's Selection Committee. He asked me if I would come to his office right away. He had something important to discuss with me.

When I got there I found several other members of the committee, including my one-time teammate and circuit colleague, Don McNeill, now a New York businessman. They were cordial but solemn.

Baker nodded toward a chair, and I sat down. "Bill," he began, "I don't have to tell you how our chances look against the Australians this year. Assuming we get that far."

"I don't know, Larry," I said. "There's always a chance."

"Well," Baker said, "we want to give it our best, anyway. To get right down to business . . ." He cleared his throat. "We've been talking about a captain for this coming trip. It's an important choice, everybody's agreed to that. Harry Hopman's certainly proved it with *his* team. They say his managing is worth fifteen points a game to the Australian players. I wouldn't doubt it. Well, we need somebody who knows the game the way Hopman does, to get that fifteen points back."

"Let's not kid ourselves," I said. "Nobody can play the game for the man on the court."

Baker brushed that aside.

"Bill, there are some people who feel that you are the man we want."

So it wasn't just my advice they wanted. I was pleased. There was no higher honor that tennis could have offered me.

"But," Baker went on, "I've got to be frank with you. There have been certain reservations expressed. There's some feeling that you don't take the game seriously enough. We don't want our boys going down there with the idea that it's one great big party. We don't want any stories in the papers except stories about the tennis."

Looking down the rank of stern faces, I felt like a twelve-year-old being sent off to summer camp for the first time. I waited until the lecture was over.

"Gentlemen," I said, "I'm flattered by the honor, but I'm also a little alarmed. If I took this job it would be with every intention of winning. Doing the best job I'm capable of. I don't think that's possible under the conditions you seem to be setting up. I'd be happy to captain the team, even though I don't relish the idea of leaving my job and my family for a month or two."

"Bill, we know it's a lot to ask a man to give this much time and effort without a cent of payment. But it's nothing we don't all do ourselves. That's tennis."

"Sure," I said. "That's not what bothers me. The point is, I don't think a Davis Cup captain can do the job unless he really is running the team. His way, not somebody else's. I have my own ideas about tennis and tennis players. Some of my ideas may not agree with everybody else's. But I'm a responsible adult — at least I like to think so. I'd like to do the job, I'm proud you asked me, but if you really want me to take it, then you'll have to trust me with it."

I sat back and waited.

Baker glanced inquiringly around the room. The committeemen looked at each other. There were a few nods, a couple of rather sheepish smiles, then Baker held out his hand.

"Thanks, Bill," he said. "The best of luck in Australia."

The gloomy reports of the team's chances proved to be exaggerated. At the end of the second day's play, at the huge Kooyong Stadium in Melbourne, the score stood, incredibly: United States 2, Australia 1. The one-point margin represented an astonishing straight-set victory in the doubles, in which Trabert and his partner, Vic Seixas, totally baffled the Australian team. The device they used to do it was one that Mulloy and I had put into practice some years before, at the suggestion of Mercer Beasley, the celebrated tennis coach.

The device was a system of signals, staged with almost theatrical effect. Before each point on our service, the net man would suddenly turn his back on the other team and flash a sign to the server, like a baseball catcher instructing his pitcher. One signal meant that as soon as the ball was served the net man was going to shift to the opposite side of the court. In that case, the server would cross in the opposite direction to cover the other side. An alternate signal indicated that the net man would stay put, whereupon the server would come to net on his normal side of the court.

Simple as it was, this scheme had the powerful elements of mystery and novelty; that sudden, unusual move by the man at the net as he wheeled to face his partner was upsetting. The Australians fell apart under the psychological blow.

The doubles victory, however, wasn't quite enough. On the final day, Trabert was beaten by young Lewis Hoad in one of the most exciting matches in recent Davis Cup history, and Seixas lost to the other half of the Aussies' boy-genius act, Ken Rosewall. We were going home covered with the glory of an unexpected near-miss, but still empty-handed.

In the locker room afterwards, we all dressed silently, getting ready to return to our hotel before the traditional victory banquet — theirs, once again, not ours.

Trabert glanced back from the mirror he was using to knot his tie. "You know something?" he said, with an expression of surprise, as if a happy thought had suddenly struck him. "We're good enough to beat those guys."

"All right," I said, "let's. Next year."

Seixas and Ham Richardson, a member of the team although he hadn't got into any of the Challenge Round matches, came forward, and we all solemnly shook hands. Next year, we decided, we would take the Davis Cup home with us.

Until the last moment, it looked as if I weren't even going to make the 1954 trip to Australia. I was just out of the hospital and still in bed after a siege of hepatitis. It had left me weak and a scary-looking yellow in color, and it had played hob with my diabetic balance. I had had to increase my daily insulin (the normal effect of any sort of infection) and readjust my diet, and I was just getting the new equation under control. Even my doctor, usually so venturesome in his approach to diabetes, urged me to play it safe this time.

"You're wasting your breath, Doctor," Nancy told him. "Willy made up his mind a year ago." She sighed. "Don't forget to call us on Christmas Day, Willy."

We had all made up our minds — Seixas, Trabert, Richardson and I — not just to go but to win, and I was as eager as any of them. I had been looking forward to Australia all year with the same optimism I had taken to Forest Hills in 1945: *This was the year.*

That frame of mind pervaded the whole trip. We guarded it in everything we said or did, as if it were a fragile piece of property entrusted to our care. Julian Myrick, a slight, dapper, vigorous gentleman then in his mid-seventies, who was accompanying us as the official USLTA representative, fell happily into step with the mood. The day we left, he presented each member of the squad with a copy of the inspirational book by Norman Vincent Peale, *The Power of Positive Thinking*, with orders to read it on the way. Myrick himself followed its precepts religiously. He was the soul of bustling good cheer, and at least once a day he found some reason to address one member of the team or another with remarks that invariably began "Now, when we get home with the Cup . . ." or "After you win your first singles match . . ." Few groups of free men have ever submitted themselves so enthusiastically to a program of brainwashing.

The facts of the situation put this cheery attitude under a certain strain. Vic Seixas, for instance, hadn't been able to beat the Aussies' Ken Rosewall in half a dozen tries, and Vic was a moody player by nature, subject to spells of worry about his physical condition and easily upset by an official's decision against him on a close play during a match. To keep him from being trained too fine and becoming tense beforehand, I held him off the courts much of the time during the weeks of practice.

Trabert, on the other hand, thrived on work. The problem here was to keep him active. Ham Richardson and I — along with the team's "colts," Mike Green and Jerry Moss — took turns against him on the practice courts, absorbing some of that excess energy.

What with the exercise, the care and feeding of tennis players, the official and unofficial social functions that are part of Davis Cup protocol, the by-now-standard requests from local diabetic organizations, and the constant assaults of the press, I was leading a crowded life. The unexpected closeness of last year's results had raised public interest to a pitch that was surprising even in tennis-mad Australia. We were in demand. I couldn't spare much attention for my diabetes, and my diabetic colleague, Richardson, was in much the same spot. Realizing that it was just this sort of circumstances that might make us both vulnerable to insulin reaction, we worked out a kind of chain-system: immediately on getting up in the morning, Tony Trabert would phone my hotel room, to make sure I was all right; then I'd call Richardson, to make sure of him.

When I phoned Nancy in New York, I was able to assure her honestly that I felt fine.

"I've got some news," she said, "that will make you feel even better. You are now a vice president. Congratulations."

"Vice president of what?"

"The company. The place you work for — if you can remember back that far."

"Honestly?"

"Dear, at transoceanic phone rates, I'm not the girl to make jokes. The chairman of the board called me. They were going to cable you, but then they decided it might be nicer if you heard it from me. Wasn't that sentimental of them?"

I hadn't expected it, although I had worked for it. After my lucky debut with the company, the first two years had been a tough apprenticeship during which commissions came hard and I might have wondered if I hadn't outsmarted myself in my deal with Tom Johnson. But since then things had fallen my way. The tennis contacts had proved every bit as valuable as I had thought they would. Now here I was with another chance to return some of what tennis had given me. A big chance.

The stands at White City Stadium in Sydney were filled with 26,000 people — the largest crowd ever to watch a tennis match. I stood at attention in the limelight of the center court while the anthems were played; shook hands with the assembled officials, the representatives of tennis and of governments; waited through the drama of Davis Cup ritual. My mind was already on the matches about to begin, trying to anticipate the situations, working out the answers.

We were in good shape. The night before, I had called in a friend to play a game of chess with Seixas, to keep Vic's mind off tennis. The luck of the draw — good luck for our side — would hold him back a little while longer now. Trabert, ready and eager to play the opener, had, in fact, drawn the first match, against Australia's Lew Hoad.

It was a contest of powerful hitters, but Tony gave it something besides muscle. A tricky wind increased the risks of a big service; we agreed that the situation called for less speed and more control. Tony, cutting down on the force of his first serve, got it in consistently. Hoad, on the other hand, faulted and was obliged to come in with an easier second serve.

From my canvas chair on the sidelines, I watched the match seesaw, first in Tony's favor, then Hoad's. Too often Trabert was being passed at the net from Hoad's backhand. I kept looking for some pattern in the Australian's game that we could anticipate. Finally, in the second set, I spotted something.

At the next change of court, I told Trabert, as I dried the handle of his racket with a towel, "Watch that backhand. When the ball comes in high to him on that side, he's hitting it straight down the line. When it comes to him low, he drives it cross-court with top spin."

Tony nodded, rinsing his mouth with water. When play resumed, he responded perfectly, anticipating Hoad's returns and cutting them off with a volley.

Still, Hoad held firm, and, after a grueling series of games in the third set, he led 7 games to 6, 40–30 in points, on his own serve. One more point would give him a lead of two sets to one — and that could finish Tony's chances.

Hoad served, deep and high to Trabert's backhand, and rushed to net behind it. Trabert returned sharply cross-court and also moved in. At close range they peppered each other with an exchange of volleys, before Hoad stepped into one and sent it murderously right at Trabert. Tony, flinging up his racket in self-defense, stabbed at the ball. Incredibly, it popped across the net. Hoad lunged and drove the ball beautifully down the line from his backhand — and out of court. It was one of those unpredictable breaks of the game, and Tony took full advantage of it. He went on to win the game, the set and the match.

Now it was Seixas's turn. Rosewall, his nemesis, had beaten him once again in an Australian tournament only a week or two before. But Rosewall, too, had a pattern: a tendency to hit cross-court off his relatively weak forehand. Seixas's tactic was to get to Rosewall's forehand as quickly as possible and move to the net, covering against a cross-court return.

Harry Hopman, seated down the sideline from me, evidently saw what was happening. I could see him earnestly giving instructions to young Rosewall during a break. Going back onto the court, Ken began to chip some of his forehands softly down the line. Another countermeasure was called for: Seixas had to avoid committing himself too quickly, had to hold back his move to the net momentarily, so that he wouldn't be caught going the wrong way and would be in position to take the chip shot.

The first set went to Seixas. In the second, he began to show distressing signs of his old habits, missing shots he should have made without much trouble, losing leads that had seemed safe. Finally, on a crucial point late in the set, Rosewall hit a ball that looked out — to just about every one in the stadium except the linesman, who called it "in." Vic came storming toward the umpire's stand, clenching his fists and grimacing in protest. I started up from my chair, thinking, *Here we go again!*

All that work, all those calming words I've been wasting on this guy during the past weeks . . .

But Vic stopped. With a gesture of impatience, he brushed his dismay aside, went back to work, and in two more sets put down Rosewall.

As we came up for the doubles, on the second day, we were in the driver's seat. Not only did we have a lead of two matches to none, but we also had a psychological edge for the doubles. The Aussies, we knew, were much concerned about the signals we had used so successfully against them the previous year. They would be set for the trick this time. Knowing that, we decided to discard it — or rather, to use it only often enough to keep the opposition guessing.

The Australians put up a tremendous fight. In the fourth set, with Seixas and Trabert repeatedly on the verge of winning the match and with it the Davis Cup, Hoad and Rosewall rescued themselves time after time. But Seixas and Trabert didn't let it shake them. Vic came strolling over to me during a change of court. "Don't worry, Cap," he said, "they're just delaying the inevitable." It was positive thinking in its finest flower.

A few minutes later, Seixas and Trabert slammed the door with the winning point. They pummeled each other happily, and I ran onto the court to console the Australians and congratulate my own players for winning back the Davis Cup.

Gamble and Glory

THAT great day in Sydney looked like the beginning of good times. It turned out that prosperity was already behind us. Our mainstay, Tony Trabert, turned pro; capable recruits proved scarce; and some of the established players who might have done the job showed little interest in sharing our underdog's role. The Davis Cup was Australia's again, and the United States was reduced to the rank of a second-class tennis power. Even people who didn't usually consider themselves tennis fans began to ask why.

I was talking the problem over one day between seasons with some of the USLTA officials.

"The worst part of the situation," I said, "is that it's going to get tougher yet. We don't just need a few players. What we need is a whole program, and it will take a while before it begins to pay off, the way it finally did for the Australians."

"If you're suggesting that we adopt the Australians' methods," one official said with distaste, "I say it's not for us."

I couldn't have agreed more heartily. I wanted no part of any program that would take kids out of high school because they were good tennis players and start force-feeding them on the game. Neither did I believe in the Australians' Spartan approach to training and discipline. I couldn't see the value of keeping young athletes penned up like Thanksgiving turkeys to make sure they were in bed on time every night and didn't ever miss a minute's practice. In spite of periodic murmurs within the USLTA about my not being "serious enough" about the Davis Cup, I continued to encourage team members to get around in the places they visited, meeting people and enjoying themselves even if it did mean an occasional late evening. As long as they stayed fit and did nothing to discredit the country they represented, I preferred to leave them on their own.

Far from discrediting their country, the boys scored their best off the tennis court. The Australian papers were so impressed with the way the Americans handled themselves in public that they always commented editorially on this sidelight of the international sports event. It was a moment of consolation to me when, after the last match ended, all the players on both teams were brought to the microphone in the center of the jammed stadium. "The Americans," as one paper remarked, "may be losing the matches, but they consistently win the speeches."

That small victory was no accident. It reflected, for one thing, the fact that all but one player on the United States teams since the war had been college-educated, while the Australians had been getting their education on the tennis courts.

I had no desire to change things. I didn't want to convert American tennis into an assembly line for the production of winning teams. It wouldn't be necessary. If we could somehow stimulate a wider and deeper interest in tennis among American youngsters, we were bound to get some winning players.

Of all organized sports, tennis is probably the most truly international. In countries where Mickey Mantle and Stan Musial are totally unknown, Lew Hoad and Pancho Gonzales enjoy the status of stars. Take a tennis racket on a vacation or on a business trip to Finland, to Thailand, to the Belgian Congo — or, for that matter, to the Soviet Union — and you'll find tennis courts and somebody willing to give you a game.

If tennis has captured public interest less in this country than in some others, it isn't because the game doesn't have some highly marketable selling points. As a participating sport, it may well be the ideal answer to a national problem that political leaders in Washington have been concerned about in recent years — the "softness" of the American public as a detriment to our national welfare. Football, baseball, basketball are all great for toughening up kids and giving them plenty of healthy excitement in the process. But what about the years after they've left school? There isn't much chance of getting twenty-two middle-aged citizens together for a rousing scrimmage. Tennis, on the other hand, is a form of exercise that a man in his sixties can enjoy just as much as his teen-age grandson, and two or four people are all it takes.

With such obvious points in its favor, tennis, I am

convinced, can be sold to the public by means of an energetic program. It would include exhibition matches in towns that up to now have had little chance to see good players in action; school activities in which tennis could profitably be made a part of the regular physical education courses; more tournaments for youngsters, to give them the incentive of a trophy.

Along with the selling job (and the organizational work behind it), there would have to be some improvement in the product in order to keep up the interest of players and fans. The game itself and the rules it operates by could stand a breath of change.

Consider the whole trend of the game during the last twenty years. In this time tennis has been dominated in turn by five players: Budge, Kramer, Gonzales, Frank Sedgman, and Lew Hoad. This is murderer's row, a group of ferocious sluggers whose games were built on the serve and volley. The one exception to this pattern who belongs in the same company is Bobby Riggs. Of the earlier players I had a chance to play against or study at close range, only Ellsworth Vines, Fred Perry, and perhaps Bill Tilden would qualify. If all these players were in competition during a single year, each at the peak of his game, the legendary Tilden, with his fine ground game, would probably rank no better than sixth. Perry, with his excellent forehand, his quickness of reaction, and above all his commanding presence on the court, might rate a notch higher. Only Vines, a slugger in his own right, would be able to crowd Budge, Kramer, and Gonzales for the Number 1 spot.

So successfully have the heavy hitters used their weapons that a large element of suspense has been shot right out of the game. Serve, volley, end of point: the pattern has all the awesome force of an artillery duel, but the element of maneuver is missing, and that is what used to give the game its dramatic pace, its rise and fall of tension.

The only way to restore this exciting element would be to make changes in the game to reduce the advantage that goes with power — reduce the size of the service court, perhaps; stall off the advance to net behind serve by requiring a player to hit one stroke off the ground before making his first volley. Whatever device might be found, even some of the heavy hitters themselves believe some sort of change is desirable.

On other innovations, the players' attitude is practically unanimous. The matter of expenses, naturally, is one. There aren't very many places nowadays where fifteen dollars a day (the present limit) will cover the cost of a hotel room, meals, laundry, and other incidentals. And tennis players can't squeeze by on tuna fish sandwiches. Like all athletes, they are steak eaters.

From the public's standpoint, one change in the game seems not only desirable but inevitable. Open tournaments, in which amateurs would be allowed to compete against professionals, simply have to come to tennis as they have to golf, in spite of the strong objections that arise within the USLTA whenever this touchiest of all subjects comes up for discussion.

The number of open tournaments could be limited at first, while the scheme gets its shakedown test. Amateurs would still be required to abide by USLTA regulations, even while competing against the pros. Prize money would be limited to the professionals; the amateur's stake would be a trophy and the challenge of proving himself against topnotch competition in the headline event.

Under these conditions a few of the best amateurs might cross the line into the pro ranks — though only a few, because there isn't room for many to make a living in the professional end of the game. Others will prefer to make their careers in other, more profitable fields. They will choose to hang on to the status that enables them to enjoy the company and fun of the clubs, where tennis is not a business but a relief from business.

Whatever happens to the individual players, the point is that the game as a whole is bound to profit. With amateur tennis at a low estate in this country, fans need some new incentive to draw them out to the courts. Open tennis would offer just that: a chance to find out, for example, whether the amateur Dick Savitt could beat professional Tony Trabert, or how Budge Patty would do against pro Pancho Segura. In tennis, as in any sport, what the public wants to see is the best; and no tennis tournament can offer the best nowadays unless it includes the pros.

Just how badly American tennis needed some sort of shot in the arm was clear toward the end of 1957, when it came time to make the annual selection of players for the trip to Australia. "Selection" isn't quite the word for the procedure we went through; it was more of a man hunt. Our choice ranged all the way from a handful of unproven youngsters to a corps of overage veterans, most of whom were unwilling to make the trip except under certain conditions, mostly impossible.

Ham Richardson, Number 1 in the United States Rankings, declined to go without his wife, and the policy of not taking players' wives was firmly established. The majority of the selection committee agreed with me that a wife added one more responsibility, one more complication, for a player whose job would be tough enough without having to keep his bride entertained. (The rule applied to the captain, too. Nancy had come to take an annual period of tennis widowhood for granted.)

Dick Savitt, unranked only because he had been playing few tournaments, but possibly the best in the world when he was playing, was another likely choice. But Savitt considered his job with an oil company too much of an obstacle, even though his boss had once told me that he himself had no objection.

Budge Patty, a player with an outstanding doubles record, insisted on a guarantee that he would be picked to play singles — a commitment I couldn't make to any player until he proved himself in practice and in the Australian tournaments that were to precede the Davis Cup matches.

We left for Australia with a team that included only one of the four leading American tennis players — Vic Seixas. The closest we had to a seasoned player for the second singles assignment was Herb Flam, a game and willing performer but one who didn't even feel up to the job himself. As one half of a doubles team, we had a player who was seasoned to say the least — my old partner, Gardnar Mulloy, still a tennis player, and a good one, at forty-four.

Two openings had been left on the squad for a pair of "colts": young players who would be going along presumably just for the ride and a foretaste of the Davis Cup atmosphere. One was Barry MacKay, a big, dark boy from Ohio with a cheery manner and a lot of raw power. On the remaining member, the USLTA's selection committee had made no official announcement up until shortly before the trip, although we had already agreed on Mike Green, a Florida boy who had made the trip previously. Aware that Mike would need some advance notice to make the necessary plans with his college authorities and his family, I called him as the take-off date approached and told him to start packing.

It was a gesture that rubbed the USLTA officials the wrong way. Davis Cup selections, I was reminded, are made by telegram, over the signature of the committee chairman. I chalked off the incident as a case of last-minute Cup jitters on the USLTA's part. There seemed to be good reason to feel jittery.

On the air route from San Francisco to Australia, Honolulu is the first stopover. Mike Todd, the engaging little dynamo of Broadway and Hollywood, was there with his bride, Elizabeth Taylor, making what was to be one of their last trips together. Todd, always on the lookout for an excuse to throw a party, immediately staged an elaborate send-off for the tennis players at Henry Kaiser's new hotel. At one point in the evening, Mike came up to me, nodded toward the group and said, "Where's your first team?"

A few weeks later, in Adelaide, Australia, as one United States player after another was being knocked out of a tournament, I found myself being asked the same question by Australian fans and reporters. Down there, I was reminded, players fought to get on the Davis Cup team. The United States, they said, was giving up the trophy by default.

If this was the way it appeared, then, I thought, the tennis public at home was entitled to an explanation. I cabled an article on the subject to the magazine *Sports Illustrated,* for which I had been writing an occasional piece as tennis editor.

I noted the absentees and their reasons for declining, and added my own conviction that they should have found some way to make the trip with the rest of us. Tennis had been good to all of them, as it had to me. It had put their names in headlines, made important friends for them, given them a start in careers off the courts. Surely they owed the game something in return. And none had ever repaid it by playing for the United States in a Challenge Round.

More than that, to be asked to represent your country was an honor. Yet we had been forced to beg, wheedle, and cajole players, and that somehow devalued the honor. It demeaned the effort of the players who had accepted and were now in Australia, doing the others' job against heavy odds.

The odds, in fact, kept lengthening. In order to qualify for the Challenge Round, we still had to get past the team from Belgium. On the match against the Belgians there was $25,000 at stake. That was the amount that the USLTA had invested in the trip and that the association would get back (along with a profit against future expenses) only if we won and thereby earned a share of Challenge Round gate receipts. Pride was at stake, too: never in the last twenty years and only twice in the whole six decades of Davis Cup competition had the United States failed to reach the finals. Yet in Brisbane that week a betting man could find plenty of money willing to argue that this time we'd never make it.

It wasn't a bad bet. In the match against Belgium, Herb Flam staggered through one victory, then succumbed to a case of nerves that nothing had been able to cure — neither practice, nor idleness, nor a doctor's care, nor a shipment of new rackets which we had flown over specially for him from California. Seixas and Mulloy were beaten in the doubles. We scraped by the Belgian team, 3–2, and were lucky to have made it at all. Now it seemed to me that we had only one possible hope against Australia: to use our one sure resource for all it was worth, and invest the rest in a huge gamble.

The fixed element was Seixas. He was our best, and psychologically he was up: At the age of thirty-four, he was planning to make this his last Davis Cup venture, and he wanted to go out a winner.

The gamble was young Barry MacKay, a player not only without previous Davis Cup experience but also without a single important tournament trophy to his credit. What he had in his favor was a tremendous serve and enthusiasm to match. In the two weeks before the Challenge Round he willingly undertook a course of preparation that was probably as intense a one as any player ever went through. In spite of some serious faults in his ground strokes, there was no attempt to change his game. That would have been worse than useless in the short time left. Aside from sharpening the equipment he already had, the preparation was largely psychological. Time after time I reminded him, "If they can't break your serve, they can't win."

Confident of his own serve, Barry could now concentrate on breaking though the opposition. He could afford to take risks to do that. He could hit for winners on the return of service; he could chip a return and go in to net. Who could tell, he just might catch the Australians off balance?

It worked out just that way. What's more, it seemed, for a while, to be paying off. In his first match, MacKay was holding his own with Mal Anderson, the fine Australian player who had won the United States singles championship at Forest Hills a few months before. Then, in the fifth set, with the score 3–4 on Barry's service, the officials called a fault on a shot that almost everybody thought was a clean ace. A moment later, MacKay broke. Seixas also lost, that day; but not before he too had carried his opponent, the world's top-ranked amateur, Ashley Cooper, right down to the wire.

Now, with the United States team in the hole, 2–0, but

with MacKay showing so well, I decided to gamble with him all the way. Shoving sentiment aside, I bypassed my old partner, Mulloy, and threw Barry in with Seixas for the doubles. It didn't work. But by the time the three-day event ended, the United States team had taken the play away from the Australian favorites and had covered itself with glory. In the last two singles matches, Seixas beat Anderson, and MacKay, the novice, mowed down the world's leading player with a dramatic show of grit and power. Australia, favored to win the cup by a 5–0 shutout, had barely squeezed out a victory by the narrowest of margins, 3–2. And each of the four singles matches was decided by a single service break in the fifth set — something that had never happened before, even in the closest of Challenge Rounds.

When it was all over — big MacKay shambling to the net to shake hands with Cooper, the Australians smiling uneasily over their narrow escape, the crowd rising in the stands of Kooyong Stadium in a salute to the losers — I stepped forward to play the role that had become only too familiar, that of bystander instead of recipient when the Davis Cup was turned over to the winning side. But in this defeat there was as much satisfaction as I had sometimes felt in the winners' circle.

During the banquet that evening, marking the formal end of the 1957 Davis Cup campaign, Barry MacKay leaned over to show me a cablegram he had received. It was an invitation to play a series of tournaments in the Middle East. He had already received other bids from tennis associations in the Philippines, Hong Kong, India,

Thailand. He was eager to play, but dubious about what the USLTA might say about his staying out of the country for such a long spell. The Association's concern was that the American tournaments would suffer if the good players were absent.

"Go ahead," I told MacKay, "and don't worry about the tennis association. I'll argue the case for you when I get home." The USLTA, I thought, would be willing to make an exception for Barry. I felt he'd earned it.

I turned my attention to the after-dinner festivities. The Prime Minister of Australia, Robert G. Menzies, was introducing me with this usual friendly banter. The year before, in a reference to my close-to-the-skull haircut, he had presented me as "that Trappist monk in white flannels." This time, adding a dig at my Wall Street activities, he described me as "a billiard ball plastered down with banknotes."

I stood up and waited for the good-natured laughter to subside. In the past, I had confined my final words as visiting captain to farewells and thanks. This time, cheered by the team's performance, I told the players and the assembled dignitaries that I considered the Davis Cup results a matter of unfinished business, and that I hoped to be back to see them about it in a year.

In both of my remarks that evening — to Barry MacKay and to the Australians — I was taking too much for granted.

The Way the Ball Bounces

I LANDED in New York just after the city had swept up the traditional litter of New Year's and was nursing its traditional hangover. In our household, the Christmas tree was still brightly lit, the packages still intact in their wrappings. Peter and Pike had become so used to waiting for Christmas until the old man came home from his annual junket across the Pacific that by now they seemed convinced other families were cheating when they opened their presents and ate their holiday dinner in December.

It was a happy reunion; the weeks of the Davis Cup trip had begun to seem longer each year. At my office, when I checked in again the next morning, papers were piled up chin-high on my desk. There were a number of extracurricular affairs awaiting my attention as well. A couple of local diabetes organizations in the Middle West wanted to know if I would be in their area at some time in the near future. If so, would I have time for speeches, visits with kids at clinics and other activities, as in the past? A letter from one of my earliest tennis circuit friends, Charley Hare, now representing a Chicago sporting goods company, brought me up to date on some details of a program we were engaged in together for promoting youngsters' interest in tennis — a nationwide program of local tournaments to be sponsored by the Junior Chambers of Commerce.

There was also the matter of a book. Now that the Davis Cup campaign was behind me, I could get back to work in earnest on the project I had started several months before: putting the story of my life and good times down on paper. There were scattered heaps of newspaper clippings to pore through, the records of tennis matches played by a skinny kid whose name was mine, all right, but whose accompanying photo often looked younger than I could ever remember having been. There were a couple of letters addressed to my parents from the diabetes clinic of Children's Hospital in Cincinnati, recording minor landmarks in my progress. There were files of letters, dated years later, from other diabetics, asking advice, congratulating me on some tennis event, or just trying to establish contact with another "one of us."

There were things to be recalled — scenes, conversations, people who had played some small but meaningful part in my life years before. All these were part of what I owed to tennis.

There were events, some of them engraved on the trophies ranged on shelves in the library and stashed away in the closets, plus some others that still cluttered up my mother's apartment — souvenirs of my mughunting days. The most important prize of all, and by far the largest part of my debt, consisted of a few unengraved words spoken by a man whose name would mean nothing to readers of either the sports page or the front page. He was a doctor who told a group of professional people and laymen interested in diabetes research: "Banting and Best discovered insulin and made it possible for diabetics to live. Billy Talbert showed them how."

What he might have added was that tennis had showed it to me.

On a Sunday morning, some weeks after what tennis people were calling "the moral victory over Australia," while I was taking advantage of some unseasonably mild weather by rolling grounders to young Pike on the terrace of our apartment, I was called to the phone. It was Victor Denny, a Seattle investment banker, who had been elected President of the USLTA a month before. I tossed the ball to Pike and hurried in, anxious to hear what the new chief of organized tennis might have to tell me and totally unprepared for what I was about to hear.

I listened, not quite believing it, then headed back toward the terrace, feeling numb.

Nancy met me on the stairs. "Bad news?" she said, reading the expression on my face.

I sat down on the stairs. "I've just been fired."

"By the magazine? The diabetes association? Which one of your dozen jobs . . ." She stopped. "You're serious."

"By the tennis association. I'm not the Davis Cup captain any more."

"You're *not* serious. Willy, it's a gag."

I shook my head. "That was Victor Denny on the phone."

"What did he say? Why? They didn't expect you to win, did they?"

"It isn't that. It couldn't be. In fact, he said everybody thought I'd done a fine job."

"Then what is the reason?"

"I don't know. All he said was that they had never intended the job to be permanent, which is true enough, and they decided to make a change." I put on a smile. "Well, I've been wanting to spend a Christmas at home with you and the boys, for a change, and if I couldn't do it by bringing the Cup home with me, at least I'll get to do it this way."

"Oh, Willy," she said, "it's such a damn shame! After all you've put into it."

Pike peered in from the terrace. "Aren't you going to play any more? I'm getting rusty."

"I'll be out in a minute," I told him. "You know," I said to Nancy, "I've been doing this job for years — all the time and the work and the trips away from home — because I felt I owed so much to tennis. And now they tell me forget it, the debt is squared, we don't want anything more from you. I ought to be relieved, but I guess my pride is hurt."

For the first time since I was a young diabetic learning my way around a cement court, I couldn't stomach the thought of tennis.

In the morning the phone started to ring early, just as I finished my insulin shot. One of my former players was calling to ask if the story in the papers was really true.

"Tell him yes, thanks for calling, and I'll get back to him later," I told Nancy, as I rinsed the syringe. There were a few drops of water left in it, and I squirted some, water-pistol style, at young Peter. He squealed, in accordance with the rules of this family game, and called to his older brother for help. I aimed a second shot at Pike as he came through the door.

"Missed me! Missed me!" he said.

"Your old man must be losing his eye," I conceded, putting the insulin kit away.

The phone kept ringing. Old tennis friends, reporters, business associates. Doc Kistner, calling from the hospital in Boston. Even some tennis officials who had, apparently, not been in on the decision and were surprised by it. Some of them had already made other phone calls themselves, in an effort to find an explanation for what had happened.

The team's performance didn't seem to have anything to do with the issue, as Denny had assured me. But there had been other complaints: I had been too "liberal" with the players (that oldest complaint of all). I had taken functions on myself that properly belonged to USLTA committees (the Mike Green affair). I had issued strong statements that ought to have come from higher sources if they were to be made at all (the criticism of players who had declined the trip to Australia; proposals for changes in tennis which I had discussed with reporters and put into print under my own byline). I had failed to co-operate with the tennis association in enforcing its rule limiting overseas play by United States players (the Barry MacKay trip).

That, at least, was the case as it was explained to me

unofficially. Officially, I was never told anything more.

Well, perhaps I had no reason to be surprised. It was as the doctor had once told me: "A little less independence wouldn't do you any harm." Even my father, who had taught me to be that way, hadn't found it easy to live with. This was what it had taken to change me from idle diabetic to eager tennis player. I could understand now what I was, but I knew I would never really change again.

As I reached my office, the phone on my desk was ringing, too. Charley Hare was on the line.

"Can't believe it, Willy," he said. "Damnedest thing I ever heard of."

"They pay the bills for the team," I reminded him. "I guess they've got a right to fire the captain."

"You've done a good job, Willy. Everybody knows it."

"Thanks," I said. "I hope the next guy does better. It would be nice if we won for a change. The hell with it, anyway. Let's talk about something else. How's Mary?"

"Fine, fine as ever." He hesitated. "Look, maybe this isn't the best time to bring the matter up, but I've worked out some of the figures on this Junior Chamber of Commerce program. The tournaments, you know."

"I know."

"Well . . . it isn't going to be easy. It'll take ten thousand dollars to run the program at the top. I mean to say, organizing the whole thing, sponsoring the follow-up tournaments for the winners from each area, all that sort of thing." He paused again. "I don't suppose you're in any mood to think about raising ten thousand dollars to promote tennis."

I swung around in my chair and stared out the window, thinking about what Charley was saying. Even through the grime and shadow of downtown New York, the day was bright and clear. The air had a false but inviting hint of spring. It was the kind of day when, twenty-five years before in Cincinnati, I would have been hurrying home from school to dig my racket out of the closet and head for the tennis courts at Coy Field.

"There are plenty of people who love tennis almost as much as you do and I do," I said. "If I talk to them, maybe they'll come through with a contribution. I ought to be able to raise the ten thousand somehow."

"Good show, Willy. I hoped you wouldn't change your mind about the program. It's really going to be a fine thing for the game if we get it going right."

"I'm sure it will."

"How's your own game these days? National indoor championship's coming up, you know. Planning to go in and show the kids a few shots?"

I could almost feel the satisfying heft of the racket in my hand.

"I'll be in it, Charley," I said.

Redwood Library and Athenaeum
NEWPORT, R. I.

———

Selections from the Rules

New fiction is issued for 7 days, new non-fiction for 14 days, and other books for 28 days with the privilege of renewal.

Books overdue are subject to a fine of 2 cents a day.

All injuries to books and all losses shall be made good to the satisfaction of the Librarian.

5 volumes may be taken at a time and only 5 on 1 share or subscription.

LIBRARY BUREAU CAT. NO. 1166.3